CIVIL SOCIETY
AT THE MILLENNIUM

Published in cooperation
with CIVICUS

CIVICUS

KUMARIAN
PRESS

Civil Society at the Millennium

Published 1999 in the United States of America by Kumarian Press, Inc., 14 Oakwood Avenue, West Hartford, Connecticut 06119-2127 USA.

Production and design by The Sarov Press, Stratford, Connecticut. The text of this book is set in Adobe Sabon.

Printed in Canada on acid-free paper by Transcontinental Printing and Graphics, Inc. Text printed with vegetable oil-based ink.

∞ The paper used in this publication meets the minimum requirements of the American National Standard for Information Sciences—Permanence of Paper for Printed Library Materials, ANSI Z39.48–1984.

Library of Congress Cataloging-in-Publication Data
Civil society at the millennium / [contributors, Marcus Akuhata-Brown
. . . et al.] ; published in cooperation with CIVICUS.
    p.   cm.
Includes bibliographical references.
ISBN 1–56549–101–7 (pbk. : alk. paper)
    1. Civil society. I. Akuhata-Brown, Marcus. II. CIVICUS
(Association)
JC337.C55 1999
301—dc21   99–34944

03   02   01   00   5   4   3   2   First Printing 1999

Contents

Foreword

When I was asked to serve on the editorial committee for this publication, I hesitated for two reasons. First, I was not sure I would be able to make the time commitment, given the nature of similar work I had seen my colleagues at CIVICUS perform in the past. Second, I was awed by the complexity of issues surrounding the concept and practice that now passes under the label "civil society."

I was not sure that I wanted to get into the middle of any "heavy duty" polemics over what civil society is, what its past role has been, what its future role should be, and many other related questions. For me, these kinds of questions belong in the realm of those who document, analyze, and store knowledge, for posterity — the academics. I was more comfortable placing myself in a particular category: that our role as civil society activists was to identify opportunities and experiment with creative solutions that confront the issues and concerns of today's more vulnerable people.

Even so, I was deeply intrigued by the challenge of participating in a unique exercise that would literally "define our name" and describe the state of civil society, globally. Although this was an exciting, albeit complex, proposition, I became more engrossed in an alternative plan for a publication that would look at the state of civil society at the turn of the millennium. The power behind this idea was overwhelming and the enthusiasm was simply infectious. We would invite experienced practitioners to reflect and write on different aspects of their work from a personal perspective. But going further to ensure that the resulting publication represented the diversity of citizens' experience and ongoing existence on the planet earth would be a feat to be admired, if it could be achieved. Readers of this final product will now have to judge whether this goal has indeed been met.

This publication builds on the impeccable standards set by the first and second CIVICUS World Assemblies. At both events, we launched high-quality publications on the life and health of civil society, which literally defy the youth of the organization. Our most recent effort, which coincides with the 1999 World Assembly, has taken a significant step in articulating the ideals to which most of us in the third sector aspire. Through the voices of outstanding citizens who share their perspectives on the health, relationships, and future possibilities for civil society, this publication presents a sound basis to debate the role that civil society should play — or more definitively, the role it will have to play in the next millennium. The author of each chapter was asked to share his or her thoughts in a private capacity. The extent of consultation and the depth of engagement that took place as the book developed, however, surely means the ideas presented here speak for many of us who want to fit into the "civil society" category.

I would like to express my heartfelt gratitude to each author who contributed to this outstanding piece of work. Besides voluntarily contributing to the body of knowledge we are building and the agenda that will emerge from here on, they have demonstrated the spirit that has gradually led to the recognition that the sector now enjoys. I would like here to single out Kumi Naidoo, CIVICUS Secretary General and Chief Executive Officer, and Rajesh Tandon, CIVICUS Chairperson, for their outstanding leadership and dedication to this publication. Contrary to my fears when I was asked to be the chair of the editorial committee, I have thoroughly enjoyed interacting with numerous colleagues in supporting this initiative.

Ezra Mbogori
Chairperson, Editorial Board

Preface

This book was undertaken during an incredibly short period of time shortly after I assumed my responsibilities as Secretary General and CEO of CIVICUS: World Alliance for Citizen Participation. Having responsibility for this project while I was trying to find my feet in what is a dynamic and exciting global movement was an immense challenge indeed.

The strategy we adopted was to invite a group of authors, spanning different parts of the world, who had a track record in several themes in which we were interested. We consciously tried to strike a regional and gender balance. While we did not attain all of our targets, I hope that the reader will give us a good pass in that regard. Unfortunately, due to the limitations of both time and space we were not able to cover all the themes that we set out initially. For example, we were very keen to have chapters looking at the role of the elderly in civil society, the location of people living with disabilities in civil society, the relation between the UN system and civil society, and several others. If we did not cover your area of special interest, we apologize most sincerely. We hope that future publications of CIVICUS will remedy these omissions.

The authors in this volume write in their personal capacities rather than as representatives of their respective organizations. This, we felt, would create greater space for critical reflection on the issues being discussed. The perspectives of the authors reflect the diversity of civil society itself. I would be surprised if any reader found agreement with all of the following chapters, but we hope that there will be a large measure of resonance. Indeed as editor, there were perspectives and emphasis taken in this publication that differed with my own. Such is the nature and openness of CIVICUS and, more generally, civil society. Every author from Australia to Zimbabwe deserves our deepest gratitude for responding to the tight deadlines that were set to ensure that this publication would be available in time for the CIVICUS 1999 World Assembly.

Several people helped to review, comment, and provide critical assistance to various chapters. Ted Howard, Heinrich "Finn" Volkhart, Ravi Thiara, Tina Choi, Annie Paul, Gary Kessler, Kathleen Lynch, Anne Firth-Murray, and Louisa Zondo all made invaluable contributions to the book, for which we are extremely grateful.

In putting together the book we were guided by the CIVICUS Board of Directors who gave valuable advice and guidance. In particular, we must thank Ezra Mbogori who served as Chair of the Editorial Committee and Rajesh Tandon, the Chair of the CIVICUS Board of Directors. Other current and former CIVICUS board members and regional advisory committee members deserving special thanks are Naima Al-Shayji, Manuel Arango, Tim Brodhead, Michael Brophy, Hugh Burroughs, Miguel Darcy de Olivera, Gonzalo de la Maza, Victoria Garchitorena, Chris Harris, Mall Hellam, Patrick Johnston, Thierno Kane, Amita Kapur, Cecilia Kinuthia-Njenga, Chimaki Kurokawa, Elba Luna, Sara Melendez, Strini Moodley, Horacio "Boy" Morales, Marek Nowicki, John Richardson, Salama Saidi, Ghassan Sayah, Peter Shiras, Sylvie Tsyboula, William White, and Eliezer Yaari.

Special thanks must go to the external coordinator of this project, Leslie Fox. Leslie, a long-time friend of CIVICUS, applied himself with dedication, patience, creativity, and professionalism. His contribution to this effort was indispensable. As was Angie Lane's, CIVICUS's Communications Coordinator, who prodded and cajoled me and everybody else involved to meet our deadlines and generally keep the project on track. Many thanks, Leslie and Angie, and well done.

Our partners at Kumarian Press worked with us with patience and professionalism and gave us a critical three-week extension when it was needed. Krishna Sondhi and Linda Beyus deserve our special thanks. This is our first publication undertaken as a joint venture. Judging from this experience, we hope it will not be the last.

Our deep gratitude goes to our various donors who provided financial support to CIVICUS. Without their support this book could not have been realized. To our close to five hundred members in more than ninety countries of the world, we thank you for your involvement and commitment to the idea of CIVICUS and for the ways in which your activity and experience shaped this book.

Finally, let me mention the obvious. Without a committed and skillful staff, this book would not have been completed on time, considering the complexity of this global enterprise. Laurie Regelbrugge (Chief Operating Officer and General Manager), Larry Slesinger (Interim Chief Operating Officer), Jo Render (Senior Program Manager), Alina

Zyskowski (BPD Knowledge Resource Group), Janet Oliver (Membership Assistant), Flo Pettigrew (Communications Intern), Kathryn Roman (Communications Intern), and Roxane Bouten (Accountant) all pitched in to help. Last, but certainly not least, Elizabeth Stoneham, my assistant, who made sure I delivered on time, even if it meant scheduling time to edit a chapter or two on an airplane or in an airport.

The project benefited from the creative energies and insightful comments and inputs of all these wonderful people, for which I am deeply grateful. Any shortcomings that remain are a result of my own inadequacies as editor.

Kumi Naidoo
Secretary General and CEO
CIVICUS

1

The Promise of Civil Society

Kumi Naidoo and Rajesh Tandon

Come Join with Us

If, like the fairy tale character Rip Van Winkle, you had just awoken after a four decade-long slumber, you might think that the world at the turn of the millennium had solved many of its major problems and that civil society was one of the principal reasons why. You would be somewhat right and somewhat wrong.

Today, we talk about civil society and its role in eradicating poverty, in promoting democracy and good governance, and in resolving social conflict and protecting human rights — among a myriad of other areas related to the human condition. It is increasingly common to see civil society organizations represented at most major international conferences, participating alongside their governments in discussions dealing with the principal social, economic, and environmental problems of the day. And these are just the more visible manifestations of a global phenomenon in which citizen-inspired associations have spread through millions of villages and communities leaving more democratic forms of governance and improved social and economic welfare in their wake.

There is sometimes a disposition among those of us involved in the movement of civil society to talk and write about it as if it were the unquestioned champion of these latter days of the twentieth century. This sometimes includes the inclination to over-glorify its accomplishments and romanticize about its innate goodness as well as its acknowledged place in world affairs. While this is a normal human tendency, it does not advance the cause of civil society in the long run. The idea and promise of civil society lies as much in its potential as it does in the very real achievements that it has produced to date. We are learning, as we go along, what our appropriate role is and how best we can contribute to the public good. Our greatest enemy is arrogance and the notion that a strong civil society is an end in itself rather than the means by which peoples express their civic side in the collective enterprise we all share. In short, the promise of civil society lies before us and we ask you to join us in the journey.

Let the Journey Begin

The year 1999 is a time to celebrate the growth of civil society globally and a time to reflect on its future development. The 1999 CIVICUS World Assembly provides a forum for its members and partners to assess civil society's previous progress, to chart its future direction, and to begin formulating appropriate strategies for achieving shared objectives. This book was commissioned by CIVICUS to help initiate this important process. More specifically, it has the goal of ensuring that the voices of its members are heard at several forthcoming international fora that are likely to discuss civil society and its future role in public life from the very local to the very global levels. In this regard, each of the thirteen essays that fall between this chapter and the concluding chapter was chosen to illuminate issues that are critical to an understanding of civil society and its emerging role as a global actor.

The thread that runs throughout this essay, and indeed much of the book, is what we termed above the promise of civil society. In 1994, CIVICUS noted the potential civil society offered to citizens worldwide to promote a better future. Five years later, we are in a position to take a closer look at the emerging trends, achievements, and challenges that civil society has faced during this period in living up to its promise. In this regard, we will look at civil society in the context of a broader global conversation in which civil society organizations (CSOs) find themselves as well as provide our conception of what civil society is and its role as a legitimate public actor from local to global levels. The essay ends with a brief road map laying out what is found in the rest of this book.

From a Local Monologue to a Global Conversation

Less than a decade ago, civil society was a concept discussed by political scientists in the sanctuary of ivory towers. Certainly, if voluntary association and associational autonomy are considered its fundamental requisites, then there was little empirical evidence of its existence outside of a handful of democracies. Even then, it was largely referred to as the third, nonprofit, voluntary, or independent sector. These terms are, generally, non-threatening to states whatever their dispositions. In the developing South, a unique form of organization emerged: the NGO, which defines itself by what it is not rather than by what it is. The term remains to this day firmly fixed in our daily lexicon. Such was the state of affairs of humankind as it approached the last decade of this millennium.

Then the walls came tumbling down. It was as if the beckoning of a new millennium led the human collective to say enough was enough. The literal coming down of authoritarian ramparts was matched by the symbolic awakening of democratic impulses in men and women from Bangladesh to Bolivia and from Uzbekistan to Uganda. The totalitarian monologue of the autocrat was replaced by a global conversation of citizens. The ensuing cacophony was music to the ear of the pluralist just as silence had been to the rule of the overlord. Listening closely, however, there was a common melody running through these many and diverse songs. Simply put, the lyrics uppermost on the minds of citizen songwriters were about how to go about addressing the same old problems in this new context. It was not surprising, however, that many of these attempts at making music were sometimes characterized by discordant notes and out-of-tune efforts. The art of making beautiful music together for the newly liberated beyond the confines of home or clan level had either never fully developed or was rusty as a result of decades of disuse.

The promise of citizen engagement was poised to breathe new meaning and life into the very notion of democracy. The tragedy of ethnic cleansing, the reality of religious intolerance, and the deepening of social and economic inequalities had found their way onto the score sheets of the music makers of the last decade. It was also the decade in which complacency seemed to descend on the older constitutional democracies and that doubts and questions began to surface about the quality and vibrancy of their institutions. In the United States, for example, growing levels of disillusionment with the political process would see ever decreasing levels of electoral participation. In some countries, questions about media monopoly began to raise concerns about whether citizens had true access to reliable information on a range of social and political choices or whether it had been replaced by a new orthodoxy reflecting pop culture rather than reasoned debate.

Notwithstanding the latter concerns, the conversation taking place among people as well as entire societies today is really about trying to determine the most effective way to create a healthy and sustainable public life. Democracy, as philosophically pleasing as it is in terms of the freedoms it posits for the citizen, is perhaps more important because of the responsibilities it allocates among and between citizens and the institutions they create to govern their relationships. As central as the citizen is to the health of a democracy, it is his or her collective manifestation either in the form of the state, market, or civil society that ultimately determines the health of public life. What distinguishes these last years of the waning millennium from the many hundreds that preceded it is the global ascendancy of democracy — if not always in practice, then unceasingly in principle.

Today's conversation is about the proper role or the appropriate balance of state, market, and civil society in public life, particularly in defining the public good and then in making it happen. This is not a discussion limited to the new democracies. It is just as heated and passionate in the old ones.

Putting the Citizen at the Center

Human development is thus a broad and comprehensive concept. It covers all human choices in all societies at all stages of development. It broadens the development dialogue from a discussion of mere means (GNP growth) to a discussion of the ultimate ends. It is as concerned with the generation of economic growth as with its distribution, as concerned with basic needs as with the entire spectrum of human aspirations, as concerned with the human dilemmas of the North as with human deprivation of the South. The concept of human development does not start with any predetermined model. It draws its inspiration from the long-term goals of society. It weaves development around people, not people around development.[1]

Civil society did not spontaneously appear one day as a realm of human interaction but has emerged over the millennia in relation to the way in which societies and their members have structured their relations to achieve collective purposes. Put differently, civil society was not the result of some public equivalent of the Immaculate Conception but rather the result of deliberate collective action to advance societal interests and the public good.

It is probably safe to say that we, as human beings, did not start out in this world with a shared blueprint or strategy guiding us to a mutually desired end-point. However, as we approach a new millennium, we appear to have arrived at a common understanding about many of the factors that go into the making of a healthy public life.

We believe that there are, in fact, a set of fundamental values and practices — some might even say universal — that have emerged over the millennia, which underlie this concept of a healthy public life — or what many describe as sustainable human development. Acknowledging that civil society has a distinctive normative dimension that derives much of its content from the world's great philosophies and religions helps us to better situate civil society today and its future role in public life.

As members of what we might call TransMillennial civil society, we think the most important of these values and practices are those associated with trust, tolerance, democracy, and civic-mindedness. These values and practices are embodied in and manifested by individuals, or in the context of this discussion, citizens, particularly in their role as the initiators of civil society organizations.

We do not use "citizen" strictly in its formal, legalistic context. For CIVICUS, placing the citizen in the center means understanding that people — individual human beings — are the fundamental civic actors. Our use of the term citizen does not exclude refugees, young people, and others whose legal status may be in transition or unprotected. People, thus, are at the center of civil society.

The following discussion takes this underlying principle of the values dimension of civil society and the centrality of the citizen to its strength as the core of a civil society strategy for participating in public life from the local to global levels.

Civil Society: A Legitimate Public Actor

To understand civil society — and particularly what needs strengthening and how to go about doing it — requires identifying its principal functions as the first step in defining what a strong and healthy civil society might look like. The attempt here is to locate civil society both conceptually and operationally in terms of its role as a public actor in the promotion of sustainable human development, the eradication of poverty, and the building of a healthy public life — whether at the local, national, or global levels.

While sustainable human development is the broad context within which civil society is being discussed, there is a tendency among policymakers and practitioners working in the field of development, particularly Northerners, to view this as relevant only in the South. Thus, the discussion of civil society and the allied concepts of social capital, democracy, and governance is considered as an interesting but academic exercise, or perhaps as the elusive magic bullet capable of delivering the poor from their misery and the rich from their obligations. Neither view does much to enlighten this field of inquiry nor makes it comprehensible in a way that has immediate relevance to improving the human condition. What is it about the concept of civil society that does have relevance and resonates in the more familiar context of our daily lives — whether we live in Belgium, Bolivia, Bangladesh, Botswana, Bahrain, or Bulgaria?

The opening quote from the *Human Development Report 1992* leads to a number of fundamental questions related to "how" and "which" human beings come to make choices about "long-term societal goals." Who, for instance, makes the decisions about the trade-off between jobs and environmental protection? Or about the share of public resources devoted to improving the conditions of the "poor" versus the "non-poor?" Or about the nature of the tax system, and how it distributes the benefits of economic growth?

This basic issue about how decisions are made and who makes them is at the center of the discussion of civil society. In fact, the broader context of sustainable human development (SHD) is only partially about civil society, or it would be under ideal conditions. SHD actually describes the conditions for a healthy public life, that is, where civil society is only one of several legitimate arenas of public action — the others being the state, market, and (some would say) democratically elected local governments related to making and implementing choices about societal goals, a process defined here simply as "governance."

At its core, when sustainable human development is reduced to its essence, it is about how human beings create a healthy public life and sustain it over time because it is able to address societal or sustainable development problems effectively. The principal issue related to creating and sustaining a healthy public life is finding the right balance between state, market, and civil society in making and implementing societal decisions. The current debate in the northern welfare or post-welfare countries is about the roles of these three public spheres in defining societal goals and then determining who best can implement programs to reach them.

This is not a new debate, although the particular issues may be, but rather an ongoing dialogue that has existed for as long as citizens have had the freedom to participate in making public choices. In the North, this has been a bit more than two centuries. In several countries of the developing South and transitioning East, the dialogue has been going on for at least several decades.

In summary, civil society's principal role is in contributing to the creation of a healthy public life as one of several spheres of legitimate societal action. In its simplest conception, civil society is the network of autonomous associations that rights-bearing and responsibility-laden citizens voluntarily create to address common problems, advance shared interests, and promote collective aspirations. As a legitimate public actor, civil society participates alongside — not replaces — state and market institutions in the making and implementing of public policies designed to resolve collective problems and advance the public good.

How Would We Know a Strong Civil Society If We Saw One?

Civil society is a contested concept. There are probably as many definitions of it as there are those who have written about it. CIVICUS's vision of civil society is rooted in our very first publication, *Citizens: Strengthening Global Civil Society,* which tied the role, functions, the very raison d'être of civil society, to the citizen and his/her centrality to sustainable human development and a healthy public life. While we acknowledge that there are many views as to what constitutes a strong civil society, we also believe that it is time for CIVICUS to begin developing its own conception, including the characteristics that define a healthy civil society. We base this decision on the simple fact that as an organization dedicated to promoting and strengthening civil society, our effectiveness in this regard requires knowing what exactly we are promoting and strengthening.

We believe the common factor that permits our vision to be translated into an operational reality is our unyielding focus on the citizen. The remainder of this section begins our quest for the answer to the question: how would you know a strong civil society if you saw one? We realize that this may generate as much heat as it does light, but as a famous mother once said, if you want to eat an omelet, my son, then you are going to have to break some eggs. Let the debate begin!

The Citizen: The Building Block of Civil Society, the Unifying Force in Sustainable Development and a Healthy Public Life

We start from the premise that civil society is not an end in itself but rather the means by which citizens advance and defend their interests in public life through collective action. As such, civil society is no stronger than the people that compose its many and diverse associations and institutional manifestations. The first attribute of a strong civil society, therefore, is a well-informed and active citizenry participating in public life through associations they voluntarily form. From this fundamental view of the relationship between the citizen and civil society, it follows that what we term as citizen organizations — the lowest level of voluntarily formed and autonomous civil society organizations — are the building blocks of civil society and, by extension, of democracy and sustainable human development.

Human beings are not just political animals concerned with power in their role as citizens. They are social beings who freely associate, when permitted, and who develop a range of relationships to address their many personal needs. Human beings are also economic beings that both produce and consume to ensure a range of material and physical requirements. Finally, human beings are natural beings, part of and yet transcending nature through their spirituality. Because the political sphere of human activity provides the broader set of rules and institutional arrangements governing these other three spheres, the citizen or political being can be considered the first among equals. As such, we can view the citizen and citizen organization as the base unit of civil society but also of sustainable development as they unify the social, economic, environmental, and political realms of human activity.

Finally, we note that it is the citizen — acting in his or her capacity as elector or elected state institutions, joining with others to form civil society organizations and forming the basic units of the market — who is able to transcend the differences between these three realms of human interaction and makes partnerships among them possible.

The Defining Feature of Civil Society: It Is a Political Concept

Civil society is linked both conceptually and practically to the promotion of democracy, to good governance, to a hybrid of the two (democratic governance), and ultimately to sustainable development. Underlying the notion of civil society is the understanding that it is fundamentally a political concept, which is what distinguishes it from other terms much in use today, including the voluntary, independent, third, philanthropic, nonprofit, or nongovernmental organization (NGO) sector. Each of these other terms describes a characteristic of civil society, but none of them provide the defining feature. In short, civil society is a political concept because it is concerned with exercising power to advance and defend the economic, social, and political interests of citizens.

It is for this reason — the potential for political action — that national governments have historically attempted to keep citizens from joining together to address their collective problems. It is for this reason too that many of the inter-governmental organizations that are owned by national governments have been hesitant to support the emergence and strengthening of civil society. And, finally, it is for this reason that market actors have supported the policies of less-than-progressive governments as well as avoided developing collaborative relationships with CSOs even when it would have advanced their own economic interests.

It has been this adversarial role, or to put it more positively, the countervailing function, that has been the defining feature of civil society's relationship to state and market actors in the past. The new political context that has emerged, marked by democracy and citizen participation, has increasingly led to more collaborative modes of relating among the sectors. It is civil society's participation in political life, in that realm of public life in which societal decisions are made and carried out, that provides the conditions for sustainable development and a healthy public life.

In this conception of sustainable development, civil society and its organizations become legitimate partners of, not replacements for, state institutions and market actors. The primary issue in formulating a strategy to promote and strengthen civil society, therefore, is how to make civil society an effective as well as legitimate partner in governance matters at the local level and beyond.

The Attributes and Dimensions of a Strong and Healthy Civil Society

As a basic premise, there is clearly little unanimity of thought about what constitutes a strong, healthy civil society; rather, as we have noted, it is a contested concept, similar to those of democracy, governance, human rights, and even sustainable development. In short, there is no universally agreed upon definition of civil society. Notwithstanding this ongoing debate, however, we see a consensus beginning to emerge on a number of the features and characteristics that underlie a strong and healthy civil society, particularly as they manifest themselves in operational terms. The following are what we consider to be the more important of them.

Voluntary Association and Associational Autonomy

Any discussion concerning the characteristics of a strong civil society must necessarily start with the set of preconditions that make it possible. The first, not surprisingly, is an enabling environment that permits both voluntary association and associational autonomy. Unless freedom of association is constitutionally guaranteed and enforced, and unless a space is carved out of public life that permits voluntarily formed associations the right to act independent of the state and market, then civil society cannot be said to exist! As such, we would go so far as to say that before

1990 civil society did not exist in large parts of the world. Working backwards from this fact, it is equally evident that the citizen, as one endowed with a set of inalienable rights, also did not exist in many countries. Unfortunately, there remain far too many countries, including some very large ones, where neither citizens nor civil society nor democracy have yet to make their appearance in a significant manner, leading to the conclusion that neither sustainable development nor a healthy public life has yet been achieved.

Institutional Pluralism

Assuming the right of citizens to be able to come together voluntarily outside of the state and market to pursue collective or public purposes, one of the principal signs of a budding civil society is in the density and diversity of associational life — what might be called institutional pluralism. The greater the density and diversity of associational life the more channels (choices) citizens have to express their interests (voices) in public life. Moreover, institutional pluralism provides citizens with overlapping membership based on their varied interests, and, thus, cuts across a range of societal cleavages (e.g., race, class, ethnicity, region) that have tended to divide rather than unite people.

The Structural and Functional Dimensions: Specialization and Differentiation

At a certain point emerging civil societies will reach a *critical mass* of associational density and diversity. When this happens, we can anticipate a process in which the structure of civil society begins to differentiate and CSOs begin to specialize in terms of the functions they undertake. If we can conceive of a strong and mature state or market — realms of human activity to which civil society is often juxtaposed — as comprised of specialized and multi-purpose organizations and institutions, then why not civil society?

The spectrum of associations comprising a strong civil society can be characterized as falling into three structural strata, each with different functions. These strata correspond roughly with the organizations' geographic scope and with their relationship to the citizen. Thus, a robust civil society generally resembles a pyramid, whose base is a vast array of primary-level organizations channeling citizen voices outward and upward in dialogue with public decision-makers. In the middle, a smaller set of intermediary associations provide support to primary-level organizations, and raise citizen voices. At the apex, one finds networks that echo the voices of these lower-stratum CSOs in national arenas. Here, there is also a cohort of specialized organizations that support civil society as a whole, providing policy analysis, training, sectoral, and other services that help amplify the "collective voice" of civil society as a partner in governance.

The Normative Dimension: The Values Domain

The final characteristic included in our conception of a strong civil society is what we term the normative dimension. This implies that civil society, as distinct from the state and market, is considered the "values" domain with a set of civic norms and democratic practices that distinguish it from these other realms of human interaction. The normative dimension is built on the foundation of social capital, or the set of values and corresponding behaviors, including trust, reciprocity, tolerance, and inclusion, that enable individuals to feel secure in entering into relationships of mutual benefit and collective action.

Social capital can thus be considered a bridging mechanism between individuals and groups and even across realms (i.e., from civil society to the state and market). From these fundamental social values that underlie individual motivation and the ability to associate together in common cause, other civic values including voluntarism, philanthropy, and public-spiritedness grow and develop, providing the glue that binds social fabric into a cohesive whole, into a healthy public life.

Simply put, civic norms, and the institutional networks that transmit them, permit individuals and even groups to transcend their personal and narrow interests and conceive of a public good to which they can contribute and from which they can benefit. Not only is social capital the currency of a healthy society, but, equally important, it underlies and promotes healthy transactions that take place in political and economic life as well. Thus, civil society can be considered the arena where many interests, often in conflict, are able to develop consensus around a set of civic norms and a collective definition of the public good.

The Art of Association

As Robert Putnam and others have noted, the denser and more diverse the web or network of voluntary associations is in any society, the stronger its ability to generate social capital and promote civic norms. At the same time, it is civil society organizations (CSOs), but particularly grassroots citizen organizations, that are the principal generators of social capital. The ability of individuals and groups to associate is a socially learned trait. The more a person does it, the better he or she becomes in associations. Citizen organizations, because they are based on horizontal relationships among equals, become the laboratories where individuals are able to test their ability to work together without fear of sanction; in fact, they are rewarded for their efforts. The notion of "human agency," or the ability of individuals to design their own futures and become empowered actors capable of realizing those futures, is first tested in the familiar setting of a group.

The Free Schools of Democracy: The Locus of Citizenship

As de Tocqueville noted more than two centuries ago, voluntary associations serve as the "free schools of democracy" where individuals are transformed into citizens as they exercise their rights within and accept their responsibilities to the group. Grassroots citizen organizations provide their members with increased potential for participating in both organizational decision-making and leadership selection, thus strengthening democratic practice and increasing the likelihood of good governance. As increasingly noted, "civil society possesses a pedagogic character since it educates individuals in the values of collective action."[2]

Ultimately, society itself benefits because the pluralism of institutions, opinions, and views that CSOs nurture prevents any single one from dominating, while it increases the knowledge and experience base from which public decisions are made and implemented. Equally important, with a high stock of social capital and the civility it engenders between individuals and groups, there is a far greater likelihood of a widespread commitment to peaceful management of social conflict. And, finally, the ability to undertake cooperative social problem-solving, a major governance function for associational life at all levels, is itself the result of a high stock of social capital.

Let There Be No Confusion about Who Belongs in Civil Society

We conclude this discussion of what constitutes a strong civil society by addressing one of the most contentious of issues, that is, who belongs to civil society and who does not. The issue is often framed by the statement that "civil society is often not very civil." In this regard, we are often referred to the examples of the Ku Klux Klan, the Mafia, and a wide range of terrorist organizations, among others. Let us examine these organizations to see if, in fact, they do belong to the ideal and strong civil society that we have constructed from our vision.

For the sake of argument, let us assume that these organizations are formed voluntarily and that they maintain their autonomy from the state and market. Some of them may even be membership-based, starting at the primary level and federating into large representative organizations that, in fact, promote and defend the interests of their members. Yet, we can only stretch this analogy so far. The one criterion that none of these organizations meets is the normative one, that is, they do not demonstrate civic values and democratic practices that include tolerance, inclusion, non-violence, commitment to promoting the public good, and so on.

Ultimately, we believe that a distinction must be made between associational life that includes all types of voluntarily formed and autonomous organizations and civil society, which narrows down this universe to those demonstrating civic norms. In other words, while associational life includes all civil society organizations, civil society does not include all organizations that comprise a society's associational life.

The State of Civil Society at the Millennium

CIVICUS's task is to create opportunities that unleash the talents of citizens around the world so that they can contribute to greater democracy, social coherence, justice, and the betterment of humanity. That is why CIVICUS is adding new initiatives to our program that are focused on mobilizing civil society participation around poverty eradication, enhancing the leadership role of women in civil society, promoting youth participation in civil society, and supporting greater corporate citizenship and philanthropy.

For CIVICUS, transforming the idea of civil society into reality is integral to our overall mission. Resting at the center of both the idea and reality is the citizen, the essential building block of civil society and, by extension, a healthy public life. CIVICUS is an institutional platform extending the voice of citizens and their voluntary associations from the very local level where they live and work to the global stage where decisions are increasingly made that touch the quality of their daily lives. This publication, at this time, is our way of ensuring that our member organizations, and the many thousands of individuals and groups they represent, are engaged in the ongoing conversation about civil society and its place in the emerging global community. It also provides us with a means for engaging our partners in government, the corporate world, and the donor community around issues that are common to each of us and ultimately, to humankind's future.

The focus of this book — civil society at the turn of the millennium —

provides CIVICUS members and partners with an organizing principle, or way of ordering our thinking about civil society and the myriad issues associated with it. We want to examine how it has evolved over earlier millennia, where it stands at this particular moment in time, and how it will participate in global public life over the next one thousand years or more. To assist us in this inquiry, we have brought together eighteen authors — respected men and women in global civil society — and have asked each of them to address topics with which they have been intimately involved as either practitioners or thinkers during their careers. In this regard, we have not only asked them to provide a thoughtful assessment of this subject area and its contribution to civil society's growth and development as we approach the new millennium, but to give us a thought-provoking discussion of its role in the coming one.

Each of the thirteen essays that make up the body of this book address an aspect, issue, or question related to civil society that helps us to better discern and analyze its underlying nature and contours as well as the many debates swirling around it. Through the optic of these individual essays, a unique perspective of civil society is depicted providing a retrospective assessment of emerging trends as well as key challenges and opportunities facing civil society locally and globally in the future. The choice of essay topics was not a random undertaking but rather the result of considerable discussion among CIVICUS members and partners. As a review of the chapter contents shows there is a logic in the choice of themes chosen for this publication.

Including this chapter and the concluding chapter, fifteen essays are grouped around several broad themes.

- The first essay, *Why We Must Listen to Citizens,* is central to the conception of civil society in which the citizen is its raison d'être. A strong, healthy civil society is not merely an end in itself, but an alternative channel by which citizens participate in public life. The essay discusses the strength and legitimacy of CSOs as public actors in terms of how well they listen to the views and opinions of their citizen members and clients before acting on them.

- The next essay, *Volunteering: Underpinning Social Action in Civil Society for the New Millennium,* discusses how civic values and practices contribute to the strength of civil society as well as how they result from citizen participation in CSOs — the art and habit of associating together. Social capital — or the norms and networks of civic engagement — is generated as people participate collectively to achieve shared goals. The better they do this the greater the stock of social capital produced. Volunteering is one of the most important dimensions of CSO activity and is intimately tied to values associated with social capital.

- The essays on *Civil Society and Indigenous Peoples*, *Women and Civil Society*, and *Youth Empowerment and Civil Society* focus on three critical social groups and the way in which civil society promotes their participation in public life and is strengthened by this participation.

- Three of the ensuing essays examine the relationship between civil society and government (*Civil Society and Government: A Continuum of Possibilities*), religion (*Religion and Civil Society: What is the Relationship Between Them*) and foundations (*Strengthening Civil Society's Capacity to Promote Democratic Governance: The Role of Foundations*). The essays look at the changing roles of these other public actors and their relationship to civil society in promoting the achievement of collective societal goals.

- The essays on sustainable development (*The Role of Civil Society in Sustainable Development*) and poverty eradication (*Civil Society and Poverty: Whose Rights Count?*) look at the role of civil society in and its contribution to the achievement of important global mandates.

- The essays on globalization (*Coming Apart, Coming Together: Globalization and Civil Society*) and global governance (*From States to People: Civil Society and Its Role in Governance*) posit a new role for civil society in terms of its participation in a range of newly emerging institutions and processes that transcend national borders but that directly affect the welfare of citizens and their communities.

- The last of these thematic essays, *New Tools — Same Values: Information and Communication Technology to Support Civil Society*, takes the view that information and technology will be the principal tools that citizens will wield in the coming millennium. Computers and the Internet, among other technologies, will permit citizens and their organizations to connect to each other and to newly emerging global institutions and processes. These tools may also make it possible to develop a truly global civil society.

Finally, we would like to note that this is not just another in the parade of made-for-the-millennium books. In fact, it links the first CIVICUS publication, *Citizens: Strengthening Global Civil Society,* produced in 1994 at the initial launching of CIVICUS, and the first in what will become the CIVICUS flagship publication, the *The State of Civil Society Report.* CIVICUS is currently developing — in collaboration with its members and several partners — a civil society index and corresponding assessment tool that will be used to measure the health of civil society in countries throughout the world in years to come. Coupled with a series of regional and global essays that address cross-cutting issues of importance to civil society, the biennial report will, we hope, take its place alongside other publications with a global mandate and audience.

Notes

1. UNDP. *Human Development Report* (New York: UNDP, 1992).
2. Alexis de Tocqueville in Richard D. Heffner (Editor). *Democracy in America* (New York: Penguin Books, 1974).

2

Why We Must Listen to Citizens

Colin Ball and Barry Knight

A New Global Agenda

For a brief period in the late 1980s and early 1990s, it seemed as if a new world was opening up. The collapse of the Berlin Wall, the ending of Apartheid in South Africa, the liberalization of regimes in South America, and the spread of "just and honest" government following the 1991 Harare Declaration by Commonwealth Heads of Government, created a new global agenda. It appeared that liberal democracy would prevail everywhere; the marketplace based on consumer choice would reign supreme; and the absence of ideological disputes would put an end to the prospect of war because there would be no basis for it. Thus the new millennium might offer a "new deal" for the world.

New Realities

This euphoria would not last for long. What broke some of it was, in a word, Yugoslavia. Once the old controls of the past were shaken off, another was laid bare — this time harder and deeper: racism. Freed from central state controls, ethnic rivalries surfaced that were fed by unscrupulous politicians hungry for power. The Balkans acted out their stereotype, and split in all manners of directions. What made it worse was that Yugoslavia had been the most prosperous of the former Communist countries, with a growing consumer economy and a thriving tourist industry.

Add to that other ethnic and racial conflicts — in Central Africa and in Asia — and it now seems that we will never be free of war. There have been ninety-eight wars since the fall of the Berlin Wall, and ninety-two of these have been civil wars within states, typically taking the form of communal violence between ethnic groups. Such conflict tends to be low-level, persistent, and resistant to formal means of intervention.[1]

As well as war, another gaping hole has opened up to spoil the prospect of a new world order. The prospect of widespread liberal democracy was based on an economic agenda, which turned out to be just what it said it was: an economic agenda. There were no ideals of progress, since we were all producers and consumers acting in accord with supply and demand. A generation brought up on H.G. Wells had believed in the perfectibility of society and of the people within it. The new order rendered such ideas meaningless because the market provided all meaning. As McDonalds opened their first restaurant in Wenceslas Square in Prague (where the crowds thronged to bring down the government in 1989), many people asked: was this a pyrrhic victory? Had the new world just been fashioned for the transglobal corporation?

The World Is a Mess

We now have to acknowledge that the world is a mess. Geography has shifted under our feet within a generation. The world has become interconnected in a way unknown in the past. The nature of transactions between people has changed dramatically, first with the fax machine and now with electronic mail. The conventional wisdom is that this is just the beginning.

It is not just technology that has changed. The last vestiges of competing ideologies have disappeared, and with them the perilous certainties of the Cold War. The new order lacks a clear balance of power. Many new nation states have come into being, while some other older states, notably in Europe, have begun voluntarily to relinquish their sovereignty.

Global capitalism has proceeded apace. Five hundred corporations control nearly half the world's resources. Of the hundred biggest economies in the world, forty-nine are nation states and fifty-one are transglobal companies.[2]

The gap between rich and poor has widened throughout the world, and there are now nineteen countries whose per capita income is lower than it was in 1960.[3] At the same time massive increases in foreign aid to poorer countries have failed to free them from the vicious circle of poverty and debt.[4]

Improvements in nutrition and in health, especially though not exclusively in developed countries, have ensured that many more of us now survive our infancy and enjoy richer and longer lives. Partly as a result, the welfare state is everywhere in retreat.

There have been seismic changes too in prevailing ideologies. Communism has retreated and Islam advanced, in its more extreme manifestations threatening the stability of some areas. Faith in the Christian tradition has declined in the West, and many have left the church. Others have taken shelter in fundamentalist beliefs, new age philosophies, and cults. Post-modern society appears in a state of flux, with the forces of danger and opportunity vying for pride of place.

Perhaps the greatest hope is a new and growing realization that we inhabit one world and that it is small and vulnerable. In part, this new appreciation of our condition has been brought about by enormous leaps in the technology of communication and in the growth of the so-called global economy, but other factors have been at work too. As a result of immigration and emigration, eighty million people now live in countries where they were not born. Another twenty million live abroad as refugees from natural disasters or political oppression. We have begun to understand that pollution knows no boundaries and that the future of our world depends on our preserving the natural environment and on our leading sustainable lives.

This is the world in which the "associational revolution" is gathering pace. Over the past decade, a striking upsurge in organized voluntary activity has taken place in almost every part of the globe. In the developed countries of North America, Europe, and Asia, and in the developing countries of Asia, Africa, the Pacific, the Caribbean, and Latin America, there has been a marked increase in people forming associations, foundations, and similar organizations to deliver human services, promote grassroots development, prevent environmental degradation, and protect civil rights. Lester Salamon has argued that the associational revolution "may constitute as significant a social and political development of the latter twentieth century as the rise of the nation-state was of the late nineteenth."[5]

The Cavalry Is Civil Society

This associational revolution is the cavalry, which can rescue us from war and from unfettered global capitalism. The concept of civil society has come to us from the East and South where democracy-seekers have thrown off oppressive regimes, and reinvented traditional, centuries-old ideas that men and women have rights to create their own communities without excessive interference from the institutions of state and church.

These political developments were followed by an upsurge in literature reminding us of our mutual responsibilities as citizens. Amitai Etzioni
put forward "communitarianism."[6] Robert Putnam stressed the importance of "social capital,"[7] Francis Fukuyama noted the value of "trust,"[8]
David Selbourne the virtues of "duty,"[9] and a variety of writers have
made the case for "civil society."[10]

In civil society, citizens participate together in their communities and
in mediating organizations, which together comprise a healthy independent sector — and are willing to dissent from established orthodoxy and
official opinion when necessary so long as they remain subject to the rule
of law. Such activity creates "social capital" — the glue that binds people
together in relationships, offering meaning to people's lives in addition to
their role as economic producers or consumers.

Civil society confers meaning, and is the building block for a good
society which values people, regardless of age, gender, race, disability, or
other aspect of social background. Civil society creates a capacity for
leadership within communities that, if harnessed and nurtured, can transform local democracy and reshape the balance of power in favor of greater
social inclusion, justice, dignity, equality of opportunity, and respect.

Using civil society in a global sense offers an opportunity for the
Northern and Western parts of the world to share an identity with the
Southern and Eastern parts. All segments of the globe have strengths and
weaknesses. As Western democracies have come to see some of their limitations, there is scope for further mutual learning based on a principle of
equality between different areas of the world. This might well replace the
old ways of one-way traffic, dating from the Bretton Woods Agreement
of 1944, where aid was the delivery vehicle. Bretton Woods said that it
was the job of the North to develop the South to enable the entire world
to become developed. This purpose, and the missionary zeal with which
it was pursued, appears increasingly unrealistic and out of place.

New Understandings Evident in World's Leading Institutions

There are signs that a new paradigm, using the concept of civil society, is taking hold. Major institutions, such as the World Bank, are
beginning to see the importance of civil society and social capital, and are
setting up social development funds in forty-five countries in the world.
The European Union has been active in creating Civil Society Development Foundations in many of the former communist countries of Central
and Eastern Europe.

Britain, displaying the last vestigial signs of a colonial mentality, has seen its role as exporting its values to the rest of the world. But this arrogant approach is changing. There is new thinking about how values can be the focus of two-way exchanges. The leading British government department concerned with international development has embraced civil society, and so has the British Council, an organization with more than two hundred offices around the world.

Western Exports of Civil Society Models

The paradigm may have changed in favor of civil society, but the methods have not. As Alan Fowler has pointed out, during the 1990s the aid system has developed a mirror view of civil society. Following the collapse of the Berlin Wall, foreign aid set out to create the institutions and organizations that produced democracy in the West with little thought to the entirely different context in Eastern Europe.[11] In Warsaw, Western technical advisors became known derisively as the Marriott Brigade, implying that they stayed at the most expensive hotels and were completely insulated from Polish life.[12] A study by Charities Evaluation Services characterized the Western input into Central and Eastern Europe as the "adoption of the adapted."[13] None of this was really surprising, as much the same approach had been taken by the Western colonial powers in many developing countries.

In doing all this, Westerners also exported their belief in infrastructure. Just as economic developers see the needs for the infrastructure of roads, railways, telephone poles and wires, electricity, and so on, civil society developers see the need for information, training, and technical assistance, opportunities for networking, appropriate legal systems, sensitive fiscal frameworks, finance, and so on.

This is essentially a supply-side model of development. The philosophy of this approach is that, providing the infrastructure is in place, civil society will develop. But just as supply-side economics fails to trickle down to poor people, supply-side civil society development fails to trickle down to communities and citizens. A study of civil society development strategies in five Central and Eastern European countries shows that the main effort has been to create organizations called NGOs.[14] Such organizations are commonly based in capital cities, staffed by young professionals, and offer a variety of programs including information, advice, training, technical assistance, and opportunities for networking. The number of people or organizations benefiting from these services is relatively small. A Webb Memorial Fellow who visited a provincial town in Romania was struck by the gap between the well-educated middle class NGO activists and the mass of the population who had no connection with NGOs.[15] Steven Sampson has shown that one of the main effects of a European program to assist civil society development in Albania has been to import terms like infrastructure development (getting a computer), program management unit (staff of an office), and sustainability (lasting beyond the grant period). Sampson points out that any Albanian wishing to make a career in civil society development must learn two new languages: English and project-speak.[16]

People

This approach leaves out the demand side. Historical studies of the development of NGO sectors show that the key factor is people who pioneer social advance. Studies of such pioneers show that they tend to act out of righteous, religious, or moral anger fired by direct perception of the need to solve a problem. Thomas Barnado, for example, the founder of children's homes in the UK, began his life's work when a child told him "I don't live nowhere." Muhammad Yunus, an economics professor at Chittagong University, tried to persuade banks in Bangladesh to lend to poor people who could offer no collateral. Ridiculed by them, he had little choice but to set up his own bank.

He began in 1976 using his own money and, in 1983, set up the Grameen Bank. His efforts have lifted one-third of borrowers out of poverty, achieved repayment rates of 98 percent, and been repeated in fifty-eight countries of the world. Pioneers are not always leading lights — that is, powerful people with connections. Just as often, they are moving spirits — local people who have had said "enough is enough, and I am going to do something about it." These people are at the core of civil society.

Pioneers tend to be slightly wayward "social" entrepreneurs who pit themselves against enormous odds, and single-mindedly pursue their goals. They can be charismatic, obsessional, and difficult in equal measure, but their contribution to development is often extraordinary.

A civil society development strategy will usually be more effective if it targets people who have a strong mission for change, and only use organizations as delivery vehicles. It makes less sense to build the delivery vehicles and wait for people to come along to drive them.

Knight and Stokes suggest the following intervention strategies for developers of civil society:[17]

Intervention Criterion	Encourage	Discourage
Policy formation	Vision-led	Funding-led
Attitude towards problems	Build on assets	Correct deficits
Medium of exchange	Energy primary	Resource primary
In the lead	Local people	External institutions
Point of intervention	Middle in at the point where locals show energy for issue	Top down or bottom up
Place	Local to global	One place primary
Organizing Principle	Mutual aid	Philanthropy
Allies	Broad support	Narrow support
Solutions required	Workable and obtainable	Effort on unchangeables
Relations with other bodies	Sharing and cooperation	Insular and competitive
Volunteers	Parity with staff	Ancillary
Hierarchy	Flat or shallow	Steep or multi-graded
Professionals	Give technical assistance	Dictate solutions
Consumer	Close relationship	Remote relationship
People	Build political leaders	Offer services
Resources spent	On action	On staff
Surplus resources	Invested	Consumed
Motives	Self interest acknowledged	Self interest masked
Coordination	Peer support & regulation	Intermediary bodies
Race, gender, disability	Equality	White, male dominance
Hours of work	Flexible	Inflexible
Identification	With the oppressed	With the powerful
Funding	Multiple & self-financing	Government
Membership	High priority	Low priority
Stance	Imperious, intuitive	Reactive, rationalist
Delivery	Power sharing	Service
Evaluation	Process/Outcomes	Inputs/Outputs

These principles of development may take us further forward, since they take account of the demand-side imperative.

In *Whose Reality Counts? Putting the First Last,* Robert Chambers suggests that central issues in development have been overlooked, and that many past errors have flowed from those with power.[18] Chambers argues that, by using the methods of participatory rural appraisal (PRA), people in many countries, both in urban and rural settings, have shown an astonishing ability to express and analyze their local, complex, and diverse realities. Often, their views are at odds with the top-down realities imposed by professionals.

To learn from citizens' voices, the Commonwealth Foundation, in partnership with CIVICUS, has since early 1998 been engaged with a major process of research and consultation known as the *Civil Society in the New Millennium* project.

In this project "civil society" is viewed as much more than the collection and sum total of formal, institutional NGOs. The project regards civil society as being about what citizens do, individually and collectively, to meet their needs and advance their own and the general human condition. It is about association, both formal and informal, with others, to do things which need to be done, which are not or cannot be done, or be done better, by the state or by the market. And, it is about connection— between citizens and their institutions of governance and between citizens and their organizations and associations.

The starting premise of the project, and indeed rationale for it, was that civil society needs strengthening from the "bottom-up." Some argue that what people do, individually and together for their own and the common good, is best left to itself, and that the best way for government, business, or other sectors of society to relate to civil society is to leave it alone, and have policies towards it that we have heard called "benign neglect." We disagree. Not only, as we have argued, is the supply-side approach to civil society not working, but many signs have emerged in recent years that individual citizens are increasingly feeling remote and disconnected from the processes and decisions which affect their lives. Benign neglect is not working either, therefore. Citizens feel more and more disempowered by trends towards globalization, competition, and individualism. In turn, the health of civil society — citizens and their collective endeavors constituting the basic fabric of all societies — has suffered. There is less association and less connection.

Through the *Civil Society in the New Millennium* project, the perceptions and experiences of many thousands of individual citizens across the Commonwealth on civil society have been gathered over the past year. The focus has, in principle but not exclusively, been especially listening to citizens whose voices are rarely heard — the "invisibles," "ordinary people." The project has been asking them three main questions:

- What is your view of a good society? How does society of today measure up to that ideal?

- In that society, who in your view should do what? What should be the roles and responsibilities of the citizens, of their government, and of the market?
- In order to achieve that kind of society, what do we need to do?

These questions are being asked in a variety of innovative ways and settings, including individual interviews, focus groups, village meetings, and through radio talk shows and phone-in programs. Since these are abstract questions, answers to them are most commonly being obtained by asking different ones, about people's experiences—their "stories," and about what they feel their needs, rights, and responsibilities are.

From all this will emerge concrete proposals. These will be placed before various fora, about steps government and other actors in society, including individual citizens and their many associations, can take to ensure that the societies in which they live are not just competitive within this globalized world. But rather, societies should be competitive, caring, cohesive, and connective, too.

Notes

1. Martin Van Creveld, *Future War* (New York: Free Press, 1991).
2. John Vida, "Environment: The Real Politics of Power," *The Guardian*, 30 April 1997, Society section, p. 4.
3. Peter Stokes and Barry Knight, *Public Policy and Civil Society* (Birmingham, England: Foundation for Civil Society, 1997).
4. The burden of a policy paper issued by the European Commission in 1996 was that the $50 billion spent under the Lome convention in the last thirty years had been ineffective, and that European taxpayers money had been misspent.
5. Lester Salamon, "The Global Associational Revolution," *Foreign Affairs*, July/August 1994.
6. Amitai Etzioni, *The Spirit of Community: Rights, Responsibilities and the Communitarian Agenda Fontana* (New York: Crown Publishers, 1995).
7. Robert D. Putnam, *Making Democracy Work: Civic Traditions in Modern Italy* (Princeton, NJ: Princeton University Press, 1993). Robert D. Putnam, *Bowling Alone, Revisiting the Responsive Community* (Princeton, NJ: Princeton University Press, 1995).
8. Francis Fukuyama, *Trust: The Social Virtues and the Creation of Prosperity* (New York: Free Press, 1995).
9. David Selbourne, *The Principle of Duty* (New York: Sinclair-Stevenson, 1994).
10. Barry Knight and Peter Stokes, *The Deficit in Civil Society in the United Kingdom* (Birmingham, England: Foundation for Civil Society, 1996).
11. Alan Fowler, *Striking a Balance: A Guide to Enhancing the Effectiveness of Nongovernmental Organizations in International Development* (London: Earthscan Publications, 1997).

12. Kevin F. Quigley, *For Democracy's Sake: Foundations and Democracy Assistance in Central Europe* (Washington, DC: Woodrow Wilson Center Press, 1997).

13. Charities Evaluation Services, *From Transition to Development: The Nonprofit Sectors in Central and Eastern Europe, 1998* (available from Charities Evaluation Services, 4 Coldbath Square, London, EC1R 5HL, enquiries@cesukl.demon.co.uk).

14. Charities Evaluation Services, *From Transition to Development: The Nonprofit Sectors in Central and Eastern Europe, 1998* (available from Charities Evaluation Services, 4 Coldbath Square, London, EC1R 5HL, enquiries@cesukl.demon.co.uk).

15. Simon Balc, *Learning Together in Bristol and Timisoara* (Newcastle upon Tyne: CENTRIS, 1998).

16. Steven Sampson, "The Social Life of Projects," in Chris Han and Elizabeth Dunn, *Civil Society: Challenging Western Models* (London: Routledge, 1996).

17. Barry Knight and Peter Stokes, *Community Development and Civil Society Foundation for Civil Society* (Birmingham, England: Foundation for Civil Society, 1998).

18. Robert Chambers, *Whose Reality Counts? Putting the First Last* (London: Intermediate Technology Publications, 1997).

3

Volunteering: Underpinning Social Action in Civil Society for the New Millennium

Margaret Bell

Why Volunteer in Civil Society?

A s we approach the new millennium it seems appropriate to review the basis for the practice of volunteering. My hypothesis is that the act of volunteering as it is practiced today comes from a pro-active model of behavior borne out of the experience of empowerment, rather than a reactive model resulting from the notion of service delivery. The latter offers a picture of plugging holes which have hitherto been filled by others, or saving governments' or other institutions' money, and it can also be expressed as "doing good." I have never heard a volunteer say they are doing so to save anyone money, or that they want to be remembered as a "good person" in the moralistic sense of the word. It has, however, often been said that people do so because they see the need for change and believe they can make a difference.

The service delivery model for me implies being caught in a net and has arisen from Victorian practices of "benevolence" that began in Europe and continued in the US, when those who "had" were encouraged to volunteer by serving those who were deserving but "had not." Smacked with the moral judgments of the times, volunteering practiced out of this model has been hindered by those and associated judgments since the turn of the last century. Well meaning but patronizing and judgmental, it neither expresses the reason why people chose to volunteer nor does it provide a raison d'être for true service within a community.

The pro-active model of seeing need for change and being sufficiently self-empowered as an individual to believe one can make a contribution and a difference expresses freedom to act, one of the choicest prizes in an environment of democratic freedom. This is the model of volunteering most widely practiced today and provides in itself a good reason to do so.

The Volunteering Tradition

To discover whether or not there is a true volunteering tradition, we must go well beyond the twentieth-century phenomenon of "organized" volunteering we see in countries such as the United States, United Kingdom, Canada, and elsewhere in Europe.

We must also go beyond the experience of the former Soviet Union and parts of Central and Eastern Europe. In this experience, totalitarianism precluded the essential component of free choice of citizens in the act of volunteering and philanthropy. Responses to these concepts are still low. The word "volunteer" can even now evoke a negative response because of the hitherto understood practice of state-demanded volunteering.

Volunteering actually comes out of long established, ancient traditions of sharing. As such, many communities have been linked by strong unwritten social pacts where people have taken as a norm the imperative of sharing their skills, time, ideas, and energy with their neighbors. They have done this in a spirit of reciprocity, something for you, and something for me, and have lived like it for their very survival, generation after generation after generation.

Such values and "volunteer practices" have long existed, side by side, in many cultures in Africa, Latin America, and in Asia and the Pacific region. Some countries in Asia Pacific have recorded histories of such living patterns for as long as five thousand years and beyond.

In the last fifty years in particular, we have seen and felt the effects of enormous diversity in social transformation. We have seen communist governments, state-led socialist governments, totalitarian regimes, and free democracies. Living has become considerably more complex, but at the core of it all and in all its continuing diversity we find the volunteer movement and the practice of volunteer effort at the heart of civil society.

In the midst of and perhaps in answer to the era of changing government regimes, business has produced varied arguments for a new order of "organizational management." Peter Drucker, an organizational management guru, turned his attention to management in the voluntary or third sector during the early 1980s. Some further attention to management of volunteering has been promulgated in the last decade. Running parallel to the management decade, a resurgence has occurred of more ancient traditions around the notion of social pacts and these have been visible by people grouping together in free forming groups to volunteer for change. We now see a proliferation of volunteers working in voluntary organizations, citizens' associations, and people's movements. Volunteers are becoming the backbone of feeding and population programs, health care, housing, environmental and ecological programs, and working in the pursuit of human rights and adult education forums also for the promotion of art, culture, and sports. Other volunteer work involves interaction across racial and socio-economic boundaries to reduce poverty and inequality and enhance the status of women.

Volunteer effort is deeply rooted in communities and civil society across the globe. It is directed towards common concerns that cannot be handled alone by families or even by the extended kinship support system, which is still very strong in some cultures.

Volunteering primarily exists at the local level. It is both managed and unmanaged. In some cultures it is most visible in "organized" ways and clearly seen as part of community life expressed at sporting events, in schools, hospitals, libraries, and in community service and cultural networks.

In other cultures it will be most active through long and unhurried meetings tapping the knowledge of local and indigenous peoples who through volunteer projects offer established methods of sustainable use of common property such as forests, waterways, hunting and fishing grounds, sacred areas, places of worship, and common festivities.

As a result of this work in many environments in the world, we are learning to respect and receive the rich traditions of indigenous organizations with their principles of natural resource management.

Since World War II, many areas of the world have been torn between arbitration regimes and revolution. Powerful volunteer peace movements have flourished and whole generations of young people in particular have demanded an end to war and/or oppression in parts of Central and Eastern Europe, in Africa, the Arab region, Latin America, and in Asia Pacific.

Volunteering today is not therefore a passive reaction to something but rather a pro-active demand for a range of different causes.

Reciprocity, Globalization, and Volunteering

Reciprocity seems to be a key word in understanding volunteering as it was once, and again as it is being practiced now with a degree of success in many cultures. In order to fulfill communities' needs for increased civic action in the future, we will do well to understand more about this idea.

We see that through today's experience of globalization, lines of trade and interpersonal and cultural relations are no longer limited by socio-economic, religious, or cultural mores. They are not even limited by distance or information. All is accessible to all through the information highway, the telephone, and the fax. What binds in these arenas is not dictated by the comfort zone of the past or the entrenched belief system of our elders, but rather the new spirit of reciprocity. Is there something in this agreement for me and something in it for you? As long as an agreement is of enough significance to both parties to remain in partnership, we do so. As long as the answer to this question remains "yes," the deal will continue, be it personal, business, or at the state level.

Reciprocity is also the trademark of the modern act of volunteering, particularly in the changing landscape of civil society and its impact on health and the viability of our world as the new millennium unfolds.

Through the volunteer movement, civil society is keenly urged to take a stronger and more visible profile in the shaping of public life in the new millennium. In so doing it has to strengthen its equal relationship with players within civil society and with governments and business everywhere.

CIVICUS, as both a principal civil society organization for solidarity and a worldwide movement within the sector and across sectors, can play this role in a significant way through massive volunteer resource mobilization at global and local levels. Volunteering is one of the strongest tools civil society has. Civil society needs to use it wisely and well to reinforce the values it wishes to draw out of communities and to build solidarity within each community of which it is a part.

Volunteering at the Core of Social Action

From local environs, particularly rural, regional, and remote areas, we are strengthened in discovering the tool of volunteering to enable us to value the concept of solidarity in civil society and to practice it across regions of the world.

We were once urged to think globally and act locally. Now, in the spirit of a renewed understanding of reciprocity and the experience of globalization, we are urged to think and act together, locally, nationally, and globally.

Volunteering lies at the core of social action in civil society. We see this in the experiences of the great challenges to our humanity today, in the aftermath of war, during natural disasters, when facing environmental degradation, and in dealing with crises created by poverty and fear, like unemployment, underemployment, increased crime rates, corruption, substance abuse, homelessness, and family breakdown.

Volunteer effort has created very important paradigm shifts during the last decade, such as:

- the work done in promoting the role of indigenous cultures as key to social and environmental transformation, rather than seeing indigenous people as a bunch of diminishing tribes to be increasingly less concerned about;

- volunteer peasant movements have formed the basis of grassroots democracy;

- trade unions have always operated through volunteer effort and have led movements for social and national change. In some cases they have put governments out of power, such as in Australia, New Zealand, and Japan;

- the women's movement has been propelled in its action by volunteer effort. It penetrates all classes and sectors of society, contributing hugely to the challenging of the male-dominated and male-oriented world view of reality;

- the need to exercise one's rights strongly motivates men, women, and children to volunteer. Through volunteer effort, people expand their choices in life, exercise self-determination, fight for good government, and strive to create a more equitable and stable social order and a better quality of life;

- volunteer effort often finds its roots and motivation in a strong spiritual power. It lies beyond what I might get, and has more to do with what I might become. In addition to the understood role of orthodox faiths such as Christianity, Islam, Judaism, Buddhism, and Hinduism, many indigenous people, and those who practice paganism, and other alternative forms of worship, offer expressions of a search for union with something outside of the self as they invoke the power of the spirits or a deity beyond, often as they struggle to protect a piece of land, the sea, or animals within it.

Perhaps two of the largest and certainly very effective civil society organizations in the world relying very heavily on the volunteer movement are the Sarvodaya movement in Sri Lanka and the Bangladesh Rural

Advancement Committee. The Sarvodaya movement in Sri Lanka, with three thousand paid professional workers and a hundred thousand volunteers working throughout eight hundred villages, strives to build democracy from a grassroots approach. The movement helps the people mobilize their own resources, especially their labor, while staying attuned to the country's spiritual and cultural values.

The Bangladesh Rural Advancement Committee (BRAC) has six thousand paid staff and many thousands of volunteers covering fifteen thousand villages of Bangladesh. BRAC offers informal functional education, family planning, health education, legal awareness, and savings and credit programs. It now has more than thirty thousand volunteer-staffed village organizations, with a membership of more than one million people, of which women account for 65 percent. These organizations have supervised the distribution of over fifty million dollars worth of credit disbursements with repayment rates of 97 to 98 percent. Volunteering in Bangladesh is not filling gaps or offering "feel-good" activities as volunteering is sometimes described in other places. Rather, volunteering is at the cutting edge where change is needed and where it is truly making a difference.

Volunteer Effort: A Tool for Change, but Not for Free

We have reflected on how the concept of globalization came to us with an announcement of hope, hope for a more equitable environment and the promise of a sustainable future. But our most urgent human problems are not becoming lighter. Instead, the rich are getting richer, the poor poorer, and there is concern that the middle class is disappearing altogether.

The promise of new technologies in the information age has been one of hope that we will be able to build a better world. Civil society, however, continues its struggle to realize the social and economic rights of our people in this contradiction of experience.

Volunteer effort, it becomes clear, can be drawn upon in communities as a strong tool to reinforce the belief that it is only through true citizen participation that we can really build a better world.

Ordinary men and women have a deep capacity and even an innate desire to organize themselves for change and for betterment of themselves and their communities. When they dare to volunteer to make a difference, this desire, together with the belief in the need for change, draws us beyond even our own survival need, into our fully intended stature in the public arena. It is something beyond, something outside of material pursuits, and is, instead, related to the enrichment of the human spirit, our own and others. It is neither the property of the rich nor the poor; it belongs to humankind and is available to all.

Volunteering is an act committed in free choice. It is a decision taken in response to our own personal value and belief system at the deepest point. The process follows a wish to change something, a free choice to consider the wish, a prizing or valuing of the personal wish and finally the decision to act upon the wish and to make it happen.

We do not have to "volunteer for good." The act of volunteering does not have a morality in itself. We could choose to volunteer for destruction, for harm, or for evil — and some do. We have the capacity to choose to volunteer as a crucial value decision to build up the earth.

Paulo Freire said: "Dialogue can only go forward when it is based on the hope of building partnership." Paulo's idea can be realized in the mandate of CIVICUS in civil society and in the motivation of the volunteer.

The modern volunteer is perhaps the new believer, that is, believing that the hungry can be fed and the earth saved from destruction we inflict upon it. The volunteer believes change is really going to happen and that I must change, you must change, and we must change together.

Volunteer Management for Future

Volunteer effort is a tool for change in civil society and volunteers, in turn, need additional tools to do their job well. Volunteers need to know they are needed. They need to be sought after, to know what jobs are required of them, and in turn, they may think of others. They need to know if there will be skills training and information about wider goals of the project. They need supervision of their work, including having it recognized and evaluated. They need to be trusted, informed, and, sometimes, transported and fed. Like others, they like it when someone says thank you.

One of the strong keys for building civil society for the future will be the deployment of competent, appropriately organized, and well-managed volunteers. Nations' action plans for building the social economy will need to give attention to developing clear policies and standards for volunteering, working to national competencies for volunteer management, and setting in place appropriate infrastructure for its establishment or continuity. Recognition of the volunteer movement in each of its communities at local, national, and global levels is essential.

Civil society needs recruitment strategies and training for those who work closely with volunteers, including civil society leaders, volunteer managers, and volunteers, themselves. Plans need to be put in place to support, measure, and evaluate volunteer effort. Recognition and celebration of volunteer effort is important, such as on 5 December — International Volunteer Day. Volunteering needs to be measured in the national accounts and recognized as an alternative to, but never a substitute for, paid work. It should be measured and valued for the contribution it makes to social cohesion, and the men and women who volunteer should be recognized and applauded for their contribution to strengthening the communities of which they are a part.

Volunteer effort can make an enormous contribution to the growing strength of ordinary citizens, which is indeed on the rise, but is yet far from nearing its true potential. Too few know how much they are really needed and instead run the risk of leading unrewarding lives, because the volunteer movement lacks both the human and financial resources it needs to grow at every level.

Volunteering Professionals

A rising tension that needs to be considered in future planning for volunteer management is that which may exist between volunteers and paid workers. Some cultures experience high tension, others little. Highly industrialized environments often negotiate working conditions with trade unions. In determining volunteering standards and policies, we find that volunteers for the new millennium need not be excluded from any area of responsibility in relation to building community. As long as individuals carry sufficient skills for the task at hand, they have a right to contribute what they have to offer.

Time given to the job is a major differential between paid and volunteer work. Time needed for tasks undertaken is to be carefully negotiated to avoid exploitation and unrealistic expectations of the volunteer. Limited time, however, does not represent limited skill, but it does represent the need to agree to definitive areas of responsibility within the framework of time available to volunteers. Managing the volunteer time of others calls for particular coordination skills to provide continuity of service. In addition to consideration for volunteers, paid workers in civil society organizations often give much of their time to tasks required and without financial remuneration. Such work therefore becomes partly paid and partly voluntary. Some "volunteers" receive a small stipend for work undertaken or villages and organizations benefit from monies earned.

Volunteers coming from abroad are sometimes remunerated at considerably lower levels than they would earn in their home countries. All are part of the volunteer movement. All work to strengthen civil society and to help it function efficiently. Volunteering professionals are those who are committed to and involved in growing the volunteer movement. It is a commitment to volunteerism grounded in values associated with civil norms that created the criteria for volunteering professionals. Such men and women may be either paid for their work; for example, the paid staff of a volunteer center or they may be deployed as volunteers. Payment is not the significant factor, commitment to excellence is. This is what causes an individual to be considered "professional" or not.

Role of Government and Business in Volunteering

Government needs to make policy about volunteering in collaboration with civil society organizations and leaders in volunteering. It needs to promote the notion and to resource its infrastructure. Then, it needs to stand back and let it happen. Government does not need to run volunteer programs because it does so badly. Volunteering is part of civil society.

In the UK, government got into policymaking and program delivery and was roundly criticized by civil society organizations (Third Sector, 6 October 94). Responsibility for volunteering was moved from the department of health and social services to national heritage in 1996. Perhaps it would have been handled with greater expertise by the national body on volunteering. In 1997, a volunteering partnership scheme replaced the two previous initiatives and a survey on volunteering published in 1998 showed overall levels of volunteering had declined.

New labor has recently introduced its "Millennium Volunteers Scheme" and its "Giving Age Initiative." It is a combination of government involvement in practice and policy with government in England having a strong hands-on role in service delivery. In Scotland and Wales, the program is more in the hands of civil society organizations, the National Volunteer Centres. The international volunteer movement will watch the intervention with interest.

Civil society organizations and volunteers throughout the world have particularly welcomed the appeal of many government members to the United Nations Economic and Social Council seeking the declaration of the Year of the Volunteer.

The government of Japan proposed the declaration following the International Association for Volunteer Effort's world conference in Japan in 1994 and was solidly supported by many governments in the ensuing three years before the United Nation's Secretary General announced the year 2001 as the Year of the Volunteer.

Governments can now play a key support role in the development of the volunteer movement worldwide by:

- working with leaders in volunteering and national associations for volunteering where they exist to establish committees at national and local levels to plan the Year of the Volunteer. Creating or supporting an appropriate infrastructure to carry volunteering into the next millennium in their countries;

- pledging to measure volunteering in the national accounts;

- creating appropriate national policy to allow volunteer activities to take place in civil society through freedom of association;

- encouraging business to become involved in supporting volunteer effort in civil society organizations by offering human and financial resources to make it happen;

- assisting leaders in volunteering from their country to attend the international association for volunteer effort world conference on volunteering 14–17 January, Amsterdam 2001;

- hosting a major recognition event to celebrate volunteering underpinning social action in civil society in their country during 2001.

Each of these steps would be supportive and collaborative, in harmony with the vision of the volunteer movement but without tampering with it.

David Korten, noted author on civil society, has said: "The 1980s saw a growing rejection of the myth that government is the sole legitimate agent for development decision-making and the management of development resources. It is now widely accepted that civil society has an essential, if not central, role in both." The same may easily be said for the volunteer movement for the new millennium, wherein government has a strong support but not a governance role.

The volunteer movement needs to design and shape its own future in close association with each nation's traditions, belief systems, and developing practices within its civil society. Government needs to walk beside this movement, promoting it and supporting its existence, but they cannot afford to walk in front, selecting poorly researched programs and projects nor behind, ignoring the strength of a movement that can greatly enhance the growth of civil society for the next decade.

Business and volunteering may not at first seem like natural bedfellows, but there is an underlying experience of reciprocity to be examined. Business needs healthy connected communities in which to trade. Unhealthy communities do not buy.

Many companies are seeking partnerships within civil society organizations to realize their corporate citizenship programs. Such programs are shaping corporate/community relations for the new millennium and "employee volunteering" looms high among the strategies companies examine to facilitate their community involvement.

"Employee volunteering" offers company employees work experience in another sector. Some take up the option by company agreement within office hours, others in their own free time but with company support for the project of their involvement.

Citizens employed in business or government and who choose to do voluntary work in civil society organizations bring with them skills, qualifications, experiences, and expertise that may otherwise be beyond the resources of the receiving organization.

Employee volunteering creates an ideal pathway for market and civil society organizations to travel together as citizens, each learning from and enriching the lives of the other.

An overriding challenge to civil society is to create enough understanding of and visibility for its organizations to be able to raise the human and financial resources needed to become a society that cares for its people. Engaging government and business in appropriately supporting the volunteer movement and its development does much to mainstream the concerns of ordinary citizens and to address breaking societal barriers and misconceptions across the three sectors.

Our capacity to volunteer for the future of civil society as a whole and for each corner of civil society in our own nations cannot become a mere set of recipes we learn from one another, or a set of stipulated services we perform. Rather, sustainable volunteer effort springs from our histories, traditions and personal belief systems. It is drawn too from our sense of spirit or national identity and comes from our cultural and artistic awareness, our own inner self. Volunteers come from living communities and return to those communities in a way that those of us who leave villages, houses, and communities every day in order to work elsewhere cannot hope to do. As such, volunteers bring an authenticity to this work that others cannot share but can indeed learn from.

The volunteer movement becomes strong in our land only when we are able to root it firmly in our own society and the customs of all our people within civil society.

Challenges for the Volunteer
Movement towards the New Millennium

Together volunteer citizens and civil society organizations are challenged to:

- Encourage the practice of volunteerism grounded in values such as reciprocity, tolerance, inclusion, and trust, usually associated with social norms. Thus, bearing in mind that the act of volunteering does not have a morality in itself, it is possible to volunteer for good or for evil. The challenge for civil society is to encourage volunteering as a choice for building the common good.

- Build meaningful relationships between volunteers of different races and between generations and women and men. To use volunteer effort to build bridges of understanding and to effect true reconciliation.

- Approach the International Year of the Volunteer 2001 to build specific ties between civil society organizations from different sectors such as health, welfare, sport, environment, people's movements, sustainable development, arts, education, trade unions, co-operatives, and human rights organizations.

- Seek new partners from academic life to research, monitor, and evaluate volunteering, and to offer volunteering opportunities through university faculties (excellent model at the University of the Philippines, 1996); and talk up, argue with, and confront the values of volunteering in the media.

- Engage governments in providing appropriate infrastructure for volunteering in their countries, and measuring it in the annual accounts.

- Work with business to create awards programs for volunteering excellence, to support a National Volunteer Week, to sponsor the celebration of International Volunteer Day and to participate in the development of employee volunteering programs. Companies may also be invited to second "volunteers for a year," on loan from business to civil society projects for special purposes.

- Select best practice education and training programs that will offer sound organizational volunteer management skills whilst building on the experience of empowering citizen participation at local levels.

In summary, there are two great challenges for volunteering in civil society for the new millennium:

- We need to find a way to build a sound citizen participatory activity base to develop volunteering in local communities that is rooted in our own traditions and cultures.

- We need to find a way to have volunteering in local communities recognized as national phenomena in all countries.

Traps to Avoid

- Seeing volunteering or the volunteer movement as synonymous with and an automatic part of the voluntary or third sector. Many voluntary organizations within civil society do not deploy the services of volunteers or believe in volunteering as a value. Volunteering is a matter of free choice. Choices to be taken by the men and women who choose to volunteer, and the organizations, movements, and associations who choose to work with them.

- Any form of imperialism or fundamentalist thought associated with the act of volunteering. Both create unhealthy dependencies. Imperialist models transfer programs and policies built for one culture and impose them on another. Often part of a notion of benevolence, such a model acts without regard for traditions, customs, need, culture, and belief systems. As such the spirit of reciprocity cannot grow and be sustained.

- Fundamentalist righteousness of any kind is a dangerous practice when associated with volunteering. Providing answers where it may only be truly feasible to question and holding people in a framework of moralistic judgment and more often condemnation. This model can only be seen as doing to rather than the liberating choice of freedom to act for.

Civil society and CIVICUS, as an organization and a movement, can foster volunteer effort. By doing so, we can do more than we do today to achieve our goal, to share more, and to become stronger.

Anywhere the act of volunteering becomes a little better understood, recognized for what it is, and called upon as an essential part of the fabric of our society, be it locally or globally, communities become healthier and more viable.

Many workers within civil society organizations feel deeply burdened by the multiple responsibilities they carry both professionally and personally. In most cases, we operate in high demand for service and low budget environs. This can lead to disproportionate fatigue, fear, and lack of energy resulting in a tendency to operate in the framework of a blaming mentality and to behave as victims.

Within civil society organizations, however, we can discover a great source of riches because we have the privilege of working with people who live and think in a spirit of optimism. This spirit binds volunteers all over the world because they are citizens who by nature see a glass as half full rather than half empty. Volunteers make a free choice every day of their lives to put something into growing our communities, just because they want to make a difference and believe they can do so. Such an attitude pervades the environment in which volunteers are found and creates a positive and healthy energy.

Through volunteer citizen participation in local, national, and global environs, we have a stronger opportunity to build a secure and prosperous future for our children and our children's children. The desire to make a difference is innate in us, and the volunteer movement is a momentum rooted in the citizens of our communities. It is one we cannot stop. Herein lies the hope we cannot fail to have and the belief we cannot fail to find.

The natural life ingredient of volunteers is to believe in a better tomorrow. We work with the richest natural resource in the world when we choose to work with them.

References

Davis Smith, Justin. *The 1997 National Survey of Volunteering*. Institute for Voluntary Research, 1998.

Drucker, Peter F. "The New Society of Organizations." In *Harvard Business Review* 70, no. 5 (1992): 95–105.

Fukuyama, F. *Trust: The Social Virtues and the Creation of Prosperity*. London: Hamish Hamilton, 1995.

Hodgkinson, V.A. and M.S. Weitzman. *Giving and Volunteering in the United States. Findings from a National Survey*. Washington, DC: Independent Sector, 1996.

Johns Hopkins University Institute for Policy Studies. Comparative Non-Profit Sector Project. Module on Giving and Volunteering. Washington, DC: Johns Hopkins University Institute for Policy Studies, 1996.

Kandil, Amani. *Report on the Arab Region*. Available from CIVICUS, 919 18th Street NW, Washington, DC. (202) 331-8518 or info@civicus.org.

Kotkin, J. *Tribes*. New York: Random House, 1992.

Latham, M. "Making Welfare Work," Bert Kelly Lecture, Centre for Independent Studies, Sydney, Australia, 1996.

Lyons, M. *Nonprofit Sector or Civil Society.* CACOM Working Paper No. 35, CACOM, University of Technology, Sydney, 1996.

Pinkerton, E. and M. Weinstein. *Fisheries that Work: Sustainability through Community-Based Management.* Vancouver: The David Suzuki Foundation, 1995.

Serrano, Isagani, R. *Civil Society in the Asia Pacific Region.* Washington, DC: CIVICUS, 1994.

Shear, J. "From Lady Bountiful to Active Citizen: Volunteering and the Voluntary Sector." In Davis Smith, Justin, et al, *An Introduction to the Voluntary Sector* (London, New York: Routledge, 1995).

Tandon, Rajesh and Miguel Darcy de Oliveira. *Citizens: Strengthening Global Civil Society.* Washington, DC: CIVICUS, 1994.

4

Civil Society and Indigenous Peoples

Caren Wickliffe

The root problems created by the domination of one cultural paradigm over another are at the heart of the indigenous experience of today's world. Until these core concerns are dealt with, the common symptoms of contact, conflict, and crisis will remain. Until the common threads of intrusion are identified, examined, and compared, there can be no attempt to reweave the cloth that forms indigenous societies.[1]

Discussing the situation of Indigenous Peoples or First Nations in a book about strengthening civil society is important because too often those who write about the state of civil society ignore the unique place of Indigenous Peoples. Probably, this is because it can not be easy to write about indigenous communities and their participation rate when all the negative statistics on crime, health status, imprisonment rates, education status, housing status, and so forth, indicate significant indigenous marginalization and disengagement, rather than participation. The reasons for this marginalization and disengagement are complex and relate to the fact that during the process of colonization, Indigenous Peoples were subjected to systematic attacks on their precolonial status and rights that in turn resulted in indigenous dispossession and the breakdown of traditional ways of life.

However, I am still critical that the theorists, in their haste to define civil society, have forgotten that Indigenous Peoples do not comfortably fit into the triangular definition of state, market, or civil society. As a collective, Indigenous Peoples occupy a different space. This space underscores the point that they were and still are sovereign First Nations or Peoples with a priori rights. In their space they manifest governmental and juridical capacity, their own form of laws and citizenship, and their own tenure systems of land and natural resource use. Individuals of indigenous nations can, therefore, be subject to two forms of competing jurisdictional power, enjoy dual citizenship, and be formally engaged or disengaged as citizens in two alternative forms of civil society.

Indigenous civil societies, at least in the countries I have studied, were traditionally collective in nature, based on kinship with predetermined social orders that dictated the division of labor and formed the basis for communal action. Before the impacts of colonialism they were societies that demanded active participation and some form of allegiance. In these societies public service was desirable and was valued for its contribution to the advancement of the collective good. Individuals in such a society had as many reciprocal duties as rights and their rank or status determined their degree of participation in decision-making. In contemporary times, there are many "active" individuals who continue to follow lifestyles that are adaptations of traditional modes of life. Alternatively, they have disengaged from these societies for a number of reasons including:

- the influence of Western values through homogenizing education systems that have undervalued or rendered invisible the history and culture of Indigenous Peoples;
- rapid urbanization; and
- involvement in the cash economy.

In comparison, the contemporary and highly or contestable conceptualization of civil society as it has evolved since the last century has a high regard for individual freedom and autonomy and uncoerced human association. As a number of theorists have warned, such values can legitimize unbridled capitalism, citizen self-interest, and selfish action as much as they can encourage public service and citizen action to defend and promote rights vis-à-vis those who have the power to deny those rights. The indigenous experience, their status, and their rights have no place in this realm, and Indigenous Peoples know it and often disengage because of it — alternatively they resist it.

Bearing in mind these differences, this chapter addresses some of the historical and legal barriers inhibiting the engagement of Indigenous Peoples in post-colonial society, including a review of the resistance they have waged to maintain or reclaim their precolonial status. Then, I consider what legal environment is needed to encourage greater participation in society while ensuring the survival of the unique ways of life of Indigenous Peoples beyond the new millennium. Finally, I review what paradigmatic shift to the state, civil society, and the market are required to ensure the survival of Indigenous Peoples and their unique ways of life.

Eurocentrism

The common experience of Indigenous Peoples colonized by the Europeans has been one of land and natural resource dispossession and alienation, oppression, marginalization, integration, or assimilation. In many cases it has been a common experience laced by human rights abuses and acts of atrocity[2] that have been supported or legitimized by governments and the legal frameworks within which they operate.

If we go back to the beginning of exploration of the "New World" we find the root cause of their common colonial experience was ideological. Countries of the European continent and Britain were the "civilized" nations in the center of the world, as it was then. Beyond these territories, there was the "void."

Into the void, the Europeans would take their notions of statehood, religion, economy, intellect, technology, creativity, imagination, innovation, restraint, rationality, honor, and ethics. These would be their tools in the creation of a new and civilized body politic, the "colonial state," governed by European values and norms. Imperial expansion through colonization would be the result. Preexisting indigenous nations and their citizens would be the recipients, by diffusion, of European civilization.

As compensation for bringing civilization, the European explorer or settler could take the resources of indigenous nations and disseminate this material wealth back to Europe. The indigenous nations could choose not to participate in the benefits of this new civilization, but they could not resist it, nor could they stop its advance. Underlying this process was an ideological belief system identified by James Blaut as "Eurocentric diffusionism." As he explains, diffusionism:

> ... is a theory about the way cultural processes tend to move over the surface of the world as a whole. They tend to flow out of the European sector and toward the non-European sector. This is the natural, normal, logical, and ethical flow of culture, of innovation, of human casualty. Europe, eternally, is Inside. Non-Europe is Outside. Europe is the source of most diffusion; non-Europe is the recipient.

European theories about the nature and state of Indigenous Peoples determined the process of colonization. Eurocentric notions of the superiority of European civilization generated these theories. By comparison, Indigenous Peoples were considered uncivilized, inferior, incapable of conducting sovereign relations and of holding full dominion over their territories.

Early theories of international law have shown that this categorization legitimized imperialism and colonization and led to the denigration of precolonial indigenous status and rights. The international legal system has been directed and nurtured like a child by the European states. It is a system that has been designed to benefit the European elite.[3] The system has supported the development of nation states based on geographical boundaries rather than the natural affiliations of peoples. The advent of the state system is a relatively recent phenomenon in history, developing only after the Peace of Westphalia in 1648. The theories of law that underpinned the process of diffusing European civilization from the core of Europe to the territories of Indigenous Peoples have included:

- the divine sanction theory, based on the religious mandate and necessity of propagating Christianity throughout the world;

- the guardianship/ward theory, which marked Indigenous Peoples as being of an alternative status — one that was unfit to found or administer a lawful state;

- the nomad theory, which argued that unoccupied or uncultivated territory, even where Indigenous Peoples who were hunters and gatherers were present, could be occupied by a colonizing state;

- the statehood theory, which defined the sovereignty over territory in Eurocentric terms;

- the *terra nullius* theory, in which territory where the Indigenous Peoples present lacked the political cohesion and sovereign capacity necessary, by Eurocentric definitions, could be colonized; and

- the impact of international law theory, in which the basic theories of European-based international law underpinned the process of diffusing European civilization outside the core of Europe to the territories of Indigenous Peoples (the periphery).

Based on these theories, the European states developed a set of rules that would clarify who held title to territory during the process of colonization. By the application of these rules, European colonizing states could undertake as many self-seeking acts as were necessary to found the best claims to territory. These acts included conquest, entering into treaties with indigenous polities, or claiming title by settlement. These acts were necessary, not to convince the prior inhabitants of the legitimacy of

European claims, but to validate claims of a colonizing European power vis-à-vis other European powers. Ultimately, continuing displays of territorial sovereignty by the colonizing power confirmed title and "might made right" on the frontiers.[4]

The imposition of the international legal system and its rules regarding territory disrupted many indigenous polities, resulting in the loss of recognition for their precolonial forms of nationhood and their international personality. This in turn made them subject to the municipal legal systems of their colonizers and resulted in their marginalization from colonial society.

The story of every indigenous nation under the domination of their colonizers and the legal systems that were used to validate this process is beyond the scope of this chapter. What can be said, is that any state that has as its core a foundation of legitimacy that can be sourced to this Eurocentric belief system, is a state that will be subject to significant indigenous challenge.

Since the establishment of the United Nations in 1945, this truth has been recognized in the UN Charter. Article one called for "respect for the principles of equal rights and self-determination of peoples." The procedures in the Charter have been used to ensure the decolonization and independence of over one hundred former colonial territories in Africa, the Caribbean, Asia, and the Pacific — territories of Indigenous Peoples. The challenge the international community now faces is how to deal with the remaining colonial territories (for example, Guam, Virgin Islands, New Caledonia) and those territories where there remain significant communities of Indigenous Peoples calling for recognition of their First Nation status (for example, French Polynesia, Bolivia, Guatemala, Mexico, Canada, Aotearoa/New Zealand, Australia, the United States). Added to these developments, in the last twenty years the voices of Indigenous Peoples have reached the international arena on an unprecedented level. With the support of modern technology, and against major opposition from many governments, Indigenous Peoples are finding each other and a unity of purpose in international, regional, multilateral, bilateral, and national forums. They are extending the boundaries of their own domestic situations to the international arena. They are searching for justice, redress for past grievances, political recognition of their unique status as First Nations, recognition of their right to self-determination, protection of treaty rights, protection of their remaining lands and natural resources, maintenance and respect for their ways of life, and protection from human rights violations.

They are challenging orthodox international law on who has the right to self-determination before the Human Rights Committee in such cases as *Ominayak v. Canada* (1992).[5] They are challenging the traditional paradigm of the State and citizen. They were a major force at international forums such as United Nations Conference on Environment and Development (UNCED) and the Convention on Biodiversity. They have taken direct action and developed their own positions through international instruments such as the Mataatua Declaration on the Cultural and Intellectual Property Rights of Indigenous Peoples. They have influenced multilateral organizations such as the ILO, the World Bank, and the Asian Development Bank.

They have also presented themselves in overwhelming numbers to directly address their issues and concerns to the United Nations Commission on Human Rights, its Sub-Commission on Prevention of Discrimination and Protection of Minorities and the Working Group on Indigenous Populations. These issues and concerns are now reflected in the Draft Declaration on the Rights of Indigenous Peoples, currently before the Commission on Human Rights. The process leading to the drafting of the Declaration marks a milestone in the history of the United Nations. This has been possible because the United Nations Commission on Human Rights, Sub-Commission and the Working Group on Indigenous Populations recognized they must address the situation of Indigenous Peoples or face continued indigenous resistance and citizen disengagement. Now, whether or not the Draft Declaration on the Rights of Indigenous Peoples is ultimately accepted by States, it is clear that Indigenous Peoples from around the globe have used the drafting process as a way of reaching a consensus on what measures are needed to preserve their status as First Nations and continue their ways of life into the new millennium.

Indigenous Resistance at the National Level

At the national level Indigenous Peoples have resisted imperialism and colonization. From their position of resistance, Indigenous Peoples have made various attempts to either disengage from the State or alternatively to reverse the impacts of colonization so as to maintain their own unique ways of life as First Nations. Three stories of colonization from former British territories and the stories of indigenous resistance are used here to illustrate this point. The stories are taken from Great Turtle Island/North America and Aotearoa/New Zealand.

Great Turtle Island/North America

The Americas were once entirely under the control of Indigenous Peoples. Before the diffusion from Europe most of North America was actually possessed and used by native communities. Brian Slattery has explained that:

> When Europeans first came to America and the Antipodes, they encountered numerous bodies of indigenous peoples, occupying definite territories to the exclusion of other groups, factually independent, sovereign within their borders, and vested with their own customary laws and political systems.[6]

Between 1400 and 1800, European colonizing states believed that it was perfectly acceptable for subjects of European monarchs to claim and colonize the territories of Indigenous Peoples, so long as the territory had not been claimed by another from the inner circle — Europe. Initially during colonization there would be dependence on Indigenous Peoples, however, once in a position of strength, the nature of the relationship between the two sovereign peoples would change. As Indigenous Peoples were considered to be "savages" or "barbarians" who, rightly, could be subjected to the rule of European monarchs, their claim to sovereignty and title to land would later be ignored, or recognized only to the extent required to guarantee peaceful settlement of the new territories.

The intentions of the Europeans to colonize, regardless of the views of the prior inhabitants, are reflected in the early letters, patents, and charters of the English monarchs granted to their subjects who would begin the dispersal to the outer circle, the New World. The colonizers sought to obtain title to territory by cession, purchase, and conquest. In doing so, they secured their authority by recognizing only certain aspects of the precolonial status and rights of Indigenous Peoples on whom, in large measure, they were initially dependent. Instead of conforming to indigenous legal systems, the colonizers applied and lived by their own laws. The following section reviews the situation of Indigenous Peoples during the period when European diffusionism was at its most rampant.

Canada

Between 1700 and 1921, there were three discernible periods of Anglo-Indigenous relations in the territories that would make up modern-day Canada. During the early years, the British Crown conducted nation-to-nation relations with Indian and Inuit polities. Treaties of friendship and alliance were negotiated on a regular basis indicating British acceptance of the inherent sovereign capacity of these peoples. During the second period, and once the British Crown was able to assert territorial sovereignty, Indian polities and their citizens were subjugated to British law and control. The third period, after Confederation, saw a transferal of power over Indian Affairs to the Federal Government and the policy of land cession by treaty. The outcome of all three periods was the gradual herding of Indian peoples onto reserves in the provinces as well as the centralization of federal control over all areas of Indian life through the Indian Act of 1876 and its subsequent amendments.

Through these successive attacks on their precolonial status and rights, First Nations adapted their modes of resistance. They have maintained their desire to be indigenous. The evidence is that the policies of assimilation, disguised as law, failed to achieve their objectives. Many Indigenous Peoples of Canada have retained their unique identity based on their precolonial sovereign status and rights.

Rather than circumscribing First Nation governments, in coming years, as the Government of Canada commences to recognize the governments of First Nations, it will face an old challenge which will require new responses. That challenge revolves around the traditional laws, political institutions, and leadership of First Nations. Over one hundred years of repressive legislation has not been able to terminate these manifestations of aboriginal sovereignty. In the urban areas, resistance by individual Indians has manifested itself by anti-social behavior resulting in increased marginalization and lack of engagement.

Indigenous resistance has forced concessions from the federal government and since 1982 Indigenous Peoples in Canada have enjoyed constitutional protection of their rights and many outstanding land claims have been negotiated and settled. While there is some recognition of an Indian self-government, the full right to full sovereignty, the development of an intentional personality, and the right to full self-determination remain to be settled.

USA

Following the American Revolution, the process of colonization was centralized and accelerated by the United States Congress. The authority of the Congress was initially provided for in the Articles of Confederation in 1777–89 and the Constitution in 1789. The power of Congress over Indian Affairs was increased with the passage of the Northwest Ordinance of 1789 and the Trade and Intercourse Acts of 1790. These statutes prevented the trade in Indian lands except under treaty of the United States. Treaty making became the most important instrument of colonization from 1790 to 1871. The treaties coupled with overt acts of war and violence were used to push Indian tribes into smaller and smaller enclaves. Today many of these enclaves form part of the modern Indian reservation system.

The mid-1800s on was an age when Indian lands were wrested from the Indigenous Peoples of America by a vicious circle of expansion, removal, allotment of Indian lands to non-Indians, BIA control of tribal governments, liquidation, and termination.

Despite the odds, the Indigenous Peoples of the USA have withstood over five hundred years of Spanish, French, Dutch, English, and American invasion. They have continued; they have survived. Their struggle illustrates the potential tenacity and longevity of indigenous resistance to annihilation or assimilation, and offers an insight into the enduring nature of indigenous belief in their own inherent sovereignty, status, rights to govern themselves, define their citizenship, and develop their own systems of land tenure and property.

In the USA, indigenous resistance has taken a number of forms. Last century, in some regions, it manifested itself in war. By the turn of the century, Indian resistance was by retreat to the reservations, but by the mid-twentieth century Indian resistance moved to the legal system through the land claims process. In the 1960s–1970s it manifested itself in the renaissance of tribal identity and the protests of the American Indian Movement. During the 1980s–1990s, with a sympathetic Supreme Court, it took the form of legal action to prevent state or federal attempts to erode Indian sovereignty or attempts to deny land and natural resource claims.

Indigenous resistance has forced concessions from the federal government. Since 1971 there have been a series of statutes passed which have been designed to devolve more power to Indian tribal governments and many outstanding land claims have been negotiated and settled. While there is some recognition of a diminished Indian sovereignty, the right to full sovereignty, the development of an intentional personality, and the right to full self-determination remain to be settled.

Aotearoa[7]/New Zealand

By the nineteenth century, Britain had decided, based on colonial office reports on indigenous political institutions, legal systems, land tenure rules, production, and so forth, that colonization in New Zealand should proceed on a "legal" basis. The British, therefore, entered the Treaty of Waitangi of 1840 with Maori polities. This was a treaty that, in the English version, actively sought the transferal of territorial sovereignty to the British Crown but which in the Maori version preserved and guaranteed Maori rights to sovereignty/autonomy and self-government over their citizens and their property. Thus, in this manner the British entered into nation-to-nation relations through the Treaty of Waitangi with Maori polities and secured the right to govern over British citizens through their guarantee to respect Maori *rangatiratanga* — the inherent sovereignty of Maori. But as in the Americas, successive colonial governments would restrict this pattern of government and Maori status and rights were diminished in order to justify indigenous dispossession of their lands during colonization.

The process of colonization was quickly centralized under the colonial government, first led by a governor, and then transferred to the colonial parliament established under the Constitution Act of 1852. Through a process of validating pre-treaty land transactions, massive State land purchases, war, land confiscation, the individualization of title resulting from the Maori Land Court process, and Maori Affairs legislation designed to facilitate further land alienation, Maori land was reduced to such an extent that today they own less than 6 percent of the entire New Zealand land base.

Although retaining only a small fraction of land, Maori remain distinct tribal peoples with their own norms and values, laws and political institutions, well defined traditional territories, and with unique claims to pre-existing status and rights. Maori have also resisted assimilation. Their campaign of resistance was accelerated in the 1970s with the rise of the Maori sovereignty movement and the Maori Land March of 1975. Occupations occurred around the country and the government of the day was forced to act. It was this Maori resistance that led to the establishment of the Waitangi Tribunal established under the Treaty of Waitangi Act of 1975 to hear Maori claims against the government. For the last twenty years Maori tribes have resisted assimilation by pursuing claims in this forum and by using the results of its work to win major cases in the Courts.

As in the Americas, the major issues of the full right to sovereignty, the development of an international personality and the right to self-determination remain to be settled. However, and unlike Canada and the United States, the government of New Zealand continues to refuse to even discuss even a diminished form of sovereignty, self-government, or self-determination.

Pathways Forward

Although I have concentrated on North America and New Zealand to illustrate the impact of colonization on Indigenous Peoples, the experience of these communities has been repeated in almost all countries colonized by the Europeans. It is possible to say, therefore, that as they became trapped within the municipal laws of their colonizers, Indigenous Peoples were subjected to systematic attacks on their precolonial status and rights, which in turn resulted in indigenous dispossession and the breakdown of traditional ways of life. Generally, these attacks were validated by colonial legislation or through the complicity of the judges. However, through it all, Indigenous Peoples resisted. They went to war, they entered into treaties, they litigated, petitioned, and entered into further treaties, and they became independent in some cases — in other cases they adapted — they were not assimilated.

The lack of protection and respect for the rights of Indigenous Peoples at the international and national levels has forced those Indigenous Peoples, who are still striving to have their precolonial status recognized, to develop new strategies for resisting their assimilation into the dominant communities of their states. It is due to the resolve of these societies to maintain their distinct political identities as first nations, that we are witnessing their call for a reconfiguration of the state. As they confront, interact, negotiate, and settle their status and rights, they are forcing states to consider a new paradigm.

Their actions are leading to total independence, or to a sharing of state power. In the latter situation they are effectively seeking a reconfiguration of the previous paradigm of state, market, and civil society to one that emphasizes the equality of the state and first nations. They are striving to see more clearly the contribution that they can make to create a more inclusive state — which, in turn, could take its place within a new, more inclusive international order. But as Indigenous Peoples reweave the cloth of their indigenous existence and as they develop the confidence to assert their self-determination, sovereignty, and self-government, the greater the threat they have become to the current conceptualization of the state, civil society, and the market.

The Role of Civil Society

When I turn to examine the role of civil society in the struggle of Indigenous Peoples I am confronted with the fact that the great bulk of citizens that comprise civil society have failed to examine their own privilege vis-à-vis Indigenous Peoples. In countries where Indigenous Peoples are now minorities, the descendants of the colonists have been and continue to be the beneficiaries of the dispossession of Indigenous Peoples. While it may be important for them to conceptualize an arena of freedom outside of the state where individuals can express a sense of freedom, autonomy, and/or voluntary association, and while they may resent the fact that they and their governments are pawns to capitalism and globalization, when confronted with the possibility of state reconfiguration in favor of recognizing Indigenous Peoples' a priori status and rights, unbridled panic and hysteria emerges. Where faced with such a threat, those who fear state oppression are the first to collaborate and run behind the state as it struggles to maintain its hegemonic power over Indigenous Peoples. Calls such as "there must be one law for all" echo through the corridors of power.

A change of the status quo in favor of a fairer division of state power remains an absolute no-no and citizen movements have grown up specifically to reinforce state, cultural, or ethnic hegemony.

Conclusion

The States, the markets, and the great bulk of civil society who occupy the traditional lands of Indigenous Peoples act no differently in denying indigenous a priori status and rights. Consequently, the greatest challenge for Indigenous Peoples and their advocates as they move into the new millennium is to overcome centuries of Eurocentric indoctrination of non-indigenous citizens. If they do not address this challenge, there inevitably will be a reemergence of ethnic or cultural fundamentalism that validates the state. A state often manifests its despotism in relation to Indigenous Peoples peacefully and by means of "democratically" formulated laws determined by the non-indigenous uneducated majority or by franchise systems that either directly exclude, as under the former Apartheid regimes of South Africa, or indirectly exclude because the systems are based on Western conceptualizations of government rather than traditional political institutions.

To meet the challenges, Indigenous Peoples/ First Nations have developed their own responses and/or they have collaborated with those few civil society organizations who have displayed a commitment to raising awareness of their concerns and to mobilize resources. In the USA, Canada, and New Zealand, for example, there are a number of citizen organizations that strive to promote and protect the remaining lands of Indigenous Peoples, their sovereignty, and their ways of life. They include the excellent work of national and regional organizations such as the National Congress of American Indians, the American Indian Movement, the Indian Law Resource Centre, the Indigenous Women's Network, the Indian Treaty Council, the Assembly of First Nations, the Inuit Circumpolar Conference, the Indigenous Peoples Bio-Diversity Network, the Native American Rights Fund, the Maori Legal Service, and the Maori Congress.

In the Pacific, where colonialism is very much an issue, they include the independence or sovereignty movements in Hawaii, New Caledonia, French Polynesia, Easter Island, Guam, East Timor, West Papua, Bougainvillea and Australia, the regional work of Pacific Association of NGOs, and the Pacific Concerns Resource Centre. All of these organizations have worked on what may be needed to encourage the reweaving of indigenous existence and ensure the continued survival of what remains of indigenous ways of life.

As we head into the new millennium, it is timely to reflect on what measures are needed for the survival of Indigenous Peoples. This will require changes to the legal environment that has reduced Indigenous Peoples' status in international and domestic law and it will also require a stronger and more determined commitment from civil society to promote and respect the a priori rights of the First Nations of their countries. The changes can be met if the following recommendations are followed.

- States to recognize their right to self-determination. How they then negotiate the manifestation of that right, either through independence arrangements, self-government structures, or legislative measures that provide special recognition is up to them. Until Indigenous Peoples have achieved recognition of their sovereign status and a priori rights, those of us who live in countries still subject to colonial rule or built from the base of colonialism cannot say we have countered diffusionism and reversed or varied the effects of colonization or that we have encouraged greater indigenous participation in the evolution of society.

- States to accept the Draft Declaration on the Rights of Indigenous Peoples as a statement of base standards necessary to ensure the survival of indigenous ways of life into the new millennium.

- States to recognize the right of Indigenous Peoples to participate as First Nations with full membership status in the work of intergovernmental agencies at the international, regional, and national level.

- States to review their national laws and policies to ensure consistency with the Draft Declaration on the Rights of Indigenous Peoples.

- Civil society to cease its collaboration with the state and the market.

- Indigenous Peoples should create opportunities to collaborate with civil society organizations that can assist with advocacy, the mobilization of resources, and education.

Notes

1. B. Goehring, *Indigenous Peoples of the World: An Introduction to Their Past and Future* (Saskatoon, Canada: Purich Publishing, 1993).
2. See for example Amnesty International, *Human Rights Violations against Indigenous Peoples of the Americas* (New York: Amnesty International, 1992).
3. J. M. Blaut, *The Colonizer's Model of the World, Geographical Diffusionism and Eurocentric History* (New York: The Guildford Press, 1993).
4. M.N. Shaw, *Title to Territory in Africa, International Legal Issues* (Oxford: Clarendon Press, 1986), 38–39.
5. *Ominayak v. Canada*, Human Rights Committee Forty-fifth Session, Supplement No. 40 (A/45/40), vol. II, annex IX sect. A, Communication No. 167/1984, 1992.
6. B. Slattery, *Ancestral Lands, Alien Laws: Judicial Perspectives on Aboriginal Title, Studies in Aboriginal Rights* (Saskatchewan, Canada: University of Saskatchewan Native Law Centre, 1983).
7. This is the North Island Maori term for New Zealand. Translated, it means "the Land of the Long White Cloud."

5

Women and Civil Society

Amani Kandil

Early in the twentieth century, women in many parts of the world first laid claim to their right to education, work, and political participation. To press their claims, these women formed their own organizations. Today, most women who achieve positions of political leadership emerge from leadership roles in nongovernmental organizations (NGOs) and other institutions of civil society.

Indeed, today's favorable climate for the advancement of women can be traced primarily to women's actions in civil society. Since the 1960s, women's groups and organizations have learned to network across frontiers. They have also had marked successes in incorporating gender perspectives into global issues such as poverty, the environment, and human safety and security. One recent example of women's successful intervention in a global issue resulting in the mainstreaming of gender perspectives is the campaign for ratification of the anti-landmine treaty. Thus, in the twentieth century, women have broadened their focus beyond anti-discrimination appeals and claims for the individual rights of women to demands for gender equality in substantive issues.

On the threshold of the twenty-first century, women everywhere have won countless improvements in their status. Yet even after a century of progress, few, if any, inroads have been made into the socio-cultural inhibitions and institutional limitations that sabotage true gender equality.

"Herstory"

The twentieth century began with limited participation of women in civil society. During the second half of the century, particularly since the adoption of the Universal Declaration on Human Rights, women have succeeded at a global level in creating a favorable climate for the advancement of their status with the adoption of a range of international instruments and the establishment of implementation and monitoring mechanisms.

Milestones in Women's Rights

1948 Universal Declaration on Human Rights

1952 Convention on Women's Political Rights

1979 Convention on the Elimination of All Forms of Discrimination Against Women

1975 Nairobi Platform of Action for the Enhancement of Women

1993 Declaration on Human Rights

1994 International Conference for Population and Development and Its Plan of Action

1995 Fourth World Conference on Women and Its Platform of Action

Conventions and declarations notwithstanding and despite some positive developments, the status of women is advancing at a snail's pace. The abolition of institutional and legal constraints curtailing women's independence has done little to uproot socio-cultural beliefs and behaviors that effectively restrict the attainment of substantive equality for women. Prominent feminists have constantly drawn attention to the ways gender biases embedded in family power relations cross over into wider social institutions and have called for the recognition of family relations in the broader discourse on governance.

In 1990, the United Nations Commission on the Status of Women evaluated the implementation of the Nairobi Platform of Action during the previous five years. It found that conditions affecting women had deteriorated in many parts of the world and particularly in developing countries. The main reasons cited were economic crisis, structural adjustment policies, growing external debt, rapid demographic growth, shrinking budgets for social services, and restrictions on women's access to education, work, and health services and, consequently, to political and public participation.

The twentieth century, in fact, has seen the "feminization of poverty," according to the United Nations Development Program (UNDP). For example, the number of rural women living in poverty increased by

48 percent between 1965–70 and the mid-1980s while the number of rural men living in poverty increased by 30 percent.

By the end of 1998, 163 States had ratified or acceded to the Convention on the Elimination of All Forms of Discrimination Against Women (CEDAW). Despite continuous efforts by women in civil society to promote and monitor the implementation of CEDAW by their respective governments, the universal application of CEDAW by the year 2000 seems highly unlikely.

In women's access to education, the economic crisis of the 1980s, structural adjustment programs, and cuts in public budgets have taken a toll. In the 1990s, females' school enrollment has dropped, especially in developing countries that do not yet have compulsory primary schooling, according to a number of studies. School budget cuts are therefore likely to hit females more than males, raising the barriers to gender equality. In 1990 there were 346 million illiterate males throughout the world — but 602 million illiterate females, UNESCO reports. Girls constitute 70 percent of the 130 million children not enrolled in schools.

Work for everyone is considered a basic right almost everywhere today. Nonetheless, the labor of a large percentage of women remains unpaid or underpaid in comparison to that of men. Men in many countries are demanding that women return to the home, insisting that child rearing is their main responsibility. Institutionally, this thinking is supported by the traditional pattern of social security, based on the notion that a woman's income is supplementary to the income of her husband, the recognized breadwinner and head of family. According to the Social Security Department of the International Labor Organization, progress toward integrating the gender perspective in social security has slowed significantly as a result of economic crises in most regions of the world during the past fifteen years. Because available data cover only labor in the formal sector, the economic participation of women at the end of this century is neither valued nor recognized. Yet women make up almost one-third of the international labor force, and women's wages are much lower than men's wages in most countries, according to UN statistics. Furthermore, women are confined mainly to inferior positions and do not have equal access to economic and technical resources.

In the field of health, women have attained some improvements. Still, half a million women die every year from childbirth and pregnancy-related disabilities, according to the World Health Organization. Most of these deaths occur, not surprisingly, in developing countries.

Women's right to political participation by voting and running for office has become recognized in most countries, but women candidates still have an uphill battle to win political positions. Precious few countries had women in 30 percent of their decision-making positions in 1995; the target set by the Economic and Social Council. Women held only 10 percent of the legislative seats in 1995, according to the World Federation of Parliaments. Political party membership by women has also declined in industrial as well as developing countries. At the same time, there is evidence in many countries that fewer women are voting.

Thus, women's struggles throughout the twentieth century have achieved some improvement in women's status and in the prominence of women's issues on the world agenda. World indicators on women's status, however, show that they still have a long way to go before gender equality is attained.

Achievements and Failures

Through women's movements, NGOs, and other initiatives women have succeeded in putting their issues on the world agenda. Networking — locally, regionally, and worldwide — has also strengthened women's voices, with positive impact on government policies and on public awareness of women's status and rights.

Feminist advocacy organizations have been particularly effective in raising questions about women's conditions, in developing women's awareness of their political and civil rights, and in influencing decision-making processes. Human rights organizations' support for and interaction with women's organizations have led to a general reformulation of the world agenda for women with equality and empowerment as priority issues. The linkage between human rights organizations and women's organization has dynamically shown the universality, indivisibility, interdependence, and inter-relatedness of human rights.

Women in civil society have also been very successful in institutionalizing women's policies. Women's issues and demands are being formulated within institutional frameworks where NGOs and associations play an important role. Women have also succeeded in penetrating political party strongholds and in institutionalizing their claims through political action. Similarly, women have gained positions of influence in labor unions and workers federations. During the past three decades, women have initiated new strategies of action to put their issues on the agendas of political parties, governments, and the United Nations, resulting in changes in domestic as well as international law. Institutional mechanisms have been put into place to protect women's ministries in government, women's bureaus, and various other structures for monitoring the advancement of women's status. Women have honed their negotiating skills through their participation in civil society organizations, in cultural, social, and political forums, and in the development, implementation, and evaluation of national action plans in many countries.

Besides successes, the twentieth century handed women in civil society a number of defeats, leaving no shortage of goals for concerted action in the coming century. One of the main failures is civil society's limited impact in changing customs, traditions, and entrenched beliefs that define gender relations. This is directly linked to the modest capacity of women's organizations to mobilize and work with women at the grassroots level. Women's organizations often sound elitist with incoherent messages that miss their audiences. Formulating a homogeneous message to reach heterogeneous groups is, therefore, their biggest challenge. This does not mean that the feminist discourse cannot appeal to the aspirations of many types of women in different socioeconomic, cultural, and political spheres. It does mean that the message has to be couched in terms that dissimilar target audiences can understand and accept. This likely means being able to raise and address concrete social and economic problems that affect poor majorities.

The extent and quality of women's participation in decision-making within formal and informal political systems presents another challenge. Is there perhaps a link between women's access to decision-making and their success in promoting women's rights? Practical experience in many countries shows that distinguished achievements in women's rights is not a prerequisite for women's participation in decision-making. Another question deserving consideration is whether women's political culture differs from that of men. Indicators do not reveal huge disparities.

Women's political participation in public life is still very limited all over the world, but there are big differences between developed and developing countries. In general, at the level of informal participation, representation of women in leadership roles is higher, but still a big dissimilarity exists between the North and the South. The economic situation and policies as well as the status of education and culture play an important role in improving or marginalizing women and their organizations in civil society.

Women's image in civil society has also been affected by their limited impact on the media, which perpetuates stereotypes that distort the real images of women. However, the last decade has seen new types of organizations dedicated to the advancement of women emerge. Many of these organizations have brought heightened awareness about stereotypes and distorted images of women in the media.

Women's involvement in local politics is still much too limited. Close involvement in local politics would simplify the establishment of links at grassroots between women and women's organizations, facilitating real change at community level. In this regard, the development of linkages between feminist CSOs with a capacity for economic analysis and the mobilization of women at grassroots level are especially important.

Thus, at the turn of the century we can see that women's organizations have managed to bring about a number of improvements in their position in society. At the same time, however, the evident shortcomings and outright failures strongly suggest the need for new strategies.

Twentieth-century Strategies for Advancing Women's Status

To achieve their goals, women have deployed four types of strategies during the twentieth century. The first, the strategy of separation, is historically linked to women's organizations and remains important today among women's movements. This is a strategy whereby an organization restricts its membership to women and focuses on women as the power behind actions and as the target and beneficiary of its activities. This tendency has come under harsh criticism on the basis that women's issues are part of societal issues and cannot be solved without contributions from enlightened and broad-minded men.

The second strategy, joining together, is exercised by organizations where men and women work in cooperation, although men usually hold the decision-making positions. The third strategy, individualism, involves a single charismatic woman who establishes, and often finances, her own voluntary organization. This strategy is quite common in developing countries.

The fourth strategy is one of subordinate assistance. In terms of this strategy, women's civil society organizations play an auxiliary role to political parties, trade unions, or huge institutions dominated by the state. In these cases, women's organizations are partially incorporated — through the women's wing of the ruling political party for instance — in the state and are not fully independent.

Why Do Women Join Civil Society Organizations?

From this look at women's contributions and activities, we can make some assumptions about their motives for joining a civil society organization. These assumptions also illustrate the important role women play in civil society.

First, the action of women in voluntary organizations is intended to create parallel points of power to counterbalance their limited participation in the legislative corpus, in political parties, and in public policymaking. In other words, women's involvement in civil society institutions and organizations is a means of influencing public policy and improving their own rights. Historically, women's organizations have been active in the struggle against colonialism and in the fight for national independence, particularly in Africa. This important role is another motive behind women's participation in civic life from the historical perspective.

Second, religion has been a major factor in shaping and defining responsibilities of women in voluntary and charity work, especially in the first half of the twentieth century. This assumption acknowledges that religion, as essential motivator of women's voluntary initiatives, opened up space for women to assume a wider and deeper role in civil society by volunteering time and contributing money through their practice of charity.

Third, the major public policy input of women's organizations is in motherhood and childhood projects. This assumption, stemming from women's traditional roles, considers motherhood and childhood favorite fields of action for women's organizations worldwide but mainly in developing countries.

Fourth, women's organizations are more powerful in societies that are not governed by strongly centralized systems. This would mean that the nature of the political system has a positive or a negative impact on the efficiency of women's organizations. In fact, this variable influences the entire range of civil society institutions, not just women's organizations.

Finally, women's participation and involvement in voluntary organizations allow them to establish parallel structures of strength at the economic and political levels, especially in the upper and middle classes. This assumption has predominated in American feminist studies that forge a link between the legal rights of women and their financial independence. Thus, women build voluntary organizations to fight for their legal, political, and economic rights.

Gender, Empowerment, and Cultural Biases

The concept of mainstreaming gender has been introduced in much of current discourse on women's status partly as an outgrowth of United Nations initiatives and partly as a natural step in the evolution of the women's movement. This concept began with the idea that women could enhance their participation in work and society through small business enterprises. However, as it has evolved in the 1990s, the concept of gender and empowerment reflects a global concern about defining the social roles of gender in different socio-cultural and political contexts. The concept is based on the idea that, although males and females differ biologically, other differences are due to social and cultural reasons proper to each society and to each historical era. Gender and biological differences do not rely on scientific or religious bases. Instead, they stem from values that see women's reproductive role as a cause to restrict them to this biological role, thus depriving them of full access to public life.

The term "sex" refers to a biological role; the term "gender" has a cultural connotation. The concept of gender gives us a tool for analyzing the structural, cultural, political, and economic factors that led to the entrenchment of discrimination. The importance of this concept lies in the possibility it offers us for reshaping and changing the social roles of gender, filling the gap created by inequality and discrimination. Finally, it will empower women to participate in the development process and enjoy the fruits of their efforts.

The emergence of the concept of gender and the increase in demands to eliminate discrimination, injustice, and violence against women were due mainly to the belief of the international community and women's civil society organizations that:

- Comprehensive and sustainable development cannot be achieved without the full participation of women at every stage and in every part of the development process.

- The values of equality, justice, and respect of human rights cannot be selective or applied only to men.

Raising women's issues under the perspective of gender and empowerment has helped to activate the role of women in civil society and has incited a qualitative change in trends of action from social welfare to empowerment. During the first development decade, women's organizations largely focused on social welfare, social services, and charitable endeavors while activities relating to developmental skills were limited. Later, mainly in the 1970s and 1980s, the focus shifted to women's economic role and the importance of providing women with economic resources such as loans and other tools of production. By generating income, women's productive activities would allow them to participate in socio-economic development. This was also seen as a way to fight poverty.

Practical experience, especially in developing countries, has proved this approach to be fragmented and of limited impact on women's lives and images. Neither has it sufficed to change ideas, beliefs, or cultures about women. However, the introduction of the gender perspective at the end of the century is likely to provoke a qualitative move towards the empowerment of women because it includes a radical, not a reformist, approach. It addresses women's issues from the grassroots through analysis of legislation, policies, values, and cultures. The gender and empowerment approach, based on the principles of equality and justice, addresses questions like women's access to basic human rights such as education, work, and health care. This approach aims at raising awareness, developing capabilities, and creating mutual understanding between males and females. This, in turn, will impel societal change that will eliminate discrimination and inequality, enhance the chances of a just distribution of resources, and provide access to political and socio-economic participation for every member of society.

The gender and empowerment approach has already had an impact on civil society. Several organizations have been established to advocate for reforms in legislation and public policy, the creation of mechanisms and procedures to assist women's empowerment, and a change of cultural values. This is a comprehensive approach, dealing with values, behavior, culture, and gender social relations.

Issues and Strategies for the Twenty-first Century

As we move into the twenty-first century, civil society organizations worldwide have identified twelve fields of concern reflecting women's issues and needs. They were agreed at the Fourth World Conference on Women in 1995 for inclusion in governmental agendas.

Issues for the Twenty-first Century

- The continuing and rising burden of poverty on women
- Inequality in access to education and adequate training
- Inequality in health care and related services
- The need to fight all forms of violence against women and girl-children
- Impact of oppression and armed conflicts on women including those women living under foreign occupation
- Inequality in participation to economic decision-making and in access to the production process
- Lack of sufficient mechanisms to enhance women's status

- Importance of guaranteeing and protecting all aspects of women's human rights
- Women and media
- Continuing discrimination against the girl-child
- Women and the economy

Judging by the strategies pursued by women during the twentieth century and their positive and negative results, no single strategy will suffice to empower women and to achieve gender equality. Women have to use multiple, multidimensional approaches and different tools to bring about the changes they want inside the political system, working through NGOs and women's movements. Logically, women should organize themselves independently from men, but to be effective, they must also be active in civil society organizations and political parties, working side by side with men.

Women's limited gains in the last three decades of the twentieth century could be jeopardized in many countries by the current economic crisis and ongoing structural adjustment policies. Compared with the hard issues raised by the economic situation, women's issues may look "soft." To ensure gender perspectives in the development and implementation of economic policies, women must take an active role in politics, beginning at the local level and extending to the national and global levels. Proper understanding of the barriers limiting women's participation in leadership roles is of vital importance to increase the leadership of women in the twenty-first century.

Women will, therefore, have to develop their own capabilities to promote their organizational and institutional power. They will also have to consolidate alliances among women to build a strong and positive role for the women's movement. Finally, they must establish links between women's movements and political women to ensure politicians' accountability for making decisions in the best interests of women's causes. At the same time, women should find ways to bridge the gap with the media, not only to further their specific interests but also to change the constantly perpetuated stereotypes, creating media-oversight mechanisms in the process.

Women will have to draw on experience acquired in the women's movements of the twentieth century to harness the energies of women in the activities and campaigns still underway. These activities include interventions for the implementation of the landmine convention, the fight against poverty, and the struggle against all forms of violence against women.

Finally, true gender equality is not yet in sight. Although civil society has put more women into leadership positions than the formal political system, a gender balance in line with demographic realities is still a far-off goal. Progressive men should therefore not be sidetracked by visible improvements and the increased number of women in leadership positions. More resources, not less, are still needed to make gender equality a reality.

6

Youth Empowerment and Civil Society

Jane Foster, Kumi Naidoo, and Marcus Akuhata-Brown

> My friends, no one is born a good citizen; no nation is born a democracy. Rather, both are processes that continue to evolve over a lifetime. Young people must be included from birth. A society that cuts itself off from its youth severs its lifeline; it is condemned to bleed to death.
>
> *UN Secretary General Kofi Annan,*
> *World Conference of Ministers Responsible for Youth,*
> *Lisbon, August, 1998*

Civil society probably needs young people much more than young people need civil society. Young people have a stake, a presence, and an influence in civil society without making any special effort. If we view our schools, our sports-fields, our community recreation centers, and, indeed, our streets, as part of what broadly constitutes the theater of civil society, then it is clear that the presence of young people strongly permeates civil society. In many developing countries, this presence will increase significantly over the next decade. According to United Nations projections, people below the age of thirty will form some 70 percent of the population in least developed countries by the year 2005. It is increasingly true, therefore, that young people are the decision-makers not only of tomorrow but of today.

Thus, there is a demographic imperative underpinning the need to nurture and enhance the decision-making capacities of young people. Participation in decision-making is an important element of the empowerment of young people so that they can realize their full potential and rise to the challenge of ensuring the continued development of their societies and countries.

This chapter explores the role of young people as a central part of civil society in the next millennium. Youth organizations, which already constitute a formal manifestation of youth civil society, have a key role in building that society and should be strengthened. Globally, there are exciting examples of youth empowerment and their participation in decision-making. However, much more needs to be done to ensure that the potential of young people is realized today and not delayed until some undefined moment in the future. Youth participation in civil society and its organizations are important bridges to young people's participation in the formal governance structures of a society.

Adults' Views of Young People

Young people can be seen as half-full or half-empty cups. The latter view, which unfortunately often predominates, ranges from the mildly negative view that young people are a risky, unknown quantity to the extreme view that characterizes them as potentially dangerous to themselves and others. The "half-full" view respects the sense of excitement and energy, the enthusiasm and freshness of approach that young people bring, and acknowledges the potential for the cup to become full, to overflow, and to spread these benefits.

If we apply this analogy to the benefits that democracy and an informed citizenry can bring, choosing the half-full cup has clear advantages. The development of informed citizenry is a process that needs to be dynamic and continual. The more that a citizenry practices democracy at the everyday level in communities, schools, and civic associations, the more skilful it becomes. The younger we are when we learn these lessons, the greater the opportunities to become highly skilled decision-makers.

Many young people have limited access to education. Yet they still have opportunities to gain skills and experiences. In developing countries, youth organizations range from formal national structures such as national youth councils to village religious youth groups and sports associations that touch the lives of nearly all young people. At one end of the spectrum, well-funded national student organizations, with an articulate, educated young leadership, advocate the interests of their members, lobby governments on education policy and programs, and form alliances for dramatic social change. At the other end of the spectrum, the village youth group in developing countries typically focused around a parent religious organization such as a mosque or synagogue. The village youth group is a focal point for young women and men in a small community. It organizes sports and social activities, and its energies are often called upon by elders to contribute to community development.

This range of organizations constitutes a vibrant, well-organized youth civil society. Young people work in teams, make decisions, raise funds, and often provide the point of intergenerational negotiation or mediation.

The benefits of diversity in civil society organizations are mainly characterized in racial, gender, religious, ethnic, or political terms. For example, peace and conflict resolution movements have examined the benefits that a gender diverse response brings. The interventions of women in resolving conflicts have often brought new perspectives to bear. We suggest that generational diversity can also enrich the responses of civil society in this and other areas. For example, there have been many examples of youth support for environmental issues and anti-racism campaigns.

Young people are a legitimate constituency in civil society, and adults need to develop a synergistic relationship with them. Yet this large, vibrant population, upon which the future health of civil society depends, does not feature in the consciousness of leaders of civil society, and can be marginalized virtually into non-existence. What message does that give young women and men about the significance of civil society and their future role as informed and empowered citizens? In the new millennium, the innovation, energy, and new ideas of young people will drive civil society in ways that we cannot yet imagine. But first of all, we have to recognize that they are a legitimate constituency of civil society.

Youth Empowerment

The Commonwealth has made important progress in identifying and promoting a new paradigm of youth empowerment. The Plan of Action for Youth Empowerment (PAYE) defines young people as empowered "when they feel that they have or can create choices in life, are aware of the implications of those choices, make an informed decision freely, take action based on that decision and accept responsibility for the consequences of that action."[1]

The rationale for youth empowerment is based on the premise that: "The empowerment of young people is everybody's business. It involves the concerted efforts of a number of key stakeholders, including governments, intergovernmental and nongovernmental organizations, the media, educational institutions, the private sector, family and community networks, youth peer groups, and, above all, young people themselves."

Youth empowerment is based on the belief that young people are the best resources for promoting their development. This definition goes beyond questions of social welfare and participation: it defines the full range of conditions young people need if they are to shape their lives and enrich their communities.

> Empowering young people means creating and supporting the enabling conditions under which [they] are empowered. These include an economic and social base; political will, adequate resource allocation and supportive legal and administrative frameworks; a stable political environment of equality, peace and democracy; and access to knowledge, information and skills.

These enabling conditions can be transcribed into the structures of civil society organizations (CSOs) as follows:

- Political will and supportive frameworks can be expressed through the mission, constitution, policy, and program priorities of CSOs.

- An environment of equality and democracy can be fostered by the development of parallel mechanisms for young people in decision-making, enabling them to participate in policy formulation, program design, and implementation.

- Access to knowledge, information, and skills can be promoted through efforts to introduce a culture and practice of mentoring, nurturing, and succession planning.

Problems and Challenges Facing Youth Participation

In the new millennium, if current trends persist, there is likely to be a growing tendency towards a diminishing role for the nation-state as we know it, and an ascending role for civil society in all its manifestations. Thus, the new millennium offers young people, youth organizations, and those that advocate for youth issues and concerns the opportunity to make tremendous progress. However, for this to happen, a few hurdles need to be cleared.

The Myth of Homogeneity

The first flaw in reasoning and approach that must be dealt with is the tendency to deal unwittingly with young people as if they were some unified monolithic group. Young people are not homogenous, even though there are many youth issues that enjoy a high level of commonality. If we are to serve fully the collective interests of young people we need to understand the various types of diversity that divide them. Apart from the obvious social variables of class, religion, ethnicity, language, and geography, there is a need to disaggregate the concept of "youth" in terms of daily-lived experiences as manifest in the occupations and activities of young people. A number of categories of young people with differing needs and concerns can be identified.[2] These categories are helpful in understanding the diverse range of issues relating to the participation of young people in decision-making:

Primary school young people: basic decision-making skills can be learned from an early age and should be part of primary school curricula. These skills can also be developed through participation in organizations such as the junior guiding and scouting movements and some religious organizations.

Secondary school young people: young people at this age are open to new ideas, concepts and possibilities, providing scope for innovative approaches to achieving social progress. A supportive environment for young people making decisions can be provided, in the school setting, by teachers and peers, as well as student representative councils, Parent-Teacher-Student Associations (PTSAs), and sporting clubs. Outside of school, support can be provided through community-based and religious youth organizations.

The unemployed: these young people often experience feelings of frustration, vulnerability, and marginalization, and can be susceptible to anti-social behavior and criminality, if societies cannot provide a social safety net to support them. The unemployed have sometimes found positive support in community-based youth organizations in the role of volunteers in literacy programs and other forms of community service. The creation of space for unemployed young people to participate effectively in such organizations allows them to grow in confidence and capabilities, and can enhance their future employment prospects.

Young workers: young people entering the work environment face many challenges, and may have a range of concerns about job security, competency levels, remuneration, health issues, and so on. In most countries, the main civil society organization for worker participation in decision-making is the trade union. However, young people may not feel confident about participating in trade unions, or see no advantage in so doing. In some countries trade unions are undertaking recruitment drives to increase youth participation.

Young people in higher education: this category of young people generally displays high levels of participation in decision making through student organizations, social movements, and youth wings of political parties. Some view such participation as essential for their career advancement, while others participate out of social commitment or political conviction.

Young professionals: these young people generally have high levels of skills, competencies, resources, disposable income, and infrastructure such as computer networks, all of which can facilitate their participation in youth and other organizations. Professional staff associations offer space for decision-making, but such participation is often narrow in scope and does not address broader youth or societal concerns. This is unfortunate, because young professionals have a great deal to offer in the development of civil society. Youth organizations should actively canvass the membership and participation of young professionals.

While each of these categories enjoys different options and vehicles for its involvement in civil society, they also have many commonalities. The challenge that faces civil society and youth organizations is to evolve programs, structures, and initiatives which are able to recognize diversity while also acknowledging and building on the substantial common ground that exists. It is also important to recognize that there are other categories of young people in special circumstances, which compound these differences. These include young people living with HIV/AIDS, refugees, street children, indigenous and minority ethnic groups, and others. The active and positive participation of vulnerable and marginalized young people is desirable and achievable.

Gender Equality

One of the main barriers to the full participation of young people in civil society is the gender division of roles that many societies have prescribed for boys and girls. As part of an agenda of maximizing the role of young people in decision-making in civil society, it is necessary to explore ways in which the promotion of gender equality can gain ground.

In many societies and cultures, girls and young women have greater demands placed on them by family and communal responsibilities. There may also be cultural restraints placed on the participation of young women in decision-making activities. It is therefore necessary to develop strategies to ensure that young women have opportunities for such participation.

Often, youth organizations tend to be dominated by boys and young men. As well as increasing the participation of young women in such organizations, there is a need to develop organizations exclusively for girls and young women. This will help ensure that they are not hindered by a predominance of males or by social and cultural barriers to their full participation in civil society. Organizations that were established specifically for young men, such as the Scouts, have opened their membership to young women.

The term "youth" is in many instances not gender-neutral. There is a tendency to associate "youth" specifically with boys and young men, which is why the term "young people" is usually preferable. Terms such as youth development, youth work, youth organizations, and so on, should refer equally, and sometimes even predominantly, to girls and young women.

Decision-making Versus Rubber Stamping

In many adult-dominated civil society organizations and processes, while a notion of youth participation in decision-making exists, all it amounts to, in effect, is a rubber-stamp of adult-driven decisions. This is an unhealthy learning process for youth leaders since they are likely to replicate these patterns when they are older. Often specific responsibilities are allocated to young people in organizations of civil society, whether it is a sporting club or an environmental justice organization where adults and young people work together. For example, during the resistance to Apartheid in South Africa, many youth leaders objected to being used simply as "pamphlet fodder," being expected only to distribute resistance media without having a say in the content.

Demystifying Concepts

The key requirements for good decision-making are an appropriate level of basic data or information, an understanding of the possible implications of the decision, and a sense of how the decision might be implemented. If we are serious about enhancing youth participation in civil society organizations, it is critical that time be allocated to ensuring that young people are equipped with the right kind of information to make decisions. Simply dumping a lot of literature on a young person and sending them away to read it will not always help. The problem is exacerbated by the high illiteracy levels and poor educational opportunities that exist in many developing countries. Attention needs to be paid to explaining "adult" concepts or language to young people so that content is demystified. Young people often have an astute understanding of common-sense environmental factors and of the informal social fabric of a particular community, which they can bring to bear in a positive manner when important decisions need to be made.

The Formalization of Youth Structures

Another challenge that confronts the project of enhancing youth involvement in decision-making is an over-reliance on formal youth structures. Statutory national youth commissions and councils, while having the capacity to influence policy and mainstream youth issues in the social policy environment, also have the potential to become gatekeepers and elite structures with little broader youth participation. Sometimes such structures can become the subject of political manipulation and intrigue. Therefore, it is necessary to develop clear guidelines about how youth participation can be enhanced at different levels through both formal and informal structures. Each society needs to explore how formal and informal processes can reinforce each other in enhancing youth participation in social processes.

Young people may find formal youth and adult organizations uncomfortable places to be. Action through alliances that enable personal expression and commitment without formal engagement is increasingly attractive. For example, the peace camps of Greenham Common (UK) attracted many young women in the 1980s. More recently, "eco-warriors" as young as eleven years old have attracted public focus to environment issues by their direct and individual actions through living in trees and tunnels.

Young people are attracted to different kinds of organizations besides traditional, hierarchical, formal institutions that mimic adult structures. Young people often gravitate towards coalitions and alliances that advocate on a single issue or support a particular platform of social concerns. These have allowed young people to be active, lend support, and take action, but not necessarily join as full members. The policymaking process may be distant and inaccessible, and input may frequently not be invited on decision-making.

Enhancing Youth Involvement in Decision-making in Civil Society

How, then, can young people and adults work in civil society organizations together in such a way that young people are genuinely engaged in decision-making processes?

Involvement in Policy Development

Clearly, involving young people in policy formulation in organizations is of key importance. Consultations with young people may require new, more interactive, and creative formats to get good responses from them. These formats can enhance adult participation. The skills in group work and group dynamics of youth development workers can be important tools in this regard. Including young people in decision-making might appear to be a costly and time-consuming exercise. However, their inclusion in the early stages of policymaking and community development enterprises is likely to deliver a higher return than if they are not consulted.

In attempting to engage young people in the social policy process, it is important to recognize that for many young people the process of policy formulation might be interpreted as a strangulating exercise. Policy processes are often slow and bureaucratic and the huge chasm between policy formulation and policy implementation can lead to disillusionment and frustration amongst the people the policy is intended to serve. For this reason, the policy process needs to be clarified to young leaders so that they are aware of the road that they are embarking on. Part of the challenge facing policymakers in the next millennium is to find creative ways in which lessons learned from successful grassroots initiatives and microinterventions can be fed into the policymaking process and thus influence national policymaking and the development of national programs.

Some civil society organizations implement mentoring programs for young people who shadow adult leaders with a view to taking over some of their responsibilities in time. This obliges adult leaders to take the time to explain why certain decisions are made and why those decisions are implemented in a particular manner. Mentoring programs provide young people with a safe environment in which they can ask questions without fear of embarrassment.

Traditional and indigenous societies sometimes exhibit very positive practices regarding young people's participation. In Maori society in Aotearoa/New Zealand it was the practice for children and young people with special talents to be identified by elders, and mentored. This mentoring could take the form of learning alongside an expert, or accompanying an elder to meetings and ceremonial events to observe and learn traditional protocols. The erosion of traditional areas of expertise and knowledge has disempowered many indigenous communities. In the process, the constructive and creative opportunities that existed for inter-generational dialogue and learning have been largely destroyed. The renaissance of indigenous language through inter-generational teaching systems provides a model that can redress this.

Young People and Leadership

The question of leadership must be addressed in exploring youth decision-making and civil society. Building leadership as a conscious strategy to enhance the quality and quantity of young people in decision-making is critical. But a question arises regarding the form and content of leadership training currently available. The curriculum of youth leadership training programs is often entirely adult-generated and driven. For leadership training to be really effective and to "practice what it preaches," young women and men need to be engaged in determining its content and evaluating it.

The trained youth development worker can ensure that young people acquire positive learning experience in leadership. This cannot be handed out by adults on an instructional basis, but requires consultations with young people to determine what roles and experience they think will be useful in developing leadership skills. Succession planning is an essential concept not only for youth organizations but also for all types of responsible civil society organizations. Youth leadership is by nature transitory; we are not young forever. It is essential to recognize that leadership must be passed on and the leadership skill pool renewed. This should be seen as a positive step and not as a drain on organizational resources. It is also important to ensure that administration and record keeping are very well handled, so that some sort of institutional memory is maintained.

Traditional youth organizations, such as the Guides and Scouts, have some excellent youth leadership and development programs which should be considered as useful tools in assisting youth leaders in becoming more assertive decision-makers.

Young People and Sports

Youth involvement in sport as a tool for development offers immense possibilities for participation, decision-making, and the development of management and leadership skills both on and off the field. In many countries, sport is a key ingredient in shaping the social fabric of particular societies and is often the preoccupation of large numbers of young people as players or spectators. Because many sports tend to be youth-dominated, which is not necessarily a good thing, it becomes critical to harness the potential of sporting bodies, as they are often a very localized manifestation of civil society. There are many communities where the only local organization is a sporting club, which becomes a source of pride and identity for a community. Sports organizations can also play a powerful role in lobbying and influencing how other civil society organizations at a local level relate to young people, and can also influence local government to put more resources into youth development.

Learning by Doing

The participation of young people in real situations provides opportunities to develop confidence, skills, and experience through "learning by doing." Together with adult program workers, young people are playing positive roles through participation in programs and organizations.

There are several key strategies for enhancing young people's participation:

- Young people should have direct involvement in the planning and design of activities that will engage young people.

- Parallel decision-making structures should be created that provide young people with a mechanism to question the organization, independent of adults.

- Networking should be developed to provide young people with opportunities to strengthen their abilities through shared learning.

- Research needs to involve young people so that they can better understand the issues they seek to address.

Adults also need to develop trust in young people and their abilities, rather than fear that participation will result in irresponsible action. Young people and adults need to create open communication in which adults listen and young people have a voice, resulting in genuine and constructive dialogue. Adults need to understand that even when young people make bad decisions, it is still a positive learning experience. The power of doing is enhanced and made more meaningful when young people can observe and measure the benefits of their decisions being implemented. The "learning" function of young peoples' organizations and their role in public policy or decision-making processes are not mutually exclusive and often reinforce each other.

Peer Support and Education

Youth activists can play several roles. Many youth organizations provide supplementary peer education and support training for young people to become informal counselors of other young people. Young people can offer peer support in such areas as health education, including sexual and reproductive health, and HIV/AIDS issues, and those who are physically violent or abuse drugs and alcohol. This is a difficult and challenging road to developing decision-making skills, but if youth leaders can stay the course, they will gain confidence in decision-making that will have life-long benefits.

Young People and NGOs

Many nongovernmental organizations (NGOs) enlist young volunteers engaged in decision-making regarding their service. Depending on the culture of the NGO and the competencies of the youth volunteer, this can often extend more broadly. NGOs can adopt strategies that consciously create space for youth interns and youth volunteers, and allocate a certain number of positions for young people. The challenge, however, is to go beyond simply creating a chance for young people to volunteer or work. Spaces need to be created for youth voices and experience to contribute towards shaping the organization's vision, policies, plans, and programs.

Parent Teacher Student Associations (PTSAs) as a Means of Learning and Participation

School governance offers many possibilities for engaging youth leaders in decision-making. Many young people spend a great proportion of their lives at school; and, the school environment provides many opportunities to enhance decision-making participation. PTSAs provide one such opportunity. The key to whether the PTSA genuinely enhances students' role in decision-making is whether the elected student representatives in the PTSA consult with the student body. Encouraging students to think about the governance of a space in which they are in the majority, a space in which they spend a substantial amount of their waking time, is a great opportunity to foster young people's involvement in decision-making about a serious issue.

Young People and Political Participation

Rethinking the Voting Age

In 1993, African National Congress President Nelson Mandela shocked the world when he suggested the voting age in South Africa should start at fourteen. Mandela used a simple logic. He noted that the struggle for liberation would not have been won but for the contributions of young people. Many children under the age of fourteen perished in the struggle against Apartheid and many stories spoke to the skill, heroism, and capabilities of young activists. Much opposition to this proposal prevented it from being implemented. But surely, if adults are willing to allow young people to go to war and if they are willing to use young people in the name of the nation, then Mandela's suggestion is not so ridiculous, as it might initially sound. Given that young people often have greater access to information than their parents, also places young people in a position that they can make fairly informed electoral choices.

It is recommended that governments give serious consideration to introducing a voting age of sixteen. By that age, many young people already have to make adult decisions, such as choosing their likely career. Furthermore, the fact that many voters aged sixteen attend school allows for basic voter education to be undertaken as part of civic education. In many countries, levels of voter turnout are extremely low, as citizen alienation from public institutions grows. If we are keen for young people to embrace electoral democracy, then it is better to start early. The school as an institutional and cultural environment has immense stature and presence, even in the poorest communities. If schools were to instill in young people the responsibilities of citizenship in general and the embracing of the electoral system in particular there would probably be fewer adults who are cynical about political life.

Youth Rights Are Human Rights

Political and social activism offers considerable opportunity for the growth of decision-making skills and the participation of young people in social processes. There is particular scope for young people to engage in lobbying and activism in the area of human rights. In taking up these issues of social justice and youth rights it is important for young people to recognize that they do not affect young people alone. Young people's rights are human rights, and by engaging in activism based on this principle, young people can advance the human rights not only of their own generation but also of all sectors of the population.

Given the high levels of materialism and individualism that current world trends reflect, it is probably more appealing to today's young people to invest their energy in causes of which they might ultimately be direct beneficiaries. However, fostering in young people a sense of community and shared responsibility could make an immeasurable contribution to increasing their decision-making ability on issues that affect their lives. It is thus imperative that adult leaders allow space for young people not only to undertake the menial tasks associated with the vision and program of this or that civil society organization, but also to engage them in the decision-making process. While many movements set up youth wings or divisions as a way to deal with youth participation, youth-adult interaction is equally important and indeed vital for better decisions to be reached and to enhance confidence and personal development.

Conclusion

In the next millennium, the impact of globalization means that the private sector and civil society organizations will address many more social issues. Demographic reality means that much of this will be done by young people, since they form a large and growing proportion of the population in developing countries. Governments, therefore, must increasingly work in partnership with the business sector, with NGOs, and with civil society at large to achieve their development objectives, and must involve young people in so doing. This needs to happen at the local, national, and international levels, since decision-making processes will take place in ways that transcend national borders.

The majority of young people enthusiastically embrace the concept of "getting involved" in activities. Their enthusiasm and energy can provide an injection of new ideas, human resources, and fresh perspectives. However, they may have different expectations to those of adults participating in CSOs. For example, because of their relatively short life experience, young people may lack the long-term view of how successful an organization is in achieving its goals or ideals. Their enthusiasm may be tempered with disappointment if they perceive their efforts are not creating the desired results in the short term. Young people and adults need to work together to keep sight of both short-term and long-term goals.

The benefits to CSOs of youth participation are clear: the full and active participation of young people provides organizations with continuity, with credibility in a whole new constituency of potential members, and with human resources for renewal of membership and leadership. Young people benefit through increased opportunities to find forums where their voices are heard, and which enable them to make a real contribution and to be acknowledged. Supportive environments that create real learning opportunities and experiences will result in personal growth, confidence, and skill development.

It is not easy to become a generationally inclusive organization. Just as achieving gender balance through the increased participation of women in CSOs and politics has required a critical examination of organizational structures, processes, and programs, so too CSOs have to examine their commitment to and capacity for youth involvement.

For CSOs, there are a number of strategies to initiating participation by young people, in addition to their direct involvement within organizations. CSOs can form alliances with youth organizations. Mentoring can be extended beyond the individual to the organizational level. Opportunities for joint activities and action with youth organizations can provide both young and adult participants with opportunities for learning and dialogue. Specific issues may require either one-off or regular dialogue sessions between adult CSOs and youth counterparts.

Notes

1. Commonwealth Secretariat, *Plan of Action on Youth Empowerment to the Year 2005* (London: Commonwealth Foundation, 1998).
2. Kumi Naidoo, "Dilemmas of a Differentiated Durban: The Politics of Youth Resistance in the 1980s," *Journal of Southern African Studies* (18) 1 March 1992.

7

The Role of Civil Society Organizations in Sustainable Development

Oscar Rojas

This chapter seeks to stimulate discussion about the role of civil society organizations (CSOs) in promoting and implementing sustainable development. Several issues will be addressed, including:

- defining the critical issues that surround world sustainability and sustainable development;

- providing an historical analysis of how CSOs and the issue of sustainability have been closely linked. A paradigm of sustainable development requires citizen participation through organizations that are well informed, capable of shaping public opinion, and capable of forming partnerships with diverse actors such as governments and the private sector;

- providing an historical perspective of the background and current debate on the role of CSOs in sustainable development;

- building the institutional capacity of CSOs as a strategy to increase and improve their role in promoting sustainable development; and

- highlighting examples of innovative work by CSOs involved in sustainable development.

Sustainable Development

Sustainable development is a relatively recent concept. It appeared in the global discourse after two decades when development was considered only from an ecological standpoint. The term sustainable development was first publicly used at a meeting held in Stockholm, Sweden, during the early 1970s. It was defined as a commitment to a more equitable form of development, characterized by intergenerational solidarity, democratic control, and citizen participation in decisions about the physical, economic, and social environment. Those who espoused "ecodevelopment" considered global progress viable because this form of development was socially just and ecologically and economically compatible. Increased awareness about global environmental concerns, however, led to the decline in popularity of the term "ecodevelopment" within more recent political-environmental discourse.

The Earth Summit held in Rio de Janeiro, Brazil, in 1992 signaled the evolution of a global environmental movement responding to a growing environmental crisis. The Rio Summit reaffirmed the Declaration of Stockholm and sought new worldwide agreements and commitments for a new paradigm of sustainable development. At the same time, this paradigm was a new contract, which required renewed levels of cooperation between governments, civil society, and businesses. This new contract respected the interests of all concerned and recognized the integral and interdependent nature of environmental phenomena.

This new paradigm provided the contextual framework for the concept of sustainable development. Opinions vary about the definition, scope, and usefulness of sustainable development and related terms. For many, the terms have different linguistic meanings: Sustained is that which is itself (that is, the ecosystem), whereas *sustainable* refers to something that should be sustained (that is, an unbalanced ecosystem). *Sustentative* refers to the efforts at reaching a state of equilibrium of a system.[1]

The concept of *sustainable development* balances the needs of current and future generations. It says that the current generation should consume enough of the earth's resources to meet their subsistence without endangering the living conditions of future generations. An implicit value is placed on balancing the use of available resources, promoting reduced consumption, avoiding excessive consumption, providing environmentally friendly standards of production, and promoting low population growth. In addition, building a national commitment to equitable sustainable development models to eradicate poverty and to promote a citizenry that respects the aforementioned rules and values is desired.

The characteristics of CSOs make them both social and civic actors.

Their values are linked to defending and promoting sustainable development. CSOs find their legitimate and true expression in these values.

Civil Society: Background

The origin of civil society as a term dates back to the late seventeenth and early eighteenth centuries. Two lines of political thought — liberal and Marxist — were responsible for coining the phrase. Liberals viewed civil society as the purest form for ordering social, economic, and political life. Conversely, Marxists viewed civil society as the arena for economic relations that determined the political order represented in the State. In other words, for Marx, civil society was synonymous with the bourgeois society.

By the mid-eighteenth century, this concept began to fade until the term civil society almost completely disappeared from the intellectual horizon. It was not until the nineteenth century, initially with Hegel, that the term recovered certain vigor and began to differ conceptually from its present antonym: the state. Alexis de Tocqueville and the economist John Stuart Mill focused the discussion on the role and relationship that civil society should play in a democracy.

These philosophical ideas bore the seal of a constant concern for ensuring individual freedom beyond or despite the egalitarian trends introduced by democracy and promoted by the state. "The trends of equality and liberty should seek their own equilibrium within a democratic context, but it is civil society that provides the necessary conditions so that individuals can express themselves freely through voluntary organizations that separate them from state control."[2]

Other scholars expanded on the concept of bourgeois domination, as expressed by Marx, by adding ideological and cultural dimensions to the original economic concept. In this context, the bourgeois hegemony over the proletariat is the product of economic relations and the cultural and political values defended by the state, thus affirming that civil society is the arena where alternative ideologies can be developed.

The concept of civil society resurfaced during the 1970s, particularly in Eastern Europe. Since then, it has gained significant ground in all corners of the globe for two reasons. First, civil society has a close relationship to the idea of mobilizing diverse actors to debate the construction of the public sphere. Second, civil society became more prevalent in discussing governmental crises and the lack of legitimacy of traditional political parties, which were rooted in representative, rather than participatory, democracy.

CSOs: Concept and Current Debate

What constitutes civil society? What is its role and purpose? These are still valid questions as we enter the new millennium. Three aspects of the political theories already discussed help broaden our understanding of the concept of civil society. First, the context of civil society as the arena where social relations occur was taken from liberal thought. Second, Marxist theory shows how economic context and relationships determine civil society. Civil society is constituted by the bourgeois. Third, the political aspect of civil society stems from the civil society/state dichotomy, as proposed by Hegel and others.

Three aspects allow the concept of civil society to involve diverse actors motivated by different goals: the *economic vision*, which is represented by guilds, business groups, and unions; the *social logic*, which is manifested through the work of nongovernmental organizations (NGOs), grassroots organizations, and associations of volunteers and ethic groups, among others; and the *political viewpoint*, which includes the subversive, paramilitary, and other armed group movements. The latter movements should be excluded because they do not respect the rules of the games and, typically, deny the existence of other sectors of society.

Based on these concepts, we can define civil society as "the totality of organizations formed by the citizens outside the State and the market (that is, for-profit sector) to support aspects of social life where a common interest exists." In simpler terms, civil society can be defined as "a society organized voluntarily as opposed to being organized through the coercive apparatus of the state."[3]

Nonetheless, the concept of civil society is complex, especially when discussed in the context of sustainable development. CIVICUS: World Alliance for Citizen Participation helps illustrate the complexity of civil society and its role in determining a plan of action for sustainable development. CIVICUS describes civil society as "men and women, in groups or as individuals, associated to do things for themselves with the purpose of changing the society in which they live." In recent decades, peoples of all classes, creeds, and races have organized themselves to defend democracy and human rights; to strive for equitable development or a better environment; to help those in need; or to improve the quality of life among their neighbors and communities.[4]

Accordingly, it is important to point out that civil society is recognized as an intermediate entity that separates the private sphere and the state. "Therefore, it excludes both individuals and families, group activities that look inwards (that is, recreation, training, or spiritual), for-profit enterprises, individual business firms, and political efforts to take over control of the state."[5]

In defining the role of CSOs in sustainable development, we must broaden the idea that the main role of civil society is to limit the power of and to exercise democratic control over the state. Indeed, we must concentrate on the role that CSOs play in offering mechanisms of association and collective defense to promote harmonious relationships between citizens and their environment.

According to Robert Putnam, the action of civil society organizations creates confidence and confers legitimacy on public life and political institutions. This results in greater economic development and helps give new content to social life. Through these means, the public arena is reconstructed as an appropriate place to deliberate collective affairs.

The public nature of CSOs helps build their knowledge- and skill-level in monitoring democratic institutions and in publicly managing the processes of citizen agreements and coexistence. In addition, CSOs are well equipped to discuss the problems related to sustainable development, including culture, the ethos, human rights, peace, and war.

Forms of Expressing the Roles of CSOs

At the end of the twentieth century, civilization bears witness to and acts on the increasing role that CSOs play in promoting and carrying out sustainable development. CSOs' role in sustainable development has had several manifestations. Sometimes, it has emphasized the participation and mobilization of individuals and groups in order to attain common social objectives. These objectives are related to sustainability of resources and government accountability and, on occasion, can be linked to community development.

There are many examples of civil society participation and mobilization in defense of the global environment. A considerable number of CSOs work on topics related to conservation and sustainable development. Other CSOs participate in the inexorable inspection of the activities of businesses, governments, and individuals whose behavior might endanger the sustainability of the planet.

A global consciousness about the dangers of the extinction of flora and fauna and public disapproval of offences against the environment has grown. This growing movement has paralleled the emergence of civil society organizations dedicated to sustainable development at the local, national, and international levels. Due to the work of CSOs, modifications in national constitutions have been made to include the concept of sustainable development. CSOs have also catalyzed changes in legislation, ranging from decrees to protect forests and create animal reserves, to sanctions against those violating environmental protection laws.

At the international level, it is important to recognize the efforts of Greenpeace. This CSO has mobilized public support against sea pollution from ecological disasters (for example, the Exxon *Valdez* incident in Alaska) and actively opposed France's nuclear tests in the Pacific. Greenpeace's efforts to mobilize public awareness and support has crossed national borders. The organization has made important contributions to creating a worldwide environmental consciousness about the value of renewable and nonrenewable resources and the commitment required from communities to maintain a healthy balance between the necessary exploitation to subsist and a respect for the ecosystems, the biosphere, and everything that depends on the sustainability of the species.

Other civil society organizations have been developed to monitor the programs and policies of socio-economic growth and the parameters of sustainability and "ecoefficiency." With the increase in the number of CSOs, the role of citizens and their organizations in surveying the environmental agendas and sustainable development programs of both the private and public sector has gained strength.

Developing countries have also benefited from the emergence of numerous civil society organizations in the developed world. Some of these organizations are dedicated to protecting and developing land masses of universal importance such as the subtropical zones of countries in Asia and the Americas and the Amazon forest. The adoption of a "green" agenda by political organizations, particularly in Europe, also points to the effect the work of CSOs has had in the field of sustainable development.

In the area of advocacy, which includes intervention and policy, the work carried out by CSOs in supporting the rights of ethnic minorities to their culture and territory, which has profound implications for the topic of sustainable development, is evident. In this context, the action of organizations that promote collaboration and dialogue as strategies for achieving peace in areas of high environmental abuse caused by warring conflicts constitutes an important contribution.

In addition, many advocacy organizations lobby before legislative bodies and other government entities to establish public policies or legal frameworks favorable to sustainable development. Within this scope of action, we can find CSOs that support processes of design, monitoring, and evaluation of local and national development plans including environmental action plans, through their participation in such organizations as territorial planning bodies.

The scope of the activities of CSOs in sustainable development is wide and far-reaching. There is consensus on the need to promote processes that create and develop the capacity of the CSOs so that they will be able to accomplish effective results in the short, intermediate, and long run. The institutional development programs for building this capacity should bring together both technical and managerial resources to promote the establishment of strategic alliances and the channeling of resources.

The issue of sustainability within CSOs frequently concerns their capacity for carrying out actions and programs with technical and managerial competency without depending on external resources but rather on the resources they generate themselves in undertaking their activities. This shift from dependency to self-sustenance is a compulsory point of analysis as well as an important requisite if an organization is truly committed to action toward sustainable development.

An increasing number of organizations in both developed and developing countries offer programs to build institutional capacity with varying methods and degrees of intensity. The common thread that runs through these types of programs is the application of participatory methodologies, based on case studies, technical assistance, and site visits and discussions. Donor organizations are also promoting capacity building within CSOs. CSOs must prepare funding proposals that are well written and thoroughly and extensively researched to meet stricter guidelines by donor organizations.

Frequently, CSOs from the Southern Hemisphere present proposals to donor organizations in the Northern Hemisphere, thus expanding the scope of both donor organizations and CSOs. These proposals represent a bid for research, intervention, or policy development that the donor organization can then accept or reject, depending on whether the proposal fits the guidelines previously established.

The contract or underwriting of agreements among CSOs and local and national governments and multilateral organizations such as the World Bank in response to burning problems related to sustainable development is another alternative used by CSOs to generate capacity within their own organizations to mobilize opinions and resources.

Innovation of CSOs in the Field of Sustainable Development

There are numerous examples of CSOs that have addressed the issue of sustainable development in an innovative fashion. These include creating viable alternatives for promoting processes to protect and preserve the environment as well as establishing environmental services and systems for sustainable agriculture production. The creation of nature reserves spawned by civil society organizations is a common occurrence in many countries in the Americas. One CSO, FES Foundation of Colombia, established Colombia's first nature reserve in the early 1980s, a long time before there was talk of sustainable development. Twenty years later, over a hundred nature reserves had been established and were being managed by civil society organizations in that country. The concept of a CSO-established nature reserve, which could have a static connotation in the sense that it maintains and preserves all that is found within specific borders, has evolved toward the idea of CSOs providing environmental services. These services have included securing forests that otherwise would be exploited for coal and establishing biosphere reserves and environmental administration zones in which CSOs have mobilized participation to implement their action. CSOs can also play a role in designing and implementing policy; promoting "ecoefficiency," or environmentally efficient production systems; creating and operating venture capital investment funds; and supporting local communities in the process of commercializing biodiversity.

At this point, it is important to define the concept of "ecoefficiency." This term is a result of the business concept of sustainable development, which bestows great importance on technology and scientific advances and which emphasizes the feasibility of sustainable growth without having a significant effect on the resource base it supports.

Ecoefficiency sets forth three aspects that should be considered for attaining continuous economic development without disrupting the resource base. Economic growth is a necessary component for development but not the only one. The efficient use of natural resources and the protection of the environment are also crucial factors in ensuring the survival of future generations. Finally, social equity is transcendental for sustainable development.

These aspects are worth highlighting for their potential to expand the role of CSOs in sustainable development, and they are manifested through the environmental services provided by CSOs. These services include the protection of watersheds, which will have a great impact on the present and future use of this resource for human consumption as well as for hydraulic energy.

CSOs have expanded their environmental services' portfolio. Services range from reforestation support and the protection of the aforementioned watersheds to the cleaning of rivers, lagoons, and wetlands as well as the protection of endangered species. Environmental services have also grown in scope of action to include financial services. These services include offering affordable and reasonable lines of credit to environmental programs and tax incentives for reforestation.

One innovative aspect that stands out is the promotion of environmentally safe production practices through the creation of venture capital investment funds. These funds support environmentally conscious businesses. The work of CSOs is being complemented by the efforts of multilateral agencies such as the Inter-American Development Bank (IADB). This institution is currently working in collaboration with CSOs in the Americas to support the creation of businesses with environmentally sound products. The first efforts were carried out in Costa Rica and Brazil and brought in revenues of about $30 million in the subsequent five years in investment for these kinds of projects. In both countries, these projects are led by CSOs.

Venture Capital Investment Funds provide support ranging from the establishment of businesses and the creation of capital funds as equity for the provision of favorable credit terms to the financing of technical assistance and backstopping of newly established businesses.

Through research and the efforts of multi-sector working groups acting as task forces, CSOs have been involved in the design and analysis of policy proposals at sub-regional, regional, and international levels. The work of a particular CSO, Centro Andino para el Desarrollo Sostenible, has provided the five countries that compose the Andean Community with the capability to make sound public policy decisions related to sustainable development. The MacArthur Foundation in the USA and the FES Foundation of Colombia funded this initiative.

In the commercialization of biodiversity, CSOs face several challenges. While educating local indigenous communities to protect the environment, they must also teach them to understand legislation and property rights with respect to natural resources. CSOs can also help these communities organize themselves to benefit from environmental commercialization in a sound manner.

Among the comparative advantages of CSOs, such as the ability to mobilize public opinion, is being able to act for the "common good." The ongoing search for answers to the problems arising from sustainable development thrusts CSOs into further exploring the area of marketing carbon. Otherwise known as carbon credits, or carbon dioxide "sequestration" of the atmosphere, these measures have tremendous potential for mitigating the greenhouse effect and other by-products of pollution by gas emissions.

The Carbon Credit projects have gained momentum as a result of the Japan international meeting on climatic changes that was held in 1997 and from a follow-up meeting in Buenos Aires in 1998. The underlying premise of carbon credits is that those businesses whose practices are detrimental to the environment should contribute to the protection of forests. Therefore, the aggregates of large factories that contaminate the environment are accumulating an environmental debt to be paid through the marketing of carbon credits. These carbon credits are used by CSOs to establish "carbon traps." These carbon traps are either large areas of protected forests or large-scale reforestation projects.

Sustainable agriculture forms the bulk of the activities of CSOs in the field of sustainable development. Indeed, they are active in the promotion of alternative systems of agricultural production that respond to the challenges of modern productivity. These alternative practices vary from extracting resources from forests, seas, and rivers to researching cattle raising and hillside farming techniques. CSOs recognize the potential of new forms of exploiting natural resources without degrading them through the application of appropriate technologies and active grassroots participation.

In this area, it is worth mentioning several innovative projects carried out by CSOs that wish to provide integral solutions to sustainable development. One well-known example is the FES Foundation in Colombia effort in establishing an Environmental Administrative Zone. This Zone works to protect biodiversity and promotes the socio-economic development of the community. Covering an area of almost 200,000 hectares of tropical rain forest in southwestern Colombia, this zone will be the focus of a series of activities to integrate the conservation of biodiversity in natural ecosystems and agrosystems. At the same time, this zone also serves as a carbon trap, thus providing a solution to forest exploitation and the degeneration of native species. This zone also seeks to integrate reforestation with sustainable agricultural production and cattle-raising practices.

Final Thoughts

A final note will be made to the monumental tasks that CSOs face in sustainable development. This chapter referred to the growing activism of citizens and civil society organizations in the field of sustainable development. Although it is difficult to establish the precise number of organizations that work on the local, national, and global levels, it is safe to assume that they number in the thousands. These thousands of

CSOs that are working on the five continents act to incorporate the theory and practice of sustainable development into their mission and vision of the future.

The brief mention of the innovative efforts of CSOs indicates that there is a global trend to protect the environment through the establishment of environmental administrative zones, carbon credits, and sustainable agriculture practices. These practices, among others, are at different stages of development around the world, and their efforts are accompanied by increasing citizen participation. Their motivation, stimulated by profound conviction, is compatible with the mission and vision of CIVICUS. CIVICUS hopes to construct a world where we are born, grow, and live in peace, frugally enjoying the natural resources and preserving the biological richness as a patrimony that grows with permanent and continuous acts by citizens. Only then can we guarantee the existence and continuity of mankind and all other species on the planet.

Notes

1. A.A. Maya, "La gallina de los huevos de oro; Debate sobre el concepto de desarrollo sostenible," in *ECOFONDO/CEREC* (Gente nueva: Santafe de Bogotá, D.C. 1996), pp. 113–114.
2. Margarita Bonamusa, Profesora-Investigadora, Universidad de los Andes en: Para qué se fortalece la sociedad, Mimeógrafo, 1996.
3. Eduardo Posada Carbo, "Ah Sociedad Civil," *El Tiempo*, Nov. 30, 1997.
4. Miguel Darcy de Oliveira and Rajesh Tandon, *Citizens: Strengthening Global Civil Society* (Washington, DC: CIVICUS, 1994).
5. Larry Diamond, "Rethinking Civil Society," *Journal of Democracy* 5 (3), 1994.

8

Religion and Civil Society: What Is the Relationship between Them?

Fritz Erich Anhelm

During the last twenty years, the history of the worldwide civil society movement reflects the history of contributions made by religious communities to the processes of participation and democratization. Having said that, there must be no illusion about the fact that religion can produce the reverse effect: the preservation of hierarchic structures and demagogic manipulation. This chapter will analyze the conditions under which religious communities can become a positive, productive factor, enabling all citizens to shape those conditions of life that reflect the ethical criteria of societies, and which are at the same time economically and socially equitable, ecologically sensitive, and culturally respectful.

In light of the present global reality, these objectives have not yet been achieved nor has the conflict between them been completely resolved. However, they have become largely accepted as orientation points in the field of civil society engagement. Consequently, when their global responsibility is under discussion, the religious communities must accept evaluation on the basis of civil society criteria, at least in respect to how they are regarded from the outside.

Religious Worldviews and How They Relate to Civil Society

Those assessing the respective self-perceptions of the major religious communities will be confronted with differing emphases.[1] To see the world as the embodiment of God and thus to invest it with holiness, to discover in its diversity the source of life, to insist on active nonviolence even in political resistance: these are the features of Hinduism that meet the current demands for ecological sensitivity, intercultural hermeneutics, and civil conflict management. Such affinities between religious interpretations of and secular responsibility for the world do not necessarily follow logically. Yet they deserve to be emphasized and consciously noted.

The worldview of Buddhism shares some common features with ecological concepts of balance and cycles. To put these aspects in such relative terms can, but need not necessarily, contradict the emphasis on human responsibility in Judaism. Ethics in this context are inextricably linked to the idea of God's justice, which also includes social, ecological, and peacemaking elements. It brings together God the Creator and the history of humanity. In Christianity, He, Himself, becomes incarnate.

The dual commandment of love for God and for your neighbor with its simultaneous eschatological (the Kingdom of God) and social reference (rich/poor), is the reason behind a view of the world based on God's unquestioned grace, solidarity between human beings, and the responsibility of individual conscience. Human action remains penultimately (that is, transitionally) oriented toward the ultimate (promise and grace). The close bond between religion and politics in Islam is based on its "realistic optimism" that humanity is capable of shaping the world once it has transcended its oblivion of God. In this respect, religion is always bound to society and politics and is anything but a private matter.

Even this short description illustrates that religious perceptions and interpretations of the world can assume contradictory features. Yet it by no means follows that an interreligious dialogue aimed at shared responsibility for the world is consequently doomed to failure. The latest attempt in this direction — the project "World Ethos" initiated by Hans Küng and Leonard Swidler, which led to a world ethos declaration at the Parliament of World Religions in Chicago in 1993 — identifies the "Golden Rule" (do unto others as you would have done unto you) as the lowest common denominator. This common basis has been criticized in two respects. On the one hand, it is said to be a "humanitarian ideal" without religious roots, thus reducing religion to ethics. On the other hand, it is said that this ideal is preformulated in Euro-American language and takes little account of other religious-cultural traditions. There are good reasons for both criticisms, but they do preclude possibilities for interreligious dialogue, which have yet to be tried out.[2]

If such dialogues are to become reality, however, they should address the problem of the inculturation of religious worldviews. Only then will we fully understand the role of religion in the lives of the faithful, the relationship between religion and society, and the differences between worldview and global responsibility. The existing claims of absolute truths, which must neither be left unaccounted nor lead to an inability to communicate, constitute a special challenge for an interreligious dialogue. They are by far the greatest obstacle of all. They cannot be overcome, but can only be identified in mutual respect and be examined for possibilities of common action against the background of existing beliefs, while recognizing that some conflicting orientations will remain.

The Different Social Forms of Religion and Their Relevance for Civil Society

Those examining the relationship between religions and civil society at the practical level will grasp its meaning less through statements of belief than through the individuals involved and their self-perceptions. In this context we can distinguish between three levels of activity: institutional, organization-related, and voluntary association.

Applied to religions, the institutional definition includes those social forms that are characterized by well-established patterns of behavior and relationships that are recognized as relatively binding. The relationship between religion and the state is thus frequently regulated by law, even though in very different ways. Religions as institutions do not really see themselves as part of civil society, often claiming a unique status. This is due in particular to their "religious quality," to claims of transcendence that elude contractual regulations. Whenever this leads to the rejection of any secular standard (for example in the form of State constitutions or human and civil rights commitments), it may create massive competition and conflicts with secular authorities. Such fundamental views can also be used for political ends or, in turn, have a tendency to lead to the use of politics, by force in the worst case.

A religious institution can be termed civil only if it at least recognizes the rules of the human rights catalogue and rejects the use of force as an element governing its own actions. It turns into a true agent of civil society only when it sees itself as part of this communication process. This, however, applies to very few institutionally structured religions.

This is different in the case of organizations that have been established by institutionalized religions with the aim of addressing specific problems and issues and that are relatively independent in their operations. Such organizations exist, for example, in the field of development cooperation and in health and education, but they also exist in many fields of advocacy and lobbying. They operate on the basis of high professional standards, yet they depend, at the same time, on extensive voluntary engagement. They are active internationally, regionally, and locally and they frequently possess large networks of their own that reach far beyond national boundaries. Since many have existed for longer than the more recent discussion on civil society and have established their own traditions, it cannot be taken for granted that they define themselves as representatives of civil society.

Some of these organizations view such categorizations somewhat skeptically because of their own religious background, but their activities are very similar to those of secular representatives of civil society. In many cases, it was a previous religious engagement (such as to eradicate poverty, in development and education programs, and in health services) that triggered such secular initiatives in the first place.

The most marked similarities between religion and the secular discussion on civil society exist at the level of voluntary association, both in terms of self-perception and the issues addressed by these organizations. They include human rights activities, civil conflict resolution strategies, peace and reconciliation services, environmental and nature protection activities, village development and education programs, health and sex education, debt remission campaigns, actions against child labor and sex tourism, and refugee and disaster relief projects. Many of these voluntary associations work on an ecumenical and interreligious basis and cooperate with secular partners. This is the example most likely to be associated with the emergence of a faith-oriented part of civil society (internationally, regionally, and locally), motivated by its religious roots, yet open to extensive cooperation. Yet, we are confronted with predominantly single-issue activities, even in those cases where international networks are formed trying to orient them towards common objectives would probably take the zest out of their practical engagement and paralyze their critical potential. Nevertheless, the discussion on civil society may serve as a frame of reference for such activities that will open up important fields of communication, especially between religiously motivated and secularly defined activities.

Interreligious NGOs as Global Players[3]

The most representative forum for the global responsibility of the religious communities is probably the World Conference on Religion and Peace (WCRP), founded in 1970. This organization has consultative status with the Economic and Social Council of the UN and is often termed the "UN of the Religions." The range of issues it addresses has expanded from its original commitment to disarmament and peace to all important fields of global concern. The "Dialogue of the Religions" in this case is clearly directed towards possibilities of sharing global responsibility, yet its decisions are not binding. Attempts are being made to maintain communication channels with the help of regional secretariats, national sections, and contact persons in many countries and through world assemblies.

Similarly to the Parliament of the World Religions, which was founded on the occasion of the World Exposition (EXPO) in Chicago, the WCRP acts separately from the religious communities within its existing institutional structure. Both the Parliament and the WCRP speak on behalf of only the individuals participating in them. These individuals represent a relatively narrow spectrum of the "official" religious communities. They are largely recruited from those sectors that are very sensitive to questions of an ethical and socio-political nature. Even if there is occasional cooperation among faith-oriented NGOs, neither the WCRP nor the Parliament of the World Religions constitutes anything comparable to a common umbrella for them all. These NGOs frequently have their own nationally and internationally active networks at their disposal, mainly on the basis of their specific religious background.

The only other association comparable to the WCRP and the Parliament of the World Religions in terms of a globally defined approach to dialogue may be the International Association for Religious Freedom (IARF). This organization is also accredited to the UN and UNESCO as an NGO, and it coalesces parts of the Christian-free churches, free religious organizations, religious humanists, and liberal movements of Buddhism, Shintoism, Hinduism, and Islam around subjects such as peace, social justice, and ecology. Consequently, this association represents a segment of the interreligious dialogue that cannot really be covered in its entirety by any of the listed organizations.

Global NGOs from Individual Religions

The dialogue between religion and civil society is sought more or less intensively even in cases where individual religions are globally present with their own organizations. For the Protestant-Orthodox section of the Christian faith and the denominational world federations (for example for the Lutheran, Reformed, or the worldwide Federation "Syndesmos," for the Orthodox Church), there exists the Ecumenical Council of Churches. Apart from its institutional membership (336 churches in 120 countries), the Council includes a wide range of organizations and voluntary associations that are inspiring and supporting its activities with their own networks. However, the relationship between member institutions and independent initiatives has frequently been a subject for discussion. The ecumenical movement, especially in its commitment to global responsibility, may receive a great deal of inspiration from this unresolved relationship.

Beyond the Roman Catholic denomination's self-perception as a world church in institutional terms, religious orders within it play an internationally important role at the organizational level. However limited their self-perception as part of civil society may be, they are engaged in many diverse social activities that, in turn, trigger further voluntary work by the laity. This lay involvement has, however, developed its own forms of organization that are not always in line with what the official church has ordered, but which form a critical potential from within the church. In all major religions, it is mainly the laity that is reaching out to the rest of society. They are the secular experts, whose expert knowledge, however, is not necessarily always appreciated by the institutionalized sections of the religious communities.

Religious orders exist in all major religions and, like the lay organizations, enjoy a certain measure of autonomy. Apart from their monastic traditions, they are constantly exerting an effect on social life. Even Sufism, which developed from purely mystic and ascetic roots in Islam in the seventh century, shows clear elements of charity today and has spread in various forms to all parts of the Arab world and beyond. The World Council of Muslim Women Foundation, founded in 1993, operates in the field of education as a global lay and nonprofit organization. This organization supports women's rights, peaceful coexistence, and interreligious dialogue. The Muslim World League/Rabita, established in 1962, is a member of UNESCO and UNICEF and has consultative status with the Economic and Social Council of the United Nations. Using its observer status in the Organization of Islamic Conferences, the League tries to bring together the different streams in the Muslim world.

The World Jewish Congress (WJC) has existed since 1936 and today has member organizations in more than eighty countries. It regards itself as the global diplomatic arm of Jewry vis-à-vis governments and international organizations and maintains offices in North and South America, western and eastern Europe, Australia, and the Middle East. Together with the World Jewish Restitution Organization (WJRO), it negotiates the restitution of Jewish property, especially in western and eastern Europe. Its own institute in Jerusalem analyzes political developments that affect Jewry and publishes a wide range of documentation on these issues.

The International Network of Engaged Buddhists (INEB), founded in 1989, has more than four hundred member organizations today that are working locally or regionally in thirty-three countries. It advocates civil conflict resolution and active nonviolence, supports dissident groups in Burma, organizes training programs for the use of adapted technologies, and represents, together with the Buddhist Peace Fellowship and the Movement for Beloved Community, the bond between Buddhist spirituality and global responsibility.

All these globally active NGOs — and this list merely represents a modest selection — constitute a world of their own, even if committed to interreligious dialogue. As global players, they always reflect the concerns of their respective religious base. In the context of the international civil society, it is in particular their hermeneutical sensitivity that is in demand as well as the ability to accept the other — both the secular and the religious.

Christian Ecumenism in a Global Context

Ecumenical Christian ethics has formulated specific orientations in the second half of this century, starting with the concept of the "responsible society," the notion of a "just, participatory, and sustainable society" and leading up to the "Conciliar Process for Justice, Peace, and the Integrity of Creation." The conciliar process, which started with the World Assembly of the Ecumenical Council of Churches in Vancouver in 1983, has tried to bring together in a binding framework of ecclesiological-ethical orientation the institutional, organization-related, and individual levels of independent associations. It has only been partly successful and has experienced a number of setbacks since the East-West conflict came to an end.[4]

This process has highlighted those issues that, in the end, set the agenda of the major UN conferences and that in the 1990s became the nucleus of growing civil society engagement on a global scale. The process of Agenda 21 initiated at the Rio Conference (1992) and its overview of economic, ecological, social, and cultural aspects of sustainable development may be regarded as the secular counterpart to the conciliar process.

Many representatives of church-related initiatives and groups that originally supported the conciliar process have now become part of a broader faith-oriented commitment to civil society. This applies to initiatives for social justice (for example, the Jubilee 2000 campaign supporting debt remission), civil conflict management, human rights activities, the protection of the rain forests, and many other issues. It applies especially to activities in connection with the Local Agenda 21.

Simultaneously, the institutional representatives have been withdrawing more and more from the conciliar process and its agenda. While groups close to the churches have become more involved in secular developments of civil society, the institutionalized churches have initiated a process of introspection that also changed their agenda. Problems related to their institutional relevance within society and to the competition between ecclesiastical self-perceptions have come to the fore. This particularly affects the church-based organizations that are closely involved with societal concerns. In their secular involvement, they frequently feel left in the lurch by the institution from which they have come, yet they still feel committed to their church roots. Their profile within civil society results from the tensions between their loyalty to the cause and to the institution.

By limiting themselves to their institutional setup, the churches will not only find it impossible in the longer term to express their global responsibility in ecumenical terms, but they will also remove the very context that provides motivation for the church-based sections of civil society in the first place. In addition, they will tend to make themselves incapable of pursuing interreligious dialogue.

This applies not only to the Christian denominations, but to all religious communities. The era of globalization calls for religious communities to face each other openly without betraying their own profile in faith. The more developed their profile, the more fruitful may be the dialogue, and the less reason they may have to fear syncretism, which is hindering such communication to this very day. Interreligious dialogue is the response of the religious communities to globalization. When this response does not exist, fundamentalism may take its place. This would mean, however, the beginning of the end of global civility.

Religious Fundamentalism and Civil Society Engagement

Fundamentalism, which aggressively claims proprietary rights on the truth, can be found at all levels: the institutional, the organization-related, and the voluntary association. Religious zeal that tries to get the upper hand by force is as old as the history of humanity. There were times when it was widespread and left horrible traces of bloodshed. When such zeal becomes tied to political objectives, charged with racist or ethnic elements, and fed by social conflicts, it may tempt entire populations to break away from any civility in the way they deal with each other.

Religion becomes a problem if it prevents the resolution of problems by absolutism. In the extreme, religious motives may even serve to legitimize criminal organizations. This is where consensus ends, where any practical cooperation reaches its limits. Terrorism — for religious or any other motives — is the worst enemy of civil society. Whenever such terrorism rears its head, the faith-oriented section of civil society must prove its immunity against it. The commitment to nonviolence and how it is handled in practice is put to the test in such a situation. It is particularly in the context of religiously motivated force that nonviolence has become the crucial feature of faith-oriented activities in civil society. The civil resolution of conflicts, therefore, constitutes one of the most important fields of activity for religious associations that regard themselves as part of global civil society. The second normative basis they share is the Universal Declaration of Human Rights, including its economic, social, and cultural aspects. The inviolability of human dignity is an indispensable requirement of any civil society engagement. This is true even if religious cults and cultures are in conflict with it, such as in the case of gender relations or the many and various forms of ethnic origin and traditions of faith. There can be no religion-specific discount in the question of respecting the other, in particular the weaker parts of society.

Fundamentalist currents in the broad spectrum of religiously oriented groups, including those willing to use force and in fact already using it, cannot be simply dismissed. It becomes even more important that the faith-oriented segment of global civil society unequivocally rejects such groups in word and deed.

"Between Jihad and McWorld" is where Benjamin R. Barber located global civil society — between tyrannical paternalisms, blood communities, and tribal cults on the one hand and the anarchic dogmas of laissez-faire capitalism and its monopolies on the other. And he states: "because he/she belongs to McWorld as a result of their needs, everyone is a consumer; those who are in search of a guardian of their identity are part of a tribe-like conglomeration characterized by either fanatical religious conviction or artificial features of gender or class. None of them is a citizen."[5]

This statement relates religion to unenlightened particularism without further ado. This is emphatically contradicted by the faith-oriented segment of civil society. It regards itself as the advocate of a participatory democratic culture and it gives it a voice in many different ways — both globally and locally.

This chapter cannot describe and acknowledge the commitment to upholding the virtues of a civil society by the many thousands of religiously motivated initiatives and groups that have developed out of voluntary association. The few examples quoted below help illustrate the spectrum of engagement in this field.

Some thirty thousand members make up the Justice, Peace, and Reconciliation Movement in Chambaland, Nigeria. It is open to all women and men from all religions, tribal backgrounds, and cultural identities and, in particular, brings together the two major religions in the region: Islam and Christianity. In addition to its educational program, it has developed projects in the agricultural and health sectors and woman economic empowerment programs at the local level.[6]

SEVA, a Hindu NGO in India, advocates civil rights, regardless of caste and class barriers, especially for the Untouchables. In addition to the organization's literacy programs in the slum areas of the largest cities, it runs health services, schools, and social facilities.

Kairos, a network of groups in western and eastern Europe and the USA, was established after the Ecumenical Assembly of Churches in Europe (Basle, 1989). It supports the victims of globalization by means of campaigns, research, and lobbying activities vis-à-vis international organizations (such as the World Bank, the International Monetary Fund, the World Trade Organization, and the European Community).

Mediating Activists is the name of some four thousand members of the Buddhist Peace Fellowship, which is affiliated with the Fellowship of Reconciliation (FOR); a global and local working association of peace groups committed to non-violence, acting on an ecumenical and interreligious basis. Peace and reconciliation activities have become a major field of faith-based associations and initiatives. Advocating and implementing human rights constitutes an integral part of all religious NGOs close to the civil society spectrum. This engagement is frequently associated with demanding democratic political rights and the right to development and conflict resolution strategies.

The Global Ecumenical Network on Uprooted People (GEN) coordinated by the World Council of Churches orients the regional ecumenical associations on all continents and the aid organizations of the Churches toward the dignity, rights, and better living conditions of refugees. It cooperates with the corresponding secular organizations and agencies internationally, and organizes an exchange of information and experience in addition to its project activities in the field.

Prospects

The early twenty-first century world is challenged to strike a bearable balance between further globalization and a new kind of regionalization that is developing in response to it. The manageability of conditions of life, the participation of individuals, and the ability to influence development trends will all determine whether it is possible to share this planet with some promise of success. The emergence of a global civil society, which is able to observe and to grasp the whole picture even at the local level, may be regarded as a gigantic learning process towards such a successful endeavor. This process has only just begun. There are still many obstacles in its way.

One of the chief obstacles is whether this learning process is in fact desired by some of the prominent players. This question does not concern the economic and political representatives only. It also concerns the religious communities. Are they willing and able to develop the spiritual basis required to accompany such a global learning process and to sustain it? The question is not about unity. It is about the ability to maintain a dialogue with each other and the world. This dialogue requires moderators to stimulate and sustain it; it also requires mediators to manage the conflicts it produces. In this respect, those who have been involved in civil society activities because of their faith have a great deal of past experience to fall back on, far more than those acting at the level of religious institutions. Faith-oriented NGOs are learning to cope with plurality, which, from within the institutions, is seen as highly threatening. They are learning to regard as an asset the complex nature of diversity. Only those who put their trust in the social competence of human beings will understand that it is up to them to use this asset in a manner that enhances justice and peace and respects nature. This is the ultimate reason for any engagement in civil society. Without such trust, diversity becomes hollow and cold, because it lacks a spiritual basis.

Trust in the social competence of human beings is admittedly an extremely fragile foundation. It needs to be carefully nurtured if it is expected to support the rest. In the dialogue, religious communities, in all their different social forms, can play an important part. Just as much as they are able to divide, to separate, and to stir up conflict and let themselves be used, or even abused, for power-political ends, they are equally able to become agents of social cohesion and integration and catalysts of an enriching diversity. This will not be their whole message. Yet, when they themselves recognize and take up the global responsibility of the religious communities, success toward global integration will be measured in terms of the religious communities' ability to discover the dialogue and to develop it further.

Notes

1. Paul Knitter, Der "einzigartige" Beitrag von fünf Religionen zur globalen Verantwortung: Hinduismus, Buddhismus, Judentum, Islam und traditionelle amerikanische Spiritualität in: *Die dialogische Kraft des Mystischen, Religionen im Gespräch,* ed. by Reinhard Kirste, Paul Schwarzenau und Udo Tworuschka, vol. 5, Balve, o.J. p. 80f.
2. Hans Küng (ed.), *Ja zum Weltethos, Perspektiven für die Suche nach Orientierung,* München/Zürich, 1995, and Johannes Rehm (ed.), *Verantwortlich leben in der Weltgemeinschaft. Zur Auseinandersetzung um das Projekt "Weltethos,"* Gütersloh 1994.
3. Information about the individual organizations in the following chapters has been retrieved from their respective homepages on the Internet.
4. On the conciliar process see: Ulrich Schmitthenner (ed.), Arbeitsbuch für Gerechtigkeit, Frieden und Bewahrung der Schöpfung mit Texten aus Seoul. Ökumenischer Informationsdienst, Wethen 1990, and on its critical evaluation: Fritz Erich Anhelm, "Von Basel nach Graz. Ein ökumenischer Lernprozeß in Europa." In *Ökumene lohnt sich. Beiheft zur Ökumenischen Rundschau 68,* Frankfurt/M. 1988.
5. Benjamin R. Barber, *Zwischen Dschihad und McWorld. In: Die Zeit issue* 42, Oct. 14, 1994, p. 64.
6. *The Emancipator,* May 1998, published by the IPRM, Gurum Nongvan, P.O. Box 281, Ganye Adamawa State, Nigeria.

9

Civil Society and Government:
A Continuum of Possibilities

Ezra Mbogori and Hope Chigudu

The Changing Role of Government

The functions and powers of governing institutions have undergone profound changes in the past fifteen years, at every level of society, from local communities to national and international arenas. Indeed, in some respects, the very definition of the role of the State is being transformed. These changes have profound implications for the government-civil society relationship, itself in a period of dynamic flux.

Political scientist Jessica T. Mathews has called this historic process a "power shift":

> The end of the cold war has brought no mere adjustment among states, but a novel redistribution of power among states, markets, and civil society. National governments ... are sharing powers — including political, social, and security roles at the core of sovereignty — with businesses, with international organizations, and with a multitude of citizens groups."[1]

This new dynamic — "cogovernance," some call it — represents the first time in the past 350 years (in the West, at least) that power is no longer concentrated in the State. The State and its instruments of government remain of central importance; but it is no longer the sole actor in determining the direction of society.

Among the most important trends and new developments reshaping the role of government and altering the relationship between government and civil society are: democratization, decentralization, globalization, governance, transnational activist networks, and sustainable development.

Democratization

More people live under democracy than dictatorship or authoritarian rule for the first time in history. The essential catalyst for this process, the end of the Cold War, unleashed democracy throughout Central and Eastern Europe, reaching as far as Africa and Latin America. Today, 118 of the world's 193 countries are democratic.[2] In the dozens of new democracies established over the past decade, civil society organizations (CSOs) play an essential role in building a "culture of democracy" in which men and women learn the practices of democratic citizenship.

Decentralization

A constellation of factors — a more politically conservative ideology in some countries, budget crises in others, and the well-documented failure of top-down development policies throughout the South — have led to a tidal wave of decentralization of state authority, programs, and services. This shift in the locus of governing power is limiting the authority of central governments in many countries and devolving responsibility and decision-making to the subnational and community levels. Increasingly, governments look to decentralization as a mechanism for improving their effectiveness. As power shifts from the center to smaller, local units, communities and regional entities are increasingly able to manage their own affairs, thus making economic and social development more sustainable through genuine ownership. In this new environment, CSOs play an increasingly important role in delivering services, helping to shape and implement programs, and mobilizing communities to gain access to basic human needs. In many countries, civil society now bears the primary responsibility for delivering human services, such as education and health care, that governments can no longer manage.

Globalization

With new international trade regimes of the 1980s and 1990s, a new, thoroughly globalized economy is taking hold throughout the world. As capitalism reaches across borders in search of markets, raw materials, and lower labor costs, transnational corporations are beginning to have an ever more profound impact on the economies of individual nations from Southeast Asia to Russia to Brazil. The implications are particularly profound for individual communities, which can be destabilized as capital and jobs move abroad. In this new economic era, *When Corporations Rule the World,*[3] what is the role of government in setting a nation's economic agenda and ensuring the economic security of its citizens and communities? According to Richard Barnet and John Cavanagh, "The fundamental political conflict in the opening decades of the new century ... will not be between nations or even between trading blocs but between the forces of globalization and the territorially based forces of local survival seeking to preserve and redefine community."[4] In this process, CSOs, place-based and representing the interests of local constituencies and communities, have a central role to play.

Governance

Twenty years ago most people thought that governance was the sole responsibility of the State and its institutions. Today, it is widely recognized that a healthy, flourishing democracy requires "good governance" — a process that is more inclusive, participatory, transparent, accountable, and responsive than in the past. The growing focus on the process of governance rather than on the institutions of government places greater emphasis on measuring the effectiveness of public policies and the use of public resources in achieving societal goals. Instead of simply the exercise of power, governance emphasizes the accountability and responsiveness of leaders to the governed, transparency in the way public decisions are made and leaders selected, and access to information so that citizens can make informed judgments and evaluate performance. Therefore, governance necessarily involves many actors outside of government — including, in particular, civil society.

Transnational Activist Networks

Since the late 1980s, and particularly since the Earth Summit in Rio in 1992, a growing network of transnational nongovernmental organizations (NGOs) has gained unprecedented influence in shaping the international agenda on issues ranging from climate change and human rights to land mines and the workings of the multilateral development banks. Through their efforts, governments have endorsed, sometimes reluctantly, international conventions that bind countries to take specific actions and produce measurable outcomes. On this new global stage, civil society organizations and NGOs have become potent players in shaping and resolving contentious international issues. States can no longer ignore the advocacy and communication powers of organized networks of transnational citizens groups.

Sustainable Development

"The 1980s saw a growing rejection of the myth that government is the sole legitimate agent for development decision making and the management of development resources. It is now widely accepted that civil society has an essential, if not central, role in both," as David Korten has noted.[6] During this period, the focus of international development programs has shifted from government-centered economic growth programs aimed at increasing GNP to "sustainable development," a perspective emphasizing a bottom-up, grassroots, people-centered approach to poverty eradication, sustainable livelihoods, and environmental protection. A recognized key to success in this process is participation — at all steps of the development cycle — of affected communities, community-based organizations, and CSOs.

These trends of the 1980s and 1990s have produced a new perspective on the role of government and the power of citizens and their organizations. The State is no longer the final arbiter of all decisions, and brute force is yielding to an enlightened approach that values the continual engagement of citizens. Even in the more democratic states, many people expect more from democracy than simply the right to enter a voting booth every few years.

The Evolving Government-Civil Society Relationship

Civil society and its organizations are inextricably bound up with government. Government establishes the legal, fiscal, and regulatory framework that defines civil society's operating space. In many countries, government is the chief funder of CSO activity. Beyond the legal and financial framework, the degree to which government is sympathetic toward the sector is a primary determinant of the extent to which civil society sees itself as a collaborator or in confrontation with government. In some settings, the relationship may be antagonistic, with government attempting to co-opt or suppress citizens groups and with CSOs in opposition to government policies and perhaps the government itself. In other countries, government and CSOs have found a broad range of ways to collaborate and complement one another's activities and agendas.

A number of observers have developed analytical frameworks to examine the ways civil society interacts with government. In various contexts, civil society organizations have served as privately supported supplementary service providers to fulfill demands for public goods left unmet by government, as complementary partners with government in public service provision, and as advocates and adversaries to prod government to make changes in public policy and to maintain accountability to the public.[7] Another framework focuses on the degree to which either the "third sector" or government is dominant in their relations, or whether a collaborative model is in effect, a partnership in which government provides the enabling environment and financing while "nonprofit" organizations help to deliver services and perform the functions that government financing supports.[8] Still another approach emphasizes a more focused set of interactions between the two sectors: legal protections offered by government; opposition to government; cooperation with government; autonomy from government, particularly financially; establishing community-controlled programs as alternatives to government initiatives; receiving formal encouragement by government through tax exemptions and other mechanisms; and efforts by CSOs to hold government accountable.[9]

Legislation and Regulation

Through its legal, fiscal, and regulatory environment, government establishes the broad parameters in which civil society and its organizations can exist. To a large degree, this framework either protects or suppresses citizens' freedom of expression, association, and peaceful assembly, both operating as individuals and through nongovernmental legal entities, that is, CSOs generally speaking and development NGOs in particular. Where the State fears the power of citizens' associations and popular movements, regulations can be highly restrictive — making it difficult, for example, to engage in advocacy, raise money, or operate without unwarranted government interference. Such restrictions can serve as significant barriers to the establishment and functioning of organizations.

Despite considerable improvement in legal frameworks for civil society organizations, many countries' laws and regulations governing their existence are still far from satisfactory. The contributions of civil society organizations to the public good are often limited by the lack of clear, coherent, and supportive regulations. The need for a more enabling legal, fiscal, and regulatory environment is almost universal.[10]

Occasionally, CSOs can mobilize successfully to head off restrictive laws. In Hungary, for example, when it appeared that the Parliament would pass restrictive CSO legislation, the Hungarian Nonprofit Information Center in Budapest translated the CIVICUS report *Legal Principles for Citizen Participation* and distributed a copy to every member as part of the debate on new laws on nonprofit organizations. In a significant victory for Hungarian civil society, the Parliament defined various types of public benefit organizations, including their rights and responsibilities, and set out rules for nonprofit business activities and public disclosure.

CSOs tend to focus on the need for governments to establish a supportive legal framework, but laws are also needed to protect the public from possible abuses by CSOs. In exchange for the right to exist as legal entities protected by law, CSOs — in their role as public actors — must follow the law and respect the rights of others. To ensure they do, the State may impose certain burdens of accountability and responsibility on them, just as it may impose similar burdens on other legal entities operating in the public realm.

Government Funding

The financial viability of civil society in many countries is due largely to government support through direct grants and contracts, tax credits and deductions, and regulations encouraging nonprofit service delivery. According to Lester Salamon, government plays a major role in financing nonprofit activity in virtually every country where a sizable nonprofit sector exists.[11]

A 1990 study conducted by the Johns Hopkins University Comparative Nonprofit Sector Project found that 41 percent of the income of the nonprofit sector — here used as a proxy for the little studied resourcing patterns of civil society — in the eight countries surveyed (the US, the UK, France, Germany, Italy, Sweden, Hungary, and Japan) came from government. This was four times larger than the share provided by private philanthropy. Few developing countries have yet become large-scale funders of local nonprofit institutions, but such partnerships have a long history in numerous places, such as India and Pakistan, and have begun to develop elsewhere as well, most prominently in Latin America.[12]

Government funding can be a two-edged sword. A government is unlikely to provide resources to CSOs that it perceives as a threat. Nonprofit organizations that do accept funds risk co-optation and overdependence. Some organizations will not accept resources from government for fear of compromising their values and the integrity of their mission. Most CSOs have to accept that, at least initially, they gain access to public resources largely on government's terms.[13]

Concerned about the negative effects of government funding, a number of civil society organizations are developing new self-financing strategies. In the United States, Pioneer Human Services, a Seattle-based service agency once totally funded by government, has become completely self-financed through its own for-profit business enterprises. In the Dominican Republic, Funredes receives 70 percent of its income from fees for services, product sales, and consulting.

Collaboration: "All Development is Local"

Supported by previously described trends toward decentralization, governance, and sustainable development — and bolstered by supportive legal frameworks and government funding — collaboration between government and CSOs is on the rise around the world. Partnerships between the two sectors, in which the State supplies financial resources and CSOs design and implement programs, are particularly strong at the local level, where civil society and local government can focus on solving concrete problems in the daily lives of citizens and communities. The nonprofit sector has often demonstrated that it can outperform government in the delivery of public services, in improving access to education and health care, and in conducting programs that generate income, eradicate poverty, and protect the local environment.

In Cebu City, Philippines, for example, the city government has established a number of programs in partnership with the private sector and citizens. The Urban Basic Services Program, for example, which aims to improve the delivery of services to the vulnerable segments of society, was jointly created by twelve government agencies, twenty-nine CSOs, including six grassroots citizen organizations.

Collaboration can extend beyond service provision and economic development into the policy and political arenas. The development of the Philippine Constitution in 1986–87 was a collaborative effort undertaken between the government and civil society. The new Constitution institutionalized "people power" and gave civil society a definite role in the life of the nation. CSOs were also heavily involved in drafting the country's National Agenda 21 (its environmental plan). In South Africa, too, the drafting of the new Constitution drew on the tradition and experience gained during the years of struggle for liberation. Public meetings were organized throughout the country, where citizens could raise their concerns and articulate their priorities for development, and CSOs conducted a public education program.

CSOs also collaborate with government in building support for democracy by encouraging citizens to engage with their governing institutions. In Portland, Oregon, the city government is financially committed and legally bound by law to solicit citizen input on matters of neighborhood planning. In Romania, the Pro Democracy Association, a non-partisan civic organization, stimulates citizens in six cities to engage government in finding solutions to local issues such as street cleaning, recycling, and playgrounds.

Advocacy and Opposition: The Political Dimension of Civil Society

If collaboration between government and civil society is on the increase in many parts of the world, confrontation also continues to be a hallmark of the CSO-State relationship.

Governments naturally welcome CSO collaboration on activities that reflect positively on the State's intentions, legitimize their policies and programs, and supplement or reinforce government action. Thus, government may look favorably on humanitarian assistance to relieve drought or famine or on programs to maintain social services such as schools and hospitals. Governments may be less welcoming, however, of CSO activities that challenge government policy.

Civil society makes a unique contribution to the democratic process through advocacy campaigns and, on occasion, outright opposition to government. In the past two decades, civil society has played an essential role in literally toppling governments from the Philippines and Panama to South Africa and Czechoslovakia. Robert Fatton, writing of civil society-State relations in Africa, argues that "Civil society is ... a constant thorn in the monopolizing of political claims of the State–a counterweight to state power and can thus serve as a critical agent of democratization." This is true in even the most developed and mature democracies, but particularly so in what Fareed Zakaria has called the "illiberal" democracies.[16] In many nations, Zakaria argues, "Democratically elected regimes, often ones that have been reelected or reaffirmed through referenda, are routinely ignoring constitutional limits on their power and depriving their citizens of basic rights and freedoms. While elections take place, the basic tenets of "constitutional liberalism" — rule of law, a separation of powers, and the protection of basic liberties of speech, association, assembly, religion, and property — are missing. In these settings, CSOs' programs of advocacy — public education, policy reform, campaigning, and citizen mobilization — are essential to the flourishing of democracy. In fact, it is this political dimension of civil society that distinguishes it from the non-profit, voluntary, third, or NGO sectors — terms of art that are often used in its place. Civil society is inclusive of these "attributes" but in addition, conveys its role in defending and promoting citizen rights in public rights.

Advocacy, at its most basic, is public action directed at changing the policies, positions, or programs of governing institutions within the public and private sectors. Although some governments may prefer that CSOs only do service work and stay out of the realm of ideas, policies, and politics, advocacy is based on the belief that building democratic societies requires discussion, debate, mobilization — even controversy. The advocacy process focuses on how ideas are advanced socially, how priorities are set, how decisions are made.

Advocacy is an essential expression of civil society, one that both defends the rights of the sector and delivers tangible benefits and results for civil society's constituencies. Indeed, as civil society has grown around the world, it has become evident that to fulfill the movement's promise, CSOs must play a strong public advocacy role — a strong political role — in raising high-level policy issues and reforming government, within nations and transnationally.

In Croatia, the Autonomous Women's House of Zagreb fights domestic violence through a public outreach and awareness campaign with a poster reading "Male Violence Against Women Is Not Just a Private Matter: Let's Recognize and Resist It!" In Belize, Spear, a political but nonpartisan organization, builds a campaign to reform the Constitution and promote expanded democratic rights for the country's citizens. In Bangladesh, the Institute for Development Policy Analysis and Advocacy launches a campaign to ban the import and indiscriminate use of a "Dirty Dozen" lethal chemicals. In Tanzania, a coalition of NGOs works to press the government to implement land reform for the poorest of the poor.

The current explosion of advocacy activities among CSOs has been fueled by three historic developments of the past decade: the process of democratization that has swept much of the world since the late 1980s; the advent of new information technologies such as the Internet, which have provided powerful new opportunities to advocates to disseminate information and mobilize support nationally and internationally; and the opportunity for local follow-up action presented by high-visibility international gatherings and events, such as the Vienna human rights conference, the Rio Earth Summit and the women's and population conferences in Beijing and Cairo. Women's organizations also have played a decisive leadership role in the growth of the global advocacy movement.[17]

Advocacy may bring civil society into conflict with the State but, paradoxically, it also relies on government to create a "safe space" where it can flourish. This includes, for instance, an agreement within a society that an important role for advocacy is holding governing institutions to account on behalf of *all* citizens; mechanisms to support nonrestrictive and robust debate on policy issues; procedures that enable groups to resist harassment from authorities; transparency in government so that the public can determine how resources are allocated and decisions made; and an unfettered and knowledgeable media educated about the role of civil society and the importance of its advocacy activities.

Over time, CSOs may move from a position of confrontation with government to something approaching power sharing. In Africa, for example, regional organizations such as the Organization of African Unity and the Economic Commission for Africa and sub-regional bodies like the Southern Africa Development Community are beginning to consult with CSOs, which used to be outside the corridors of power and decision-making.

CSOs may also find themselves at loggerheads with government on some policies, while collaborating on others. The South African NGO Coalition (SANGOCO) recently worked in partnership with the government ministry responsible for drafting a new law to govern operations within the nonprofit sector. But even as it did so, SANGOCO learned that the same ministry was going to broaden access but reduce support levels to children living in poverty. The NGO coalition, even though they supported the de-racializing of the benefit, aggressively fought the new proposed level of the benefit while maintaining a working relationship with the ministry on the legislative issue. The government eventually increased the benefit by 25 percent from what they had originally offered.

Increasingly, transnational advocacy and organizing networks are putting pressure on governments. Coalitions of CSOs from many countries, as well as individuals, join together to challenge policies and violations of basic rights and freedoms. These cross-border CSO networks have been instrumental in such areas as the successful international campaign to ban land mines, opening up the North American Free Trade Agreement (NAFTA) to environmental and labor concerns, and influencing negotiations on global environmental conventions. The skillful use of new information technologies has been critical to the success of many of these transnational advocacy efforts and has caused important changes in government policies and tactics. Observers credit the use of the Internet by CSOs with having limited the Mexican government's response to the Chiapas rebellion of 1994. Mexico's foreign minister, Jose Angel Gurria has been quoted thus: "The shots lasted ten days and ever since, the war has been ... a war on the Internet."[18]

Elsewhere in Latin America, the CSO Casa Alianza, the Latin American branch of Covenant House, works to serve and protect the lives of street children in Mexico, Guatemala, and Honduras. Bruce Harris, of

Casa Alianza's Legal Aid Offices, describes how "electronic advocacy" is used in the defense of children:

We have developed a list of several thousand people (and growing) from many, many countries around the world who are concerned for the plight of the street children. When an incident takes place which requires international pressure (for example, the murder of a Guatemalan street child by a policeman or the "social cleansing" murders of six street children in Honduras) we immediately send out an e-mail message to the thousands of people on our list. We explain what has happened, and ask them to send a short, polite message to government officials (we give them e-mail addresses for the Guatemalan or Honduran authorities). Within hours, the President of Guatemala or the Minister of Foreign Relations receives hundreds of e-mail messages from around the world asking for investigations. Often it is the first time that these politicians have heard about the incident, and the simple fact that they then call the head of the National Police puts a priority on the case for investigation.

Toward an Expanded Government-Civil Society Relationship

[W]e have not created the foundations of a genuinely evolved civil society, which lives on a thousand different levels and thus need not feel that its existence depends on one government or another or on one political party or another.

—Václav Havel

Democracy is not just a way of selecting leaders; it is a mode of life that grows out of a thousand individual initiatives. Throughout history, social organization has been based on the assumption that most people need to be ruled and only a few are capable of ruling. Democracy is a revolt against this idea. At its purest, it is the audacious belief that all humans are or can become capable of governing themselves.

—Erazim Kohak

This brief discussion of the relationship of civil society and government has focused on how that relationship is expressed in democratic states. These nations have made tremendous strides in positioning civil society as a stronger partner with government, as a powerful voice to influence government policy and performance, and as a social force to be reckoned with. Increasingly, the views of CSOs and the interests of their constituencies are, at the very least, considered in the decision-making process within government.

But if we focus not simply on the institutions and mechanisms of government, but on the underlying principles of democracy, and ask "what is the relationship of civil society to the process of democracy?" a new set of challenges and issues presents itself.

Whatever else it is, democracy — whether at the local, community, or at the large-scale national level — is not simply about occasional elections and "participation," but about who decides. In all countries, from the developing nations of the South to the industrialized North, few serious observers would argue that citizens' groups, neighborhood associations, community-based organizations, and other expressions of civil society actually "decide." This does not mean that their voices are not being heard and that they are not consulted. But in most settings and at most times, the most important decisions affecting the fate of communities and nations, and the lives of citizens, are simply not made by the civil sector. Civil society may have won the right to participate in some aspects of government, but power resides elsewhere.

There are, however, a growing number of exceptions to this rule. These occur at the community level, where citizens and their organizations are becoming involved in governing as an expression of their commitment to civil society. In these cases, civil society organizations are beginning to assume responsibility for exercising public authority, and as they do so, are involving citizens in local "political life" in ways that go beyond the mere act of occasional voting. By engaging citizens in local institutions that have the power to determine important issues within the community, these efforts help people become the kinds of citizens that democracy needs. These are citizens who are concerned not only with their own well-being and the well-being of their intimate circle, but with the public interest of the larger political community.[19] In short, they build institutions of real democratic governance that are available to average citizens.

A prominent expression of this form of "co-governance" is occurring today in Porto Alegre, a Brazilian city of 1.3 million people. Here, citizens and their neighborhood organizations engage as equal partners with government in an ongoing municipal participatory budgeting process to determine the distribution of city funds for street paving, sewer investments, school construction, and so on. The main goal of the participatory budgeting process is "to encourage a dynamics and establish a sustained mechanism of joint management of public resources." By breaking from an authoritarian tradition in the formulation of public policy, the process encourages "the direct participation of the population in the different phases of budget preparation and implementation, with special concern for the definition of priorities for the distribution of investment resources."[20] Through this mechanism, citizens and their civic associations are assuming civic responsibility, learning the skills of democracy, and building strong democratic communities, communities in which large numbers of citizens participate in the act of governing.

It is this possibility — extending the sphere of influence of non-governmental actors beyond confrontation and collaboration with government, and into the arena of actual governing and building strong democratic communities — that will transform what we have known in the twentieth century as the third, non-profit, or voluntary sector to a true civil society partner in the coming century.

Notes

1. Jessica T. Mathews, "Power Shift," in *Foreign Affairs,* January/February 1997.
2. Sondra Myers, ed., *Democracy Is a Discussion II* (New London, CT: Connecticut College, 1998).
3. David Korten, *When Corporations Rule the World* (West Hartford, CT: Kumarian Press, 1996).
4. Richard Barnet and John Cavanagh, *Global Dreams: Imperial Corporations and the New World Order* (New York: Touchstone Books, 1995).
5. Jessica T. Mathews, "Power Shift."
6. David Korten, *When Corporations Rule the World* (West Hartford, CT: Kumarian Press, 1996).
7. Dennis Young, "Complementary, Supplementary, or Adversarial? A Theoretical and Historical Examination of Nonprofit-Government Relations in the United States," in *Nonprofits & Government: Collaboration and Conflict* (Washington, DC: Urban Institute, 1999).
8. Lester Salamon, "Government-Nonprofit Relations in Perspective," in *Nonprofits & Government: Collaboration and Conflict* (Washington, DC: Urban Institute, 1999).
9. See *Legal Principles for Citizen Participation* (Washington, DC: CIVICUS, 1997); and Robert Bothwell, "Indicators of a Healthy Civil Society," in *Beyond Prince and Merchant: Citizen Participation and the Rise of Civil Society,* edited by John Burbridge. Institute of Cultural Affairs International. Brussels and Pact Publications, NY.
10. See *Legal Principles for Citizen Participation*; and Robert Bothwell, "Indicators of a Healthy Civil Society."
11. Lester Salamon, "Government-Nonprofit Relations in Perspective."
12. Lester Salamon, "Government-Nonprofit Relations in Perspective."
13. Gonzolo de Maza, Richard Holloway and Fadel N'Diame, "Public Resources from Government," in *Sustaining Civil Society: Strategies for Resource Mobilization* (Washington, DC: CIVICUS, 1997).
14. *Governance for Sustainable Growth and Equity,* UNDP, 1998.
15. Robert Fatton, Jr. "African in the Age of Democratization: The Civil Limitations of Civil Society," in *African Studies Review,* Vol. 38, No. 2,

September 1995.

16. Fareed Zakaria, "The Rise of Illiberal Democracy" in *Democracy is a Discussion II* (New London, CT: Connecticut College, 1998).
17. "Public Advocacy: A Cornerstone of Democratic Society. *CIVICUS World,* May–June 1998.
18. Jessica T. Mathews, "Power Shift."
19. Some of the ideas contained in this section have previously been developed by Stephen Elkin in *City and Regime* (Chicago: University of Chicago Press, 1987).
20. Boaventura de Sousa Santos, "Participatory Budgeting in Porto Alegre: Toward a Redistributive Democracy," in *Politics and Society,* Vol. 26, No. 4, December 1998.

10

Strengthening Civil Society's Capacity to Promote Democratic Governance: The Role of Foundations

Volker Then and Peter Walkenhorst

A Global Perspective on Civil Society

As the turn of the millennium approaches, optimists herald the "global associational revolution."[1] Pessimists claim that voluntary action and associations, which de Tocqueville considered to be the foundations of democracy, are eroding and that citizens of old Western democracies are "bowling alone."[2] Neither perspective may represent the whole truth, but both are relevant observations about contemporary society.

In a globalizing world our frame of reference is shifting. It is clear that processes of societal development in the North, South, East, and West are inextricably linked. Analysts in the old Western democracies are expressing concern about important changes in the structures and development of social capital in these societies. However, civil society has been blossoming elsewhere. For example, it has been reinvigorated in Eastern and Central Europe as both a cause and consequence of the great political transitions underway since the dismantling of the Berlin Wall. But transition processes are not limited to the last decade in Europe. Today an unprecedented number of viable democracies exist, raising the prospects and responsibilities of civil society globally.

While the concepts of civil society and democratic governance claim universal validity, globalization carries new challenges. Long-standing divides between the North and the South have not withered away. As a consequence, governance in a global context is increasingly about the art of reconciling the old distribution challenges between the haves and the have-nots with the new issues of sustainability.

Sustainability is far more than just an ecological concept. In the context of global governance it also aspires to the peaceful coexistence of very different cultures and value systems. This requires achieving balance in a world of intermingling cultures and endogenous cultural resources. Global governance is also inherently an issue of the viability of social systems and of strategies that could potentially prevent what some portend as an inevitable "clash of civilizations."[3]

People have responded to this dramatic global and local change through new or strengthened associations. This "associational revolution" has spawned organizations seeking to strengthen social ties, articulate reciprocally shared norms and values, and to promote and conduct civil society activities globally. Tentative norms of reciprocity are yielding trust. While critical to global development, the viability of this trust is also questioned.

With more and more civil society actors entering the stage, locally and globally, the question of national and global governance needs to be considered in a different light. Civil society organizations are indispensable in their intermediary function. They involve citizens in institutions and activities that mediate vertically between the macro systems of society and the individual. They may also be extremely valuable in mediating horizontally between adherents with conflicting norms and values. Nonetheless, civil society institutions represent particular constituencies, they organize around and articulate particular interests and value systems, and are thereby fundamentally subject to the pluralism of modern societies. They cannot necessarily claim to represent the common good. They produce public goods, but they ultimately must be subject to democratic reconciliation and balance.

It is important to keep in mind that there is a standard against which the development of civil society must be judged: the democratic nature of interaction between civil society actors. Civil society can provide many public goods but it cannot govern. It can organize many voices in today's world but it cannot thrive without a system of democratic governance that balances the voices, guarantees fundamental rights, and empowers those who would otherwise be powerless.

A credible discussion of civil society necessarily addresses state-civil society relationships. There are three distinct dimensions of these relationships: 1) the level of constitutional rights; 2) the level of political problem-solving, decision-making, and service provision; and 3) the level of financially empowering civil society to provide services to the community.

In this analysis, we concentrate explicitly on the *last* of these dimensions. The other two are implicitly important when considering the relationships between and among philanthropic foundations and civil society.

Financing Civil Society: Sources of Civil Society Revenue

As integral members and partial financiers of civil society, charitable foundations are playing important roles in the growth, development, and spread of civil society and the "associational revolution." Private philanthropy — individual donors and philanthropic foundations — provides a mechanism for channeling ideas and funds through civil society to activities promoting the public good and civic norms. The most common kinds of foundations are private foundations, individual or family foundations, community foundations, and corporate foundations. Most of these foundations are established with an endowment; that is, funds that belong to the foundation and allow it to pursue its charitable mission over a long term. These foundations are integral to civil society due to the experience and networks they gain through their funding activities and through their relationships with civil society organizations.

Contrary to most current expectations, the nonprofit sector only receives a limited portion of its total revenue from private philanthropy. Recent findings from the Johns Hopkins Institute for Policy Research's comparative nonprofit sector project indicate that, on average, private philanthropy contributes only about 11 percent of the nonprofit sector's total revenue (the average is based on nineteen countries for which data is available). Philanthropy does not provide more than 35 percent of the nonprofit sector's finances in any country. In fact, studies indicate that countries with a large share of philanthropic revenue in the nonprofit sector are those with a very small sector that has emerged recently (Romania, 35 percent; Slovakia, 23 percent; Hungary, 18 percent; and Czech Republic, 17 percent). Private philanthropy can and does play an important and stimulating role for the emergence of the nonprofit sector. It can act as a catalyst, but it cannot support a viable and growing sector on its own. Private philanthropy simply does not have sufficient resources to support civil society's ongoing programs and services.

There are other strategies for building the emerging nonprofit sector. Overall, fees and charges represent the largest share of nonprofit sector income (47 percent), and this finding is consistent with two different interpretations. In countries with a very young sector, this situation reflects the unavailability of other sources of income and indicates that the sector is still relatively small. Examples include Mexico (85 percent), Peru (68 percent), Spain (49 percent), and most of the transition countries in Central Europe (54–56 percent average). In countries with a highly developed nonprofit sector this substantial revenue from fees and charges reflects the strong market position of the sector as a service provider — a sector that supplies many (public) goods and services that are in great demand. Examples of countries with this situation include Australia (62 percent), Japan (62 percent), and the United States (57 percent).

Another strategy for developing a strong nonprofit sector is particularly evident in European countries where the sector relies heavily on public funding and acts as an agent, spending considerable amounts of public funds. Ireland leads this group of countries with public funds representing 78 percent of nonprofit income. Germany, Israel, the Netherlands, and even the "liberal" United Kingdom rank between 64 and 47 percent. This pattern of nonprofit sector financing "reflects the tradition of subsidiarity built into European social policy, a tradition that acknowledges the important role of the state in financing social welfare services, but turns extensively to private, nonprofit organizations to deliver many of the services that result."[4]

When public grants and contracts constitute a major share of civil society revenue it typically is an indicator of a relatively large nonprofit sector in that country. More active and interventionist approaches to public policy and services, particularly evident in developed countries, rely on spending public funds through intermediaries. For example, the nonprofit sector receives considerable amounts of money as third-party payments from public health care and social security programs. The same pattern is increasingly evident in support of arts and culture programming.

If one analyzes the sources of revenue by field of activities or spending, the pattern clearly shows that professional and business associations, cultural and recreational activities, environmental issues, and development and philanthropic organizations are basically fee or charge driven. By contrast, health care, education, social services, and civic or advocacy issues rely heavily on public funding. When volunteer contributions in time and kind are accounted for, philanthropy becomes the dominant source of incoming resources for several of these fields: environment, civic and advocacy, philanthropic intermediaries, and social services.

This reveals that a distinction needs to be drawn between traditional public goods financed by the state that are now being provided by nonprofits and other civil society organizations on the state's behalf and more recent developments in civil society relating to participation and "voice" issues in public policy formulation. For the latter issues — those relating to public awareness, participation, and voice — we find that advocacy, civic, and environmental organizations are increasingly confronting government action with articulated citizens' positions. While it may be an oversimplification, the activities of civil society organizations are often categorized as relating to direct service provision or to public policy and advocacy.

The State and Civil Society

The Johns Hopkins project invites some interpretative speculation. It seems to indicate that public funding put into operation through the principle of subsidiarity provides substantial support for civil society, thereby increasing the sector's viability. Providing public goods through civil society organizations implies that a country has a regulatory framework that allows, and maybe even encourages, civil society organizations to be established. It implies further that patterns of self-organization and citizen participation are given a chance to develop and structures of reciprocity may be nourished in their growth — that is, moving beyond self-interest to mutual benefit through collective action.

Yet the data also reveal challenges to political governance resulting from globalization, mobility, media, and other communications, increased transparency, cultural exchange, and educational progress. Inherent in all these processes is an increasingly articulate demand and opportunity for citizen participation. Civil society organizations give a voice to and venue for this desire for participation. Public funding can empower this level of democratic expression. But the state ultimately needs to be aware of the need to strike a balance between the public policy decision-making processes in a democratic political system and the way in which services are delivered, both through state funding of intermediaries and through self-organization of citizens. Civil society has a role in both arenas.

This relevance of civil society to policy formulation and service provision is reflected by the increased interest that international organizations, particularly those established inter-governmentally, express towards civil society.

For example, United Nations conferences increasingly involve the "grassroots" level of civil society organizations, hoping to get their support in implementing political issues that would otherwise be far more difficult to be put into action. The World Bank is working to engage the foundation sector through many different channels, although the foundations are rather puzzled by the demands that this huge international organization puts on its humble capacities. The Commission of the European Union has addressed the nonprofit sector in a special communication in which it is trying to assess both the capacity of the sector and the conditions for its sustained growth.[5]

Public policymakers including the above-mentioned institutions of international public policy now realize that the civil society is not just an actor that can be prompted to fill gaps that state interventionist policies cannot fill. There is growing awareness that empowering the nonprofit sector specifically and civil society more broadly in their own rights can be a worthwhile strategy for improving living conditions in many of our countries.

Therefore, deliberate mutual learning activities are beginning. Such efforts will alert the civil society to the limitations inherent in demanding public funding (or trying to feed itself on EU programs or World Bank support which has not developed extensively anyway) and will alert public policymakers to the autonomous and diverse character of civil society.

Foundations and other civil society actors can never assume the state's roles regarding services to which citizens can claim a legal entitlement. They can only bring additional wealth and implementation capacity to the reality of our contemporary society — wealth not measured solely in terms of funding but in a whole range of innovative and pluralistic options for how to organize the modern commonwealth of societies.

Civil Society and Private Funding: The Growing Role of Foundations

Civil society implies that autonomous actors exist and engage in self-organized activities to express their own vision of the world and their work towards achieving this vision. By its very traditions, civil society is the twin of a truly liberal perspective of the world — a world in which responsible, active citizens make contributions to the public good and the community. A society of responsible citizens is the distinct result of a long process culminating in articulations and practices that protect the basic legal qualities of a citizen; meaning, above all, that human rights are guaranteed and enforced. It is through constitutional achievements that citizens have options for how they contribute to society. Among the options open to them is the right of free speech as well as the right to associate. In addition, modern democratic constitutions guarantee the possession of private property and the free disposal thereof. In this constitutional tradition, the different legal qualities of a citizen are complementary and serve as the mutually reinforcing foundations upon which civil society rests.

While some forms of civil society activity rely heavily on participation and involvement, others rely on private resources made available through philanthropy. Philanthropy is an instrument for devoting private funds to public purposes. Private foundations are an important form of organized philanthropy in modern societies today. It is quite natural then, perhaps even inevitable, that foundations are emerging as complementary institutions in countries in transition to democracy. Their development is less dependent on accumulated wealth than it is on the emergence of a constitutional political system. Foundations were established in European countries such as Spain and Portugal in the early years of their democratic transformation. Transition countries, such as Taiwan, South Korea, South Africa, countries in Central and Eastern Europe, and many Latin American countries, have seen their foundation sectors grow substantially in the last decades, even though these sectors may still be small.

Notwithstanding the fact that foundations are among the oldest existing social institutions, it is empirically evident that both the number of private foundations and the size of the sector have experienced a period of sustained growth in recent years, a trend that many expect to continue in the future. This growth is due both to the political transitions towards democracy in the last two decades and to the unprecedented accumulation of wealth in the "old" democracies of the Western world. A long period of peace and economic success allowed for the accumulation of private wealth to a degree that almost necessarily made foundations boom.

Although little is known about the exact size of the foundation sectors around the world in solid empirical terms, with the exception of the United States, there can be no doubt that foundations are becoming increasingly common all over the world. Observing the rapid growth of the foundation sector in countries as different as the United States, Japan, Germany, Italy, Sweden, Turkey, or Brazil, some observers have even stated that "foundations in many countries — and not only in the United States — represent essentially a late twentieth century phenomenon. Perhaps we will soon have to recognize that the key to understanding the future of foundations lies not in the past, but in the present."[6] Understanding the growing number and importance of foundations in contemporary societies requires an investigation of their key social functions and the genuine sources of their legitimacy in contributing to society. What role do foundations play in the development of civil society and democracy, and what is the basis on which their activities gain public acceptance and legitimacy?

Kenneth Prewitt[7] offered startling insights on foundations that challenge some of the conventional legitimacy arguments foundations cite in describing their sector's contributions to society. There are four standard arguments for the legitimacy, special value, and role of foundations: the redistribution capacity of foundations, their efficiency as a producer of public goods, their acting as an agent of social change, and their substantial contribution to pluralism in society.

To perform a redistributive function effectively would require that foundations allocate their program spending to the lower strata of society, on the assumption that their funds originate from the society's wealthiest strata. While this performance is difficult to assess empirically, it is obvious that a considerable amount of foundation spending does not necessarily favor the lower classes. Therefore only a portion of total expenses is actually redistributive. But even if foundations did serve a redistributive function, the argument would still require foundations to be more redistributive than tax-based state expenditure. Without substantial evidence to back these claims, foundations must base their legitimacy on different grounds.

Another traditional argument justifying foundation activities asserts that foundations are more efficient in their work than comparable efforts undertaken by the government or through public agencies. The allegedly better cost-benefit ratio and results of tax-exempt foundation funding compared to funds spent by the state or other nonprofit agencies, has, however, never been proven convincingly in practice. Moreover, the lack of distinct accountability mechanisms, such as shareholders, customers, or voters who can withdraw their contributions or support, undermines the efficiency argument as the basis on which the legitimacy of foundations rests.

A third argument for the special value of foundations suggests their notable role as agents of social change. Because of their independence, flexibility, and continuity, foundations claim to have a unique capacity to bring about desired social change. Although foundations can legitimately claim many changes in their respective fields of activity, these interventions normally do not reach a scale that would provide the kind of broad legitimacy needed to justify their activities. Or, to put it differently, foundations have been actively involved in most of the significant societal transformations in the last several decades, but they generally were trying to catch up with social, political, economic, or technological forces far more powerful than any they could have put in place. The environmental movement, feminism, the rise of civil society and the nonprofit sector, and the new information and communication technologies are a few examples that illustrate the fact that foundations are involved in major transformation processes they did not generate.

Even if foundations could bring about major social change, this would not be a sufficient basis for legitimacy because major societal changes are usually highly controversial and, therefore, are likely to encounter strong opposition from those interests and parties that are not served by those changes. Thus, the notion that foundations serve as agents of social change is a weak argument for public acceptance and legitimacy.

A final line of argument suggests that foundations contribute to the society's pluralism, an essential ingredient of democracy and civil society. Although private foundations constitute only a small share of the overall number of nonprofit organizations, they are in a singular position to promote the diversity of civil society activities. As philanthropic entrepreneurs they can facilitate new trends and developments, or they can support constituencies and interests that are ignored or neglected by the market and the public sector. In other words, foundations have a unique opportunity to expand and nurture the natural diversity of civil society organizations and, thus, to make a lasting contribution to pluralism.

According to Prewitt, this potential for promoting pluralism constitutes the strongest argument upon which to base the legitimacy of foundations. "Not redistribution, not efficiency, not even social change (though some amount of all those occur) but an ongoing and lasting contribution to the pluralism of practice and thought and via that contribution a deep commitment to the principles of tolerance and openness that flow from pluralism"[8] is the strongest argument for a viable foundation sector in civil society.

Transparency and Accountability

Foundations conduct their affairs within the overall context of civil society and with special status — such as tax exemptions — granted through the regulatory framework. Consequently, public acceptance of their work depends not only on what they actually do but also on how the public perceives their activities. Public perception is based largely on the transparency and accountability of individual foundations as well as that of the sector as a whole. At a minimum, transparency means a comprehensive information policy that meets the legitimate needs of the public for information on all aspects of foundation activities. A lack of foundation transparency and openness to the public fosters misperceptions, misunderstandings, and mistrust. Therefore, foundations should ensure that their activities are transparent to the public, whether this emerges from a sense of moral obligation, enlightened self-interest, or responsibility for the sector as a whole. In fact, there is a growing tendency among foundations and foundation associations to develop and adopt voluntary codes of conduct as an effort in self-regulation.

An expanded understanding of public accountability has changed considerably the way foundations define themselves and their program priorities, especially in the United States. Responding to critics and to the principles of participatory democracy voiced by the different social movements since the 1960s, private foundations have tried to reposition themselves in public discourse by becoming more open, accessible, and responsive in their relations with grantees and with the general public.[9] This development represented an important shift in the self-definition of foundations. Having been viewed traditionally as private funds privately managed for public purposes, foundation representatives now espouse the notion that foundations are de facto public trusts to be operated for public purposes.

Of course, it would be an exaggeration to suggest that foundations act as if they were public trusts. But there can be no doubt that changing public expectations have had a lasting impact on the way foundation missions and programs are designed and negotiated. Private foundations, individually and collectively, are not immune from social expectations and public pressure. On the contrary, the experience of the United States shows that foundations respond to social change. Their objectives cannot be determined in full by a founding donor or self-defined mission. In view of fundamental changes in society, politics, the economy, and civil society, foundations have to reassess over time their program strategies, their mission, and their contribution to society in general.

Foundation-Grantee Relationships

If foundations perceive of themselves more like public institutions acting in and on behalf of a pluralist society, this carries implications for their responsibilities regarding their spending and their grantee relationships. This approach makes foundations the "gardeners" of civil society in providing funds for many civil society activities to grow and to expand their capacities. In this regard, foundations have an organization-building responsibility: they can be prime consultants if they think of themselves as empowering institutions.

To perform this vital task of empowerment, foundations have an array of increasingly complex options and models for organizing foundation-grantee relationships: power relations, marketplace, contract, solidarity, and partnership relations.[10]

Perhaps the simplest approach is for foundations to provide the resources of the rich to the needy, understanding their activities in a rather patriarchal way. The basic question here is where responsibility for the outcomes lies. In this simple approach, this responsibility is most likely to be placed with the grantee only.

To pursue a more balanced relationship, foundations may act as buyers of "products" or services available in a market of civil society institutions competing for funding. The inherent challenge in this approach relates to the viability of civil society institutions in a longer term, given that funding is usually granted on a temporary and limited basis.

The same holds true for the contract model. While a foundation is likely to be more interested in building the capacity of the organizations it funds, it still acts on a temporary and selective basis.

Situations in which the foundation becomes an active partner in delivering outcomes shift responsibility increasingly towards the donor in that a considerable part of the project development is usually internalized into the foundation organization. The more a foundation feels a responsibility not only for the success of its immediate programs but for the long-term effectiveness of its funding, the more likely it is that the foundation develops into a cooperative actor that jointly develops and designs its programs with partners in civil society. Thus, the most complex and sophisticated foundation-grantee relationships may result in a joint venture or strategic alliance. Such relationships are based on shared values and common goals as well as respect for others. They require building trust and jointly developing conflict-solving mechanisms and project steering operations conducive to the best interest of the quality of the project. The most basic assumption of this collaborative model is that choices — alternative options — exist for both sides and their joining forces is based on deliberate choice.

Foundations acting responsibly in an increasingly complex, pluralistic social environment can play the role of capacity builders. They can evaluate and consult civil society organizations and their fellow actors in civil society, thereby providing a kind of "testified statement" on issues of quality management in civil society organizations. This makes foundations agents of professionalization. They provide an impetus towards professionalism in a field in which many volunteers multiply the potential effectiveness of what funding can achieve.

To perform appropriately and effectively, foundations must be aware of the important role their own mission plays. Their view of how the world should be or how it may evolve is pivotal in bringing attention to the funding prospects in new fields. Foundation support can have a seismographic function: it can even prompt and reinforce issues making their way onto civil society's agenda. They can be discoverers of new social trends. In regions such as Central and Eastern Europe or Latin America, foundations play an important developmental role.

Foundations and Their Role in Building Civil Society and Democratic Governance

Private foundations are genuine actors within civil society. They have contributed to the rise of civil society organizations and activities all over the world and are likely to play an important role in the future development of the nonprofit sector. A viable, sustainable civil society depends not just on a steady flow of income but also on the longer-term assets of foundations. Viable democratic governance depends somewhat on a state realizing that civil society — vibrant associational life with a public purpose and guided by civic norms and practices — can be both a partner and an expression of subsidiarity that favors citizens taking action in their own right. In a pluralistic and increasingly complex world, the well-being of communities depends on their own action and participation. There is both an increasing "market" and a growing public policy interest in this development. In a global world, the network of civil society institutions becomes ever more important.

Notes

1. Lester M. Salamon and Helmut K. Anheier, *The Emerging Sector Revisited: A Summary* (Manchester, UK: Manchester University Press, 1996).
2. Robert D. Putnam, "Bowling Alone: America's Declining Social Capital," *Journal of Democracy* Vol. 6, No. 1, 1995.
3. Samuel P. Huntington, *The Clash of Civilizations and the Remaking of World Order* (New York: Simon & Schuster, 1996); Peter L. Berger (ed.), *The Limits of Social Cohesion: A Report of the Bertelsmann Foundation to the Club of Rome,* Boulder, CO, 1998.
4. Lester M. Salamon and Helmut K. Anheier, *The Emerging Sector Revisited.*
5. Commission of the European Communities, Communication from the Commission on Promoting the Role of Voluntary Organizations and Foundations in Europe, Brussels 1997.
6. Helmut K. Anheier and Stefan Toepler, eds. *Private Funds, Public Purpose, Philanthropic Foundations in International Perspective* (London: Center for Voluntary Organizations,1999).
7. Kenneth Prewitt, "The Importance of Foundations in an Open Society," in Bertelsmann Foundation, ed., *The Future of Foundations in an Open*

Society (Gütersloh: Bertelsmann AG, 1999).

8. Kenneth Prewitt, "The Importance of Foundations in an Open Society."

9. Kenneth Prewitt, "The Foundation Mission: Purpose, Practice, Public Pressures," in Bertelsmann Foundation, ed., *Foundations in Europe* (Gütersloh: Bertelsmann AG, forthcoming).

10. Bruce Shearer, "Grantmaking or Partnership," in The Protestant Academy at Loccum, ed., *Foundations and NGOs as Agents of Change* (Loccum, Germany: The Protestant Academy at Loccum, 1999).

11

Civil Society and Poverty: Whose Rights Count?

Caitlin Wiesen, Geoffrey D. Prewitt, and Babar Sobhan[1]

At the turn of the millennium, we are confronted with both old entrenched forms of poverty and deprivation and rapidly changing new forms of inequality and exclusion. The end of the Cold War and the promise of a peace dividend for development has not materialized. In its wake, we have experienced intransigent civil strife, rising ethnic conflict, and tensions. Health gains that were translating into longer lives and declining infant mortality are being offset, if not nullified, by the HIV epidemic. The unfettered market, which has generated tremendous wealth for the privileged, has also demonstrated its capacity to generate new poverty on an unprecedented scale.

By contrast, and perhaps in reaction to stark and growing inequalities, we also face a world where the voice of civil society has never been stronger. The global arena is perhaps where the coming of age of civil society has been most spectacular, bringing advocates and activists for poverty reduction to forums that were once the exclusive domain of representatives of the state. Isagani Serrano describes the phenomenon as "countless small circles of citizen power from below growing into powerful civic movements that are becoming a leading edge in shaping development as we move into the next century."[2] Lester Salamon argues that this "global associational revolution" of citizens power, is potentially "as significant to the latter twentieth century as the rise of the nation state was to the latter part of the nineteenth century."[3] In this wake, civil society has been called upon to shoulder an increasing share of the responsibility for eradicating poverty. There is a sense of expectancy with eyes focused on civil society to deliver where the state and market have failed.

? The emergence of civil society, with the vast array and diversity of organizations it represents (people's organizations, trade unions, women's associative movements, churches, non-governmental organizations, etc.) is having a profound impact on how poverty is perceived. In the past, there has been an overwhelming focus on poverty as a condition or plight and the poor as objects to be targeted rather than agents of their own development. Starting with the notion of "the poor" — civil society has given a face, texture, and voice to people living in poverty as a complex and richly divergent population with important assets to bring to development. It has recast the perception of "the poor" as people and leading actors in breaking the processes of their impoverishment rather than passive recipients of aid.

Above all, civil society reminds us that people living in poverty are citizens of society with rights and entitlements to claim the benefits of development. Squarely set within the context of citizen's rights, poverty eradication takes on a rich tradition of international human rights law that recognizes the political, civil, social, economic, and cultural dimensions of deprivation. As such, civil society is changing both the understanding of poverty and the imperative for its eradication from fulfilling basic needs as an act of charity to fulfilling rights to which citizens are entitled (as a societal obligation). Most recently, no doubt spurred by the fiftieth anniversary of the Human Rights Declaration in 1998, many UN agencies have been trying to advance a rights-based approach to development and poverty. Today, civil society has been at the forefront of putting a rights-based approach to poverty and globalization to test.

Civil Society: Shaping the Poverty Agenda

Civil society has become a force for challenging existing policies and institutions to work for the poor, and in so doing, is reshaping the rules of the game. Civil society organizations have articulated and projected the aspirations of people living in poverty, which in turn is shaping an emerging global consciousness. Often they serve as the unofficial moral sense of nations, closely monitoring how governments and donors meet their obligations and commitments. Their role in meeting the basic needs of deprived populations through improved service delivery is broadly recognized, but their major influence on the understanding and practice of poverty eradication within a rights-based approach is barely acknowledged.

Development practice since the 1980s has been driven by the neoliberal orthodoxy and the so-called "Washington Consensus," which effectively equated development with liberalized trade, macroeconomic stability, and getting the prices right. It gave little regard to how assets were distributed within society and its impact on people living in poverty. Civil society has reminded us that poverty is about people and their rights and entitlements as citizens. As such, poverty is a political and social phenomenon.

The Asian financial crisis and the speed with which it spread have brought this point home with disturbing clarity. Policy-focused civil society organizations (CSOs) have argued that the cost of what was essentially a private sector failure has fallen disproportionately on the poor. Some individuals within the international financial institutions (IFIs) now share this view. According to World Bank Chief Economist Joseph Stiglitz, "We have an international economic architecture which has led to more frequent crises ... While there is much talk about pain, the poor have absorbed more than their fair share."

The overwhelming focus on the financial dimensions of the Asia crisis masks the fact that it is above all a social and human crisis. Millions of people were thrown into poverty overnight, and decades of development gains vanished. As Nicola Bullard from Focus on the Global South aptly put it, "Reform of the global financial architecture is now on the agenda, but instead of thinking about architecture, we should be thinking about the people we are building it for."[4] Basic issues are at stake: how we value people and their right to development free from poverty; how the duties, responsibilities, and costs should be apportioned among sectors and actors; and what alliances and relationships should be (re)drawn between citizens and governing institutions to put people back at the center of development practice. These questions highlight the need for reforming the "global social architecture" — the structure of relationships between State, market, and civil society actors — to ensure that the poor reap the benefits and not just the costs of globalization.

Civil society has been at the forefront of a shift in our understanding of poverty from meeting needs or development requirements to fulfilling citizens' rights and entitlements. Citizen entitlement to human rights is a radical concept. As described by Dileep Padaonkar, the Universal Declaration of Human Rights (UDHR) and its subsequent conventions, treaties, and agreements, is a seminal achievement of humankind that "for the first time in history ... set a benchmark to judge the conduct of government toward their citizens."[5] In an era of rapid economic globalization, there is a question of how these covenants can be used and expanded to judge the conduct of the market and hold its actors —

transnational corporations (TNCs), trade consortia, and the like — accountable for citizens' social and economic rights.

"The fundamental importance of integrating poverty eradication within a human rights framework is the potential it creates for shifting priorities in the political economy of resource allocation and distribution in favor of people living in poverty."[6] This has been vividly demonstrated by civil society in its use of human rights declarations, bills, and conventions to advocate on behalf of people living in poverty as citizens with rights and entitlements to the benefits of trade, debt reduction, and macroeconomic policy. All these domains once were the exclusive privilege of State and market actors. The most effective use of human rights instruments is perhaps the successful battle to stop the Multilateral Agreement on Investment (MAI), explored below.

Civil Society in a Globalizing World

At a time when globalization appears to have been reduced to expanding economic liberalization, civil society organizations have insisted that markets be designed to serve the needs of people and not the other way around. At national, regional, and global levels, this has manifested itself in numerous innovative and creative approaches that aim to insert people into the debate on the values and rights of citizens in a global future.

The Multilateral Agreement on Investment

The recent negotiations on the Multilateral Agreement on Investment illustrate how concerns of the market and the rights of corporations seem to drive current development practice. The MAI would have required national governments to accord foreign corporations the same rights and opportunities as local companies. At the same time, national governments would have lost the right to direct and regulate the type of foreign investment coming into the country. The agreement would also have given TNCs the right to sue national governments for compensation for lost profits due to local laws or regulations that did not conform with MAI provisions. The MAI negotiations were conducted largely between State and market actors with little or no involvement of citizens. The Third World Network, Council of Canadians, and other international and Southern CSO movements mobilized opposition to the MAI that is largely credited with stopping the agreement from going forward.

CSOs in both the North and South have argued that the MAI fails to address the concerns of the groups that will be most affected by the treaty: citizens, workers, and small producers in developing countries. The Polaris Institute has called for a reworked MAI that is grounded in mutually reciprocal rights and regulations.[7] It argues that the MAI undermines the basic rights and responsibilities that are contained in the UDHR. CSOs have lobbied against the negative impact of the MAI on the rights of citizens which are embodied in the Covenant on Economic, Social and Cultural Rights and the International Covenant on Civil and Political Rights. Furthermore, the 1974 Charter on Economic Rights and the Duties of States recognizes the political sovereignty of nation states to protect the public interests of its citizens. The charter works on the principle that TNCs have social obligations and enter into an implicit social contract that guarantees respect for the rights of workers and the environment, based on the premise that capital formation is a social process. As opponents of the MAI point out, society is organized around three interlocking principles of citizens' rights, state obligations, and corporate responsibilities. Any discussion on the future form of global governance needs to be grounded in these principles.

Making Debt Reduction Work for the Poor

The international debt crisis has been at the center of a heated debate between the global financial institutions and development activists for much of the 1980s and 1990s. Discussions have focused on the question of how to reduce the debt-service payments of highly indebted poor countries without canceling the entire debt. Several international civil society networks have been campaigning in Organization of Economic Cooperation and Development (OECD) countries for a moratorium on outstanding International Financial Institutions (IFI) and private bank loans, if not outright cancellation. Organizations such as Oxfam International have pointed out that repayments are stifling opportunities for debtor countries to make the investments in human capital that would enable them to break out of their cycle of low growth and increasing poverty and inequality.[8] In several African countries' debt-service payments now exceed net official development assistance (ODA) transfers. This situation is having a catastrophic impact on debtor countries' ability to allocate resources to health and education at the levels agreed upon at the World Conference on Education for All in Jomtien, Thailand (1990) and at the World Summit for Social Development (WSSD) in Copenhagen (1995). The series of United Nations-sponsored conferences of the early 1990s have proved highly influential in establishing basic agreements on human development. Oxfam International argues that converting debt spending into human development investments would make it possible to address these human development deficits and to achieve many of the targets set at the World Summit. For instance, according to the 1997 *Human Development Report*, transferring debt repayments into social sector budgets could have financed health investments capable of saving twenty-one million children's lives and provided education for ninety million girls and women.[9]

More recently, the Jubilee 2000 campaign has brought together a diverse range of civil society actors to press Northern governments to ensure that over a billion people do not enter the new millennium weighed down by the burden of unpayable debt. The campaign has argued that the impact of third world debt needs to be analyzed in terms of its impact on the basic rights of citizens and their ability to access basic social services. The appointment of the UN Special Rapporteur on the Effects of Foreign Debt has been an important victory for civil society campaigners.

Challenging Structural Adjustment: SAPRIN and SAPRI

Civil society opposition to World Bank/International Monetary Fund (IMF) structural adjustment policies (SAPs) has directed attention to the impact of macroeconomic policies on people marginalized from mainstream development efforts. Although most resistance to SAPs has been at the country level, a recent initiative links together movements from several different countries. The Structural Adjustment Participatory Research Initiative Network (SAPRIN) is a worldwide network of civil society organizations examining the impact of SAPs on the poor.[10] The network works with citizens' groups in more than a dozen countries to organize public processes to determine the real impact of World Bank- and IMF-supported economic reform programs and to chart a new course for the future. The network grew out of SAPRI, which has brought together the World Bank, government, and civil society in eight to ten countries.

In El Salvador, CSO activists have argued that privatization of public services cannot be viewed as a series of isolated and "neutral" measures, but should be seen as a chain reaction in which the privatization of one service impacts numerous other services and sectors. Participants at the first SAPRIN national forum described a makeshift approach in the design and implementation of privatization measures, which has resulted in private monopoly structures, contradicting World Bank recommendations on privatization. In Hungary, SAPs have exacerbated an already fragile system of social delivery in the aftermath of the collapse of the communist system. The government's social expenditures in Hungary had fallen in both real and nominal terms, limiting both the quality and the scope of these services. Public spending on health care has been reduced to a level, which places it sixth from the bottom out of twenty-six budgetary sectors. This has caused the health system to rely on outdated equipment and places it twenty years behind Western European technology. In the area of education, cuts in public expenditures radically cut teachers' salaries and led to the dismissal of 8,600 teachers, critically undermining the viability of the education system.

Beyond providing powerful testimony to the human costs of adjustment, the SAPRIN has been carving out space for the voices of citizens to be heard in policy debates normally conducted exclusively between governments and the IFIs. For the first time, macroeconomic policymakers are being challenged to incorporate the views and opinions of communities.

Holding the Players Accountable

UN conferences have been highly influential as a galvanizing force for the emergence of global citizens' movement. The Social Summit in particular was an important turning point in the approach to tackling global poverty. It helped to shape an emerging consensus that viewed poverty as a denial of human rights, not simply as a plight or condition. Social Watch has argued that the commitments made at the Social Summit cannot and should not be viewed as expressions of good intentions between diplomats, but as obligations undertaken by state leaders on behalf of their citizens.[11] This notion of poverty eradication as a fundamental obligation of nation states and the global community as a whole is an important reconceptualization of poverty.

Three important civil society initiatives are mobilizing communities and global citizens to maintain pressure on governments, multilateral agencies, and the private sector to ensure that the eradication of poverty and inequality remain central to the global agenda. They are: Social Watch[12] Eurostep's "The Reality of Aid"[13] and the Women's Environment and Development Organization's "Beyond Promises."[14]

Social Watch is a coalition that has brought together a broad range of civil society actors to monitor progress in meeting goals and commitments made by States at the Social Summit and the Fourth World Conference on Women (FWCW). The coalition publishes a yearly assessment of progress, using an "Index of Fulfilled Commitments." More important, it also acts as a force for local action. NGOs and CSOs involved with Social Watch contribute to the assessment and produce and share local studies with other actors at the local level. These reports form the basis for an ongoing discussion with national governments.

"Beyond Promises" assesses the implementation of the Beijing Platform for Action established at FWCW by surveying national governments and NGOs, while the "Reality of Aid" monitors international aid. The latter report argues that too often aid commitments have been used reactively to respond to crises that could have been avoided had governments and the international community acted proactively to maintain a commitment to aid. The report monitors whether national governments meet the 0.7 percent of GNP target for overall ODA and encourages investments in basic social services for people living in poverty. At the WSSD, donors and governments pledged to devote at least 20 percent of aid flows and budgetary allocations, respectively, to social sector spending. This goal has become an important benchmark for CSOs monitoring commitments to poverty eradication.

Making Space for the Voices of the Poor

At the national level, CSOs have also begun to reorient their work to focus less on service delivery — although this remains an important aspect of their work — and more on questions of empowerment and conscientization. The transition to democratic systems of government around the world has challenged CSOs to find new ways of working with and mobilizing the State at both national and local government levels.

In South Africa, CSOs have led efforts to ensure that poverty eradication is seen as a national priority and to ensure the participation of the poor in national decision-making. A new constitution made an explicit commitment to gender equality that also fell under the purview of the Poverty Hearings. The 1996 census provided stark evidence that Apartheid had exacerbated poverty and inequality in South Africa and showed that the normal project approach of development NGOs could not have a meaningful impact on poverty. This led the South African NGO Coalition (SANGOCO) to push for a coordinated campaign to address poverty, emphasizing forging partnerships between NGOs, other CSOs, government agencies, and other actors.

The War on Poverty Forum (WOPF) is an attempt to create space for the poor themselves to become agents for social change. SANGOCO brought together a broad range of different actors from the government and civil society to address the multidimensionality of poverty in South Africa. A significant aspect of the forum was to "initiate and sustain participatory policy dialogue around poverty eradication." A series of hearings were convened around the country in 1998 — conducted in local languages — and around ten thousand submissions on the experiences of the poor were collected. At the local level, NGOs, church groups, and CSOs came together to mobilize communities to work on creating a genuinely participatory agenda for poverty reduction. At the national level, important relationships were formed with government ministries and other institutions with responsibilities for protecting the rights of the poor. WOPF created the National Plan of Action for Poverty Eradication, which was launched on the International Human Rights Day on 12 December 1998. The plan is seen as a first step in creating a new consciousness that poverty eradication cannot be treated separately from national development and should be at the forefront of all government action.

Another example of how development NGOs are moving beyond a simple service delivery approach at the grassroots to challenge the distribution and allocation of resources comes from Bangladesh. Proshika MUK, one of the country's largest development NGOs, has been conducting participatory rural appraisal (PRA) exercises on the national budget since 1997. The purpose is to link the micro experiences of the poor and the macro policies of government. To combat the view that poverty is something that happens to others, Proshika follows up on the PRA exercise with a national seminar to which senior government officials, policymakers, and other key actors are invited. The seminar serves as an important advocacy tool by challenging government officials — including the prime minister — to talk about how national budgetary priorities will affect poverty reduction efforts. It reinforces the key message that as long as poverty and deprivation exist, the chances for sustained economic growth remain limited.

Together these initiatives are important attempts by civil society to ensure that the rights of people living in deprivation are not forgotten in the headlong rush toward economic globalization. Thinking about poverty in human rights terms challenges the development community to rethink the notion of the poor as a "distant" other. Reducing poverty to concerns about resource mobilization and improved service delivery represents a far more manageable proposition for the world than thinking about it in terms of rights and entitlements to the benefits of development. But that is precisely the challenge that civil society is attempting to take up. The examples discussed are critical demonstrations that we live in an increasingly connected world where poverty cannot be isolated from overall societal well-being.

New Forms of Governing Institutions and Alliances

Civil society has brought the power of collective citizen action into both the national and global arenas and with it a fresh understanding about poverty. At its most fundamental level, poverty is about people — their rights and relationship. This perspective is having far-reaching consequences in the practice of development. In grounding the issue of poverty in citizens' rights and entitlements, civil society has demonstrated how the rich body of standards and principles embodied in human rights declarations and conventions can be effectively used to leverage development benefits for people living in poverty. They have used the law to question the nature of inequities of governing institutions and have raised anew the questions of relationships and accountabilities between state obligations, citizens' rights, and corporate responsibility. Above all it has been shown, that without the mobilization of citizen action, the noble aspirations of the UN human rights conventions and declarations remain just that — aspirations.

The spirit and force of collective citizen action when coupled with the rights and space provided by the United Nations together create a powerful alliance for redrawing a different kind of globalization. This paper argues that while the focus of attention has been on the reform of the "financial architecture," what is called for is a corresponding reform of the "social architecture" or structure of relationships between actors. Only reforms of this magnitude will ensure that the benefits of economic globalization are more equitably distributed, and undertaken in accordance with human rights conventions and standards. Together, the collective challenge of the UN and civil society at the third millennium is to re-vision a world of more equitable relationships where the rights of the citizen rather than the market are at the center of development practice.

Historically, civil society has been able to look to the United Nations as a (i) court of appeals for unrepresented rights at the national level; (ii) custodian and builder of standards and principles; and (iii) necessary manager of global public goods. While the UN certainly provides the forum for the debate on globalization and its impact on social and economic rights, it has been criticized for not providing a high level decision-making body in the event of a social and economic crisis.

With the financial crisis in East Asia, Brazil, and Russia, the private sector was able to muster multi-billion dollar bailouts through emergency high level meetings of the IFIs, G-7, and vested commercial interests. In stark contrast, there was no comparable high-level decision-making forum for dealing with the human and social crisis that ensued which plunged millions of people into poverty, nor set of reserves to be tapped for the unforeseen shock and insecurity that followed.

The UN Security Council could in theory provide a high level of decision-making forum to mediate global social crises. However, it is constrained by its narrow interpretation of security in terms of military threat. The UN has been criticized for straying from the broad vision of security intended by its founders:

> The battle of peace has to be fought on two fronts. The first is the security front where victory spells freedom from fear ... No provisions that can be written into the Charter will enable the Security Council to make the world secure from war if men and women have no security in their homes and jobs.
> (Statement at UN Founding Meeting in San Francisco, 1945)

The 1994 *Human Development Report* introduced the concept of "human insecurity," which recaptured its original intent as more than just a military threat but a social and economic threat as well that could be manifested as hunger, disease, crime, repression or hurtful disruption of daily life.[15] It advocated creating a UN Economic Security Council, or expanding the mandate of the existing Security Council, to provide a decision-making forum at the highest level to treat issues of world insecurity such as global poverty. Such a forum could treat the social and human crises brought on by economic globalization. The time is ripe to revisit these proposals in the context of a review of the global social architecture.

"We the People..."

Equally important is the question of representation at the UN. The UN needs to revisit and update its interpretation of who represents "We the people ..." as stated in its Charter. When it was drawn up, States were considered the sole representatives of their citizens. It is time to recognize more formally the role civil society plays in reflecting the rich diversity of society often excluded from the development process and policy debates at both national and global levels.

There is an unparalleled opportunity and momentum to empower the Millennium People's Assembly in the year 2000 (which is intended to run in parallel with the UN General Assembly) with the formal recognition it deserves. The details of how the People's Assembly (comprising organizations of civil society) would relate and interact with the UN General Assembly (comprising governments) could set an important global precedent. It is not clear at this stage whether a People's Assembly will be convened or whether the more comfortable formula of a parallel NGO Millennium Forum will be used.

At stake for the UN is the need to democratize its institutions and expand its system of governance to formally recognize the valuable global role played by civil society. This will not be easy. While there is a groundswell of support within the UN for such expansion, there are also pockets of resistance. In turn, the currency of civil society as a critical actor in the global arena is based in no small part on the perception that it reflects the diversity of society and provides a voice for people who have been marginalized or excluded from the benefits of society. Formal recognition of civil society's role through representation in UN decision-making bodies would increase demands on civil society to be accountable to the constituencies and voices they are perceived to represent. Not all elements of civil society are civil, however, which raises the question of standards of representation and accountability of civil society in the context of a People's Assembly or other UN forums.

However, standard setting is not without risks. Advocates maintain that some standards of CSO accountability to the people and institutions they represent is necessary in order to maintain the credibility and currency that civil society has garnered over the past years. Yet, it could risk a backlash that precludes the participation of less organized CSOs, thereby reinforcing the status quo of more sophisticated policy-oriented CSOs in global governing debates and forums, further driving a wedge in a growing and potentially dangerous divide.

Issues of Social Architecture

If civil society and the UN are to play a decisive role in reshaping the social architecture of governing relationships, rules, and terms of engagement, a number of questions need answers, revolving around issues of representation, capacity, and recourse in case of crisis. Four issues are critical to the debate.

1. Balance must be struck between the spirit of collective citizen action and the power of their political voice as a countervailing weight in policy debates at local and global levels, and the desire for formal representation in governing institutions. At question is the degree to which the political spirit of civil society might be compromised or diluted if formalized into a system of global representation. Ultimately, it means finding the right mix of direct

representation and autonomy that will enable actors of civil society to promote an effective citizen-centered agenda both from within and outside of global governing bodies.

2. The increasing complexity of our world and the speed with which fundamental changes in development occur place enormous demands on civil society to negotiate with a much broader range of actors than in the past. To effectively advocate for the rights of citizens in a world of rapid economic globalization will require new sets of skills and capacities. Sophisticated civil society research and policy institutes have emerged with considerable knowledge, skills, and political acumen in socio-economic rights-based work, making them effective advocates in international and national debate. Civil society organizations — from the global to the local — must similarly build their skills and capacities to effectively mediate the rights of citizens in poverty.

3. The principles and standards for redrawing state, market, and civil society relations along more equitable lines are already largely present in the Universal Declaration of Human Rights and International Conventions on Political and Civil as well as Economic, Social, and Cultural Rights. However, much remains to be done in expanding the concept of burden sharing. The human rights conventions and declarations overwhelmingly place the onus on the role of the State as the principal custodian of citizens' rights. While the notion of individual and collective responsibility has been invoked to call into question international agreements such as the MAI, much more work is needed in recognizing and clarifying the responsibilities of TNCs, trade consortia, and other key market actors in a globalizing world. Much remains to be done in developing the needed benchmarks for measuring progress and compliance and a compelling system of incentives to effect real change.

4. The UN needs to revisit the principles it values and upholds in practice. This should involve a review of its institutions to ensure that they include the needs of people living in poverty, as represented by civil society organizations, and reflect an expanded concept of human security that provides recourse to a high-level decision-making forum for handling social and economic crises as they emerge. Integrating the concept of poverty eradication within a rights-based framework introduces new conceptual parameters and approaches to the issue of poverty whose

implications on policy and programming initiatives need to be carefully examined. If a rights-based approach to poverty is to be taken seriously, staff capacities for negotiation, policy analysis, and programming in this domain will also have to be developed.

Conclusion

The case for poverty eradication has been made as: (1) a moral imperative — an act of charity for those less fortunate — rooted in the culture of philanthropy; (2) "good business" — or enlightened self-interest which sees the poor of today as the markets of tomorrow; and most recently as (3) a human right and societal obligation to fulfill. The one common and constant thread throughout these iterations has been the concept of poverty as a problem that could be remedied within the boundaries of countries. It was seen as the province of public action. Even on an international level, addressing poverty was perceived as a role ascribed to the official aid system.

This situation has been significantly altered by the forces of globalization, which can transmit shocks of all kinds (economic, environmental, cultural) from any level (local, national, regional, global) to any other level. These shock waves have become more numerous, complex, sudden, devastating, and immediate in their consequences. They aggravate the asymmetry between the time frames used to reduce human poverty (which requires decades of consistent macro- and micro-level efforts) and the time frames within which markets' loss of control can hit. Above all, the crises of globalization show that markets can rage out of control and recklessly undercut social and political systems. When globalization and markets challenge fundamental ethics — social justice, human rights, and equity — it is time for the global community, individually and collectively, to seek remedies.

There is a need to effect a shift in how the concept of poverty eradication is held in trust by the global community, to rethink the nature of relations among actors and institutions, and to assess what kind of global compacts are needed to mediate the roles and responsibilities in sharing in its cost. New forms of national and global governance — rules and institutions — are needed, based on principles of justice and inclusiveness. Not all actors in global governance are equally involved: civil society is often formally left out, and national governments are increasingly marginalized or stripped of authority. The responsibility traditionally vested in governments for guaranteeing and protecting rights now largely escapes the realm of public action.

Existing international human rights instruments provide a good set of principles upon which to build a different kind of governance in the age of globalization. They represent the core values of equity (social justice) and equality (of opportunity) around which people-centered development must be based. But a fundamentally different system of institutions and rules probably needs to be elaborated. Not only governments, but a number of relatively "new actors" (TNCs and trade consortia) as well as more conventional players (IFIs, but also the UN system) that have been largely left out of the debate on responsibility, need to be held accountable. The challenge is that the most powerful actors do not lend themselves easily to regulation. Some degree of accountability should also apply to civil society if it is to genuinely share the responsibility of making decisions on national and global governance. A rights-based approach to governance would require, at a minimum, a considerable strengthening of the existing human rights treaty bodies, which currently lack authority over the "new actors," and critically, lack the capacity and resources to adequately address these new sets of issues. These bodies would probably need to be "reinvented" as an integral part of a system of institutions that need to be created if the governance of globalization is to bring about a more equitable society where the rights of people living in poverty are upheld and respected.

Such a goal would have appeared unthinkable only a few years ago. However, crises are often the only vehicle for changing the minds of decision-makers, and the events of the last few years have provided ample opportunity which civil society has been seizing and using with considerable impact.

Ambitious though it may appear, this agenda for the reform of the social architecture — the set of governing relationships, rules, and institutions — is the agenda that civil society and the UN have begun. It will require a continuous effort to push for a system of global governance that is based on principles of justice and equality. Principles negotiated and agreed through five decades of human rights progress now need to pass the test of globalization: for whom and at what cost? In this endeavor, civil society and the UN share a collective role in progressively recreating a system of more equitable relationships where people living in poverty are given the lead and the resources to break out of impoverishment.

Notes

1. This essay was written by Caitlin Wiesen, Geoffrey D. Prewitt, and Babar Sobhan from the Civil Society and Participation Program (CSOPP) at the United Nations Development Program (UNDP). The views expressed in

this essay are those of the authors alone, and do not necessarily reflect the views of UNDP Executive Board, Administration, or the countries that they represent.

The paper benefited from the advice and assistance of a number of people. In particular, the authors would like to thank Thierry Lemaresquier, Barbara Adams, Rebecca Rios-Kohn, Thord Palmlund, and Hamish Jenkins for providing valuable comments on earlier drafts.

2. Lester M. Salamon, "The Rise of the Nonprofit Sector," *Foreign Affairs* Vol. 73, No. 4, 1994.

3. Salamon, "The Rise of the Nonprofit Sector."

4. Nicola Bullard, "The Economic Necessity of Social Justice," in *Social Watch Annual Report 1999* (New York: Social Watch, 1999).

5. United Nations Development Program, *Overcoming Human Poverty* (New York: United Nations Development Program, 1998).

6. Hamish Jenkins, United Nations Nongovernmental Liaison Service. *Human Rights Approaches to Development*, NGLS Round-Up, n.d.

7. R. Jayaraman, and R. Kanbur, "International Public Goods and the Case for Foreign Aid," Kaul Inge et. al. (eds.), *Global Public Goods: International Cooperation in the Twenty-first Century* (New York: Oxford University Press, 1999).

8. Polaris Institute, "Toward a Citizens' MAI: An Alternative Approach to Developing a Global Investment Treaty Based on Citizen's Rights and Democratic Control." Discussion Paper, 1998.

9. Oxfam International, "Debt as Barrier to the World Summit Targets." Submission to the UN Commission on the Rights of the Child.

10. United Nations Development Program, *Overcoming Human Poverty*.

11. SAPRIN Country Reports: Bangladesh, Ecuador, Ghana, El Salvador, Hungary, Uganda.

12. Social Watch, *1999 Annual Report: Montevideo, Uruguay*, 1999.

13. United Nations Development Program, *Human Development Report*. New York: United Nations Development Program (annual publication).

14. ICVA and EUROSTEP, *The Reality of Aid: An International Review of International Aid* (London: Earthscan Publications, 1996).

15. WEDO, "Beyond Promises: Governments in Motion One Year after Beijing 1996," New York, 1996.

12

Coming Apart, Coming Together: Globalization and Civil Society

Isagani R. Serrano

A Millennium Party of One

Sometime in October 1999 we will be welcoming the six billionth member of the human family, in time for a grand millennium party. The question is whether people will be in the mood or have the means and energy for such a rare celebration.

The world is in turmoil. Gloom, doom, and uncertainty are probably apt words to describe the mood at the end of this millennium. Three years ago things seemed more certain. Not anymore. Everywhere people are busy securing their lives against the effects of a pervasive crisis situation. We also have not figured out the full impact of the Y2K bug. The greater part of humanity is unsure what blessings to count and what to expect tomorrow. Already many have been thrown back to the basics of survival. Russia and Indonesia are threatening to fall apart. China and Brazil are under severe stress. Japan, the second wealthiest nation, is stagnating and cannot figure its way out of the impasse. Dark clouds hang over Europe. The miracle economies of Southeast Asia are no more miracles. Countries big and small are hurting and struggling to keep their societies whole.

For much of the world, July 1997 will be remembered as the watershed year that heralded the doom that followed. What started out as a mere money problem in Thailand spread like wildfire that no power on earth seemed able to contain. What normally would have been a localized crisis quickly reached worldwide proportions and now threatened the global system itself. The metaphors generated by this phenomenon were fearsome — a meltdown, a financial Titanic, a contagion, a bubonic plague, a wrecking ball.

It seemed to many of us that some were luckier than others. The current global crisis appeared unique in that there seemed to be only one winner — the US. The rest were either losers or deeply scarred. In his January 1999 State of the Union address, President Clinton proudly spoke of the exiting century as the American century and predicted that the next one would be American too. True enough, the twentieth century began with the US emerging on top of falling empires, seemed to proceed with the US presiding over much of what transpired, and is now ending with the US standing alone, triumphant. As *Time* magazine extravagantly claimed, the world owed much to America, in particular to the three wise men and financial heavyweights — Alan Greenspan, Robert Rubin, and Lawrence Summers — who composed what the magazine called an all-American committee to save the world.

Thus it would seem to many that at millennium's end only one nation has enough reason to party. But can the US forever continue to be blessed in such a manner, people ask, while so many societies are collapsing all around? Present trends seem to suggest that it will probably remain standing should there be a global crash tomorrow. To the disillusioned majority it appears that with all the blessings of prosperity and power the US is by far the most stable society in the world although it has its own share of social divides and burdens within. Following the financial meltdown the US was in a position to use most of the money in circulation to buy what it wanted at a bargain to continue financing its high consumption. There are those who feel that it is home to a comparatively small population comfortably settled in a living space whose abundant natural endowments have been largely preserved at the expense of others, that it has monopolized the greater part of the world's resources and energy, and that it has the modern technology to continue expropriating the carrying capacity of this planet, even stretching its pursuits to the moon. It has the most sophisticated communications technology to project the American dream, values, tastes, and lifestyle globally — symbols of the good life even the proud Chinese would find hard to resist. And anytime it chooses to throw its weight around it can count on its possession of the most powerful weapons of mass destruction, so powerful as to reduce this world to smithereens. Name it, America has it.

The rest of us will have to keep body and soul together while a few might still have the spirit to toast and kiss at New Year's Eve. It makes one wonder where globalization has taken us.

Globalization Has a History

Considering all of the above there is a real danger of turning globalization into a straw figure to be blamed for everything that has gone wrong. But it would be foolish to blame all our present miseries and troubles on globalization. By the same token we cannot attribute to globalization all the good things resulting from greater openness and interdependence among nations, societies, and peoples. Like many things in life globalization has many sides to it. Positively, it may simply be taken to mean a process of overcoming barriers to the free movement of goods, people, and ideas.

The temptation to retreat, to be more wary about further opening up, is strong. Already there is growing appreciation of the protectionist measures undertaken by Malaysia, China, and to a certain extent, Chile. But disappointment with globalization can be stretched beyond mere retreat to the "safety" of one's borders. Already some angry nations have been agitating for a kind of stonewalling that glorifies narrow nationalism. To demonize globalization is just as wrongheaded as the pre-1997 tendency to hold it up as though it were God's gift to humanity.

Globalization has been with us for much of modern times, perhaps even much earlier on. It is a continuing human story of how otherwise isolated and distant societies get connected or divided by a host of driving forces beyond the control of ordinary citizens and their institutions. Erstwhile settled societies came into contact with one another in the course of satisfying their basic need for food, clothing, shelter, and whatever it is they value in life. In this sense it is a process as old as human existence itself. Long before the birth of settled societies ten thousand years ago people had been roaming the globe in search of food and better climes. Our great, great ancestors appeared, out of necessity, to lead a "global" lifestyle as restless nomads until they invented agriculture and learned to settle down.

Fixing the beginning of globalization can be tricky. We can mark it from the rise of ancient civilizations in China, India, Middle East, Africa, and Meso America. Or from the time of the earliest empires whose dominions spanned continents. Tracing the spread of great religions can also give some useful insights about how diverse races and cultures came to be bound by a common faith. Transborder wars and conflicts, a dominant feature of much of human history, also have globalizing elements in them. The demand for resources, energy, and new knowledge has also driven the human species to the farthest, highest, and deepest reaches of this planet, and even farther on into outer space.

The history we are talking about may be long or short depending on our reference point. Two million years from the origin of the human species is certainly too long. Ten thousand years ago when agricultural societies first emerged is also long enough. Two thousand years from the birth of Christ seems like ages as well. But think for a moment in terms of lifetimes or generations of say twenty to thirty years when a parent would reproduce a parent replacement. Then our ten thousand years is only about four hundred generations, our last two millennia only about eighty parent lifetimes.

One other way of imaging our history, a favorite among environmentalists, is the twenty-four-hour metaphor. If we take the whole span of human existence as the cycle, then so-called civilization, beginning with the invention of agriculture and the emergence of settled societies ten thousand years ago, would only cover the last three or four minutes on our clock. If we use the same twenty-four hour metaphor on this ten-thousand-year-old civilization then the industrial age of scientific inventions starting around the middle of the eighteenth century involves only the last thirty-five minutes.

It is just amazing how the world was made much, much smaller in such a brief span of time. In a succession of two hundred parents we have gone from the Stone Age to the space age, from using fire to cook raw food to inventing the nuclear bomb to burn the entire planet. In eighty generations we have gone from using the donkey, the mode of transport of Christ's parents, to using the car as a high point in personal mobility. In the same span of time we have shifted from the cart to the car, to the locomotive, to the ocean liner, to supersonic jets in order to move goods and people around the world. We have given up on the postman on horseback for the handy cell phone to reach a friend ten thousand miles away. We can now beam a uniform message through cable television to reach 100 million people at one go in an instant. In twenty generations we have gone from using the galleon to circumnavigate the globe to sending the first spaceship to the moon.

And continuing in the metaphoric vein in the last thirty-five minutes of our twenty-four hour clock we have been using coal, oil, natural gas, metals, and minerals as though they come from bottomless pits and with little or no regard at all to the fact that these fossil materials cannot be renewed nor replaced in our lifetimes. We have mined the forests, the deep oceans and have caused countless plants and animals to disappear forever . In the same brief span of time we have poisoned the air we breathe, the water we drink, the soil that gives us food. In the last two minutes of our twenty-four hour clock, we have waged two world wars against each other with devastating human and ecological costs without parallel in all of human history. In the last few seconds we have seen how gazillions of money can be moved around the world, in and out of national economies, by a mere tap of the computer key. We have just seen how one collapsing economy can push the world economy to the verge of destruction. Modern society, as we know it, is no older than twenty generations. Probably younger if we count from the transition of natural order society to civil society during the Enlightenment period, around the beginning of the second half of this century. Indeed much younger even if dated from the beginning of the industrial age around 1750. This modern civil society is a creation of the industrial age that is vastly different from all civilization that preceded it. We can see this difference in at least two areas. First, in the process of wealth creation and, second, in the growth of our numbers.

For much of human history basic changes took a long, long time to happen. Societies were settled in areas so far apart from each other in such a vast landscape that one knew nothing about what was happening in other locations. Periods of transition from stone to metal to the steam engine took long intervals. Back then it was too hard to live and too easy to die. In contrast modern society runs on high gear and quick acceleration. Transitions come in rapid and shortening doubling time, as happened from the invention of the steam engine to the discovery of electricity and nuclear fission to our present digital world. Our great ancestors walked long distances for days on end to reach the next community, today's car riders and jet setters take only a few hours to get to the next city destination in another country. Today's science and technology has enabled us to live longer lives, even to tinker with life by modifying our natural genetic make-up.

Modern society has transformed beyond recognition what was there once only in its natural, pristine form. Precious little has remained untouched and beyond the reach of human activity. It seems virtually nothing will remain forever unknowable and impossible to modern humans driven by the obsession to grow and acquire more. In 1900 the world economy was valued at $600 billion. It now grows by more than this amount in just two years. On average, the additional economic output in each of the last four decades has equaled the total output from the beginning of civilization until 1950. Within this century the global economy has increased twenty times, and nearly five times since 1950 from $4 trillion to about $20 trillion.

Like the global economy, world population has also been growing exponentially. It took two million years, until 1825, for the world population to reach one billion. Our second billion was added after one hundred years, the third billion in thirty-five years (1925–60), the fourth billion in fifteen years (1960–75), the fifth billion in twelve years (1975–late 1980s). We will hit six billion by October 1999. During the next twenty-five years our numbers shall have grown between a low projection of 8.1 billion and a high of 11.6 billion.

We are a modern society of six billion men, women, and children thinking, believing, and doing different things. We are six billion people interacting with each other and with our surroundings in millions of different ways. These interactions result in diverse outcomes both intended and unintended to make our modern history.

We want to make sense of the complex modern society that we have now. We want to understand why things happened the way they did. We want to know who did the changing and how. We want to understand the philosophy and values behind the action, what forms of institutions and means of organizing were devised to bring about the changes. We look back to our past because we want to understand what people who lived before us did to make our world of today, to learn from what they did as we make our present world which in turn will be our children's history and their starting point for creating their own story.

Building a Civic World

The day will come when every village, town, city, and country on this planet will become more safe, more healthy, more egalitarian, more sustainable. These villages, towns, cities, and countries will become models of sharing and caring, of equal opportunity and inclusive participation, of a kind of living that is worthy of human dignity and is attuned to nature's limits. People, goods, ideas shall be free to move anywhere. No hell below us, above us only blue skies. Though we may still be different people of different colors believing, thinking, doing different things, all this diversity will merely enrich our lives; these dividing lines won't exist and the world might look as it does when we look at our planet through a telescope from outer space. Come that day the world will live as one.

All this sounds pretty much like an impossible dream, similar to the message in John Lennon's song "Imagine" and the song "Age of Aquarius" by the Fifth Dimension. Quite a number of songs, poetry, and prose echo the same message. Daily around the world this message gets projected through radio and MTVs and other forms of modern communication. The message they convey continues and never fails to get the sympathy of millions wherever they may be. It might not be too much to say that this is a message shared universally.

Just try contrasting this vision with the scenario drawn up by Marx and Engels in their *Communist Manifesto* of 1848.

Modern industry has established the world market. All old-established national industries have been destroyed. They are dislodged by new industries whose introduction becomes a life and death question for all civilized nations, by industries that work up raw material drawn from the remotest zones, industries whose products are consumed, not only at home but in every quarter of the globe. In place of the old wants, we find new wants, requiring for their satisfaction the product of distant lands and climes. All fixed, fast-frozen relations are swept away, all new-formed ones become antiquated before they can ossify. All that is solid melts into air, all that is holy is profaned, and man is at last compelled to face, with sober senses, his real conditions of life and his relations with his kind.

Forget for a moment that these stirring words were penned by communists. But remark that the words of these authors were taken as marching orders by more than half of humanity, who dared to reorganize and rebuild their societies around those ideals no matter the cost and consequences. Forget about who actually said those words, and you might think you heard the World Bank president Wolfensohn or some bankers and economists at the last Davos World Economic Forum saying something similar.

Or take the wrecking ball metaphor of the most successful money game player of all time, George Soros. In his latest book, *The Crisis of Global Capitalism,* Soros zeroed in on what he calls market fundamentalism as underlying the current world turmoil. Market fundamentalism is the wrecking ball that has knocked down one country after another in the recent Asian and global crisis. To George Soros, capitalism need not look elsewhere for the causes of our present troubles. The problem is within capitalism itself. With almost a ring of religious faith to it, this belief says that market forces left to their own devices and allowed to move freely without any fetters will make our world the best ever place to live in. There will be occasional imbalances all right, but eventually things will end up in a state of equilibrium without any interference from anyone. It is a belief that attributes all virtues to the market and mostly evils to the state. George Soros is no communist, in fact he admits openly to being a staunch opponent of Soviet communism and any form of totalitarianism. Soros is a profound believer in Karl Popper's concept of open society. He is convinced that no one can ever be in possession of the ultimate truth, that the world we have is an imperfect one and cannot be made perfect. Soros asserts that runaway capitalism as symbolized by the behavior of market fundamentalists will put all our strivings toward an open society and a stable one-world economy in grave peril.

The process of globalization has brought us within touching or wrecking distance of each other, literally and figuratively. Setting aside for the moment the horrible stories that attended this process we now have before us a modern world that has more than enough accumulated wealth to sustain us even if we work less hours and spend more time for leisure. We have more than enough to feed, clothe, house, educate, lengthen the life, and expand the freedom of movement and choices of every man, woman, and child now living and yet to be born. We can use this accumulated wealth to pay back social dues and start off the greatest ever social-leveling process. And probably there will be more left to clean up the mess we have caused our environment.

Or we can just watch things take their own course and leave the wrecking ball be. If nothing else, the current crisis should be a wake-up call. It should make us realize that as tightly connected as we are, a minor glitch in one part could trigger a breakdown in the whole system. We live in a closely interconnected world where we have just seen how a country like Russia which does not trade with Latin America and is located on the other side of the globe could crash and bring down Latin America, if not the whole world.

The civilized world has come this far, and still remains divided. The civic world is yet to be. We may not have enough time to build it. The writing on the wall at the end of two thousand years is so clear and compelling. We can hang on to each other like brother to brother, like sister to sister or we will all go down together. There is no individual way out of our present mess. We can and must come together or be torn apart and perish together.

The Need for a New Scaffolding

In building a civic world the first tall order is to change our thinking and value system. But what sort of thinking and values must change? We are talking here of modern society or societies which total six billion people believing, thinking, valuing, and doing different things. True, some ideas and judgments came out much stronger than others and turned out to be the most crucial in guiding and shaping human actions. The dominant institutions that we see today have been built around them. Until they are questioned and changed it will be business as usual come the third millennium.

The ways of thought underlying modern society and the collective as well as individual behavior of its citizens have their origins in Western thought that were shaped about twenty, or less, generations ago. The key figures were French philosopher Descartes and British physicist Newton. This essay makes no pretense about understanding the scope, depth, and complexity of their ideas and their consequences. For our purposes here, caricatures and metaphors may do.

Cartesian thought doubts the existence of everything, including the existence of the questioner. The logical end of this endless questioning is the reduction of the world to its ultimate particle. Think about the cosmos and begin untangling it into composite solar systems, these solar systems into separate worlds, and each world into its smaller constituent parts, and each part into its minutest particle, till you hit the atom. But this atom is not the end, it has to be split further till we hit real dead end where fission can go no farther. This analytical way of thinking gave birth to complex mathematical formulas based on which we can supposedly explain anything, from the amoebae to the solar system. Thanks to Rene Descartes, humanity has a method to explain everything. The problem is, this mode of thought has deconstructed everything and we are at a loss how to put the parts back together. For his part, Newton gave us the laws of mechanical motion, the perpetual dynamic of causes and effects. Around his physics was built the modern machine that grows endlessly and now behaves like Soros wrecking ball.

These two European philosopher-scientists laid the foundation for the scientific revolution that created the modern world. They cannot be held responsible for everything that has happened for far too many actors have contributed to the outcome. But their influence has dominated and continues to dominate to this day. We are not about to give up on analysis or mechanics, they are still very much needed. But the ways of thought represented by these two great men of the sixteenth century cannot continue to be the ways of thought that guide human action in the twenty-first century. They were suited for the era of endless growth that brought unparalleled prosperity alongside equally unprecedented but terrible consequences to our society and our environment.

We need a philosophy and science of fusion, as it were, to survive and create a global entity without exclusion. We need a world view and method that will enable us to bring more solidarity in our divided world, more sharing and caring instead of cold-blooded scientism and destructive competition. We need a philosophy of life that will make us more sensitive and caring for the things around us, for things that sustain our lives through to the next generations. The new world we are trying to build needs a fundamentally different consciousness, though its features are still being debated and its shape still evolving. However it is fashioned, this new consciousness should enable us to learn to live together despite our extreme diversity, it should be able to help us build a global society where everyone has a dignified place at the table. This new consciousness should be able to steer us into actions that help to restore our depleted and polluted environs.

Our modern world has been built around the prince or the merchant, or both. The first is symbol of the state, the second economic enterprise. Both made good use of the ideas of philosophers, scientists, economists, academics, and technical specialists to construct and run the institutions of global governance and the world economy. They may be some cuts above the rest of us but they are just like you and me with the same genetic make-up, the same basic needs but maybe different desires. They were just lucky to have been favored by the convergence of factors and events, for being in the right place at the right time. We, ordinary mortals, have judged them from varying standards as either great successes or miserable failures. They have had their day.

The prince and the merchant have a place in creating a civic world. But they cannot continue to dominate and run things the way they did in the past. Change they must, and in ways that are worthy of the citizens of a new world. They have the means and the institutions, which if reformed can enable a faster, less bloody, and more civilized transition to a civic world.

So far the crowning achievement of the prince has been the establishment of the United Nations. This is the only global institution that can approximate global civil society. But the UN itself is under siege. The Universal Declaration of Human Rights which proclaims the basic rights and freedoms of peoples (note, not nations) has been more honored in the breach than compliance. Too many times the UN has proven helpless to prevent the occurrence of things that divide us, to stop powerful or stubborn nations from pushing their weight around and calling them to account for their uncivilized behavior. On many occasions it could not even carry out its own resolutions or sanction those who would constrain their implementation. If the UN is our metaphor of one-world it certainly falls short of the mark. Still it is the only common platform which can provide the most inclusive space for the voices and concerns of all the world's citizens. But if its most powerful members continue to behave as they have been doing, the UN will be an obstacle to the process of building a civic one-world.

Judged as even more wanting than the prince, the merchant has much more reforming to do. Though the new consciousness is already beginning to rub off on him (business leaders like politicians are mostly men), the merchant is hardly in a position to reverse the tide of self-destruction of the world created in the image of capital. Driven by the bottom line and an obsession to acquire more he will always lead us to a situation where there are only a few winners and so many losers. He is a slave to destructive competition, which one can win only by continuously externalizing nature and marginalizing human labor. The merchant who has some concern for a more civil and civic world will have to realize that there are limits to growth. He must be able to demonstrate in action that business activity, in order to succeed, need not discount people and our future. And that internalizing social and ecological costs also makes good economic sense in the long run.

There are civic princes and civic merchants too, and their numbers are slowly but steadily growing. This is nothing strange. Goodwill and humanity may be found in strange quarters and are not a monopoly of so-called NGOs and other civil society organizations.

Civic people can be found and can develop anywhere — in government, in business circles, in the local community, in all social institutions. They are the people who believe that the way toward a new civic one-world, though rocky, entails inclusive participation, gender equality, redistributive justice, civic initiative, concern for the common good, solidarity, and caring. They are the promoters of a new consciousness and civic action needed for the new millennium. They understand why paying our social and ecological dues now and not later will make for a sustainable society that is vastly different from what we have now.

Civic mindedness as embodied by citizens, prominent or ordinary people, like you and me, have come a long way from the time of Plato's exclusive city. They were the opposing voices to the monarchs and popes during the Enlightenment, the leading advocates of the emerging civil society of that time. They were the opponents of the prince who caused wars and sent men (lately women, too) to the frontlines. They were the activists behind the most powerful social movements of modern times. They were the alternative voices of the 1960s who dared think and do things the Establishment did not want, from smoking marijuana to anti-war mass demonstrations. They were the voices of citizen participation in an era when decisions affecting our everyday lives at home, in the neighborhood, in the workplace, in schools, churches, and parks were nearly monopolized by the prince and the merchant.

These new citizens are yesterday's and today's alternative voices celebrating and shaping the coming new age through their songs and poetry, through voluntary association and communal living, through caring and sharing for each other. They are the brave ones who lay their lives on the line to bring down dictators and corrupt governments, to stop companies from further hurting our already degraded environment. They are the leading social activists challenging distant and highly centralized institutions of power in order to restore sovereignty to the hands of ordinary people.

Fast Backward to the Future

If we look back to the first settled societies or the more recent enlightened feudal societies in the middle ages when there was less created wealth but more caring, our modern society is way, way beyond recognition. The process of creating a one-world, particularly during the last decade, seems to be leading nowhere near that goal. Rather, globalization is leading us to where no sane person wants to be — to the brink of global collapse.

This amazing process has been presided over mostly by the prince and the merchant, whether civic-minded or uncivilized. And look at what they and the so-called globalization process have made of us — a world more divided, more insecure. They had their chance and blew it.

The clock must be turned backward, and fast. There is no time to lose, the wrecking ball is upon us wreaking havoc everywhere like nothing we have seen before. Governments cannot lead, they are lost and almost completely helpless, they can only do crisis management at best. Corporations are resigned to fatalism because they are trapped in the hole of market fundamentalism.

But we have the civics with us to show us the way out — fast rewind — to a more secure common future. Civics are a bunch of activist idealists in a great hurry. They are in a great hurry to put a stop to runaway, negative globalization. Therefore, everything they think and do is intended to derail and reverse such a destructive process. Civics are a driving factor for the creative disintegration of the present system. They want to build smaller worlds — small defensible spaces where everyone will have a better chance to participate — and on this basis create a united world. Their shortcomings, their insolence, and impatience are of little consequence to what they want our world to be.

With these modern or postmodern citizens we have a fighting chance to achieve a radical turnaround. They will accelerate the process of teaching us to live together, of really uniting, before the wrecking ball succeeds in tearing our world apart.

13

From States to People:
Civil Society and Its Role in Governance

Miklós Marschall

> Citizens are at the center of the global drama unfolding today.
> They are the leading actresses and actors in building global demo-
> cratic governance and human development ... The security of
> our common future lies in the hands of an informed, inspired,
> committed, engaged citizenry.[1]

In *Citizens,* the inaugural publication of CIVICUS, Rajesh Tandon and
Miguel Darcy thus summarized their faith in the power of ordinary
citizens to oversee governance processes around the world. In the last
two decades of the twentieth century, this conviction has become the
credo of countless global, regional, and local civil society initiatives.

The twentieth century has seen ideologies that were at odds with
everything civil society and citizenship represent. Not without some grati-
fication, we note that the same century that witnessed lethal mass
manipulations seems to be departing with an unprecedented civic revival.
A "happy ending" for the bloodiest century? Not quite. Nevertheless, we
have reasons to be optimistic.

The way we go about handling our lives, concerns, and conflicts seems
to be changing. A "power shift" has taken place in the collective management of our affairs at every level: global, regional, national, and local.[2]
New "non-state" actors — a multitude of citizen organizations — have
become part of the processes and institutions we call "governance." This
change, this shift in governance, is one of the most intriguing phenomena
that will determine the way humankind starts the next millennium.

What exactly is governance? Governance is the sum of the many ways individuals and institutions, public and private, manage their common affairs, control resources, and exercise power to achieve public purposes.[3] Governance includes:

- *processes and rules* for channeling conflicting or diverse interests into cooperative action

- *institutions and regimes* with power to monitor and enforce compliance and sanction noncompliance

- *informal arrangements* that people and institutions have agreed to and are willing to follow

We have recently seen an acceleration of change in the processes, institutions, and arrangements by which we organize our lives from the local to global level. The shift in governance can be described by three major areas of change: globalization and communication, civil society networks, and norms and ethics.

Globalization and the revolution in communication and information technologies have brought fundamental changes to the overall system of sovereignty. The sovereignty of nation states as supreme authorities over all matters within their geographic boundaries, and as the sole actors in the international relationships, has been substantially and visibly weakened. As Jessica T. Mathews put it:

> National governments are not simply losing autonomy in a globalizing economy. They are sharing powers — including political, social, and security roles at the core of sovereignty — with businesses, with international organizations, and with a multitude of citizens groups, known as nongovernmental organizations (NGOs). The steady concentration of power in the hands of states that began in 1648 with the Peace of Westphalia is over, at least for a while.[4]

In Mathews' opinion, "the clash between the fixed geography of states and the nonterritorial nature of today's problems and solutions . . . strongly suggests that the relative power of states will continue to decline."[5]

Regional, Subregional, and Local Levels of Governance Have Gained Power

National governments turned out to be too big to deal with the diversity of issues directly affecting people's day-to-day lives. Cities and regions as quasi-autonomous entities entered the global market as competitors.

By their very nature, local governments are closer than national governments to the "life sphere" of people. Thus, local governments can facilitate civil society and benefit the most from increased citizen participation. Civil society networks have sprung up — local, national, and transnational — manifesting an unprecedented decentralization of power into the hands of citizen groups, associations, and NGOs. Indeed, a *network society* is on the horizon, where traditional hierarchical structures are being complemented, and replaced in some cases, by diffused, horizontal structures of decision-making. As Jessica T. Mathews said in her seminal article: "Networks have no persons at the top and no center. Instead, they have multiple nodes where collections of individuals or groups interact for different purposes."[6] Civil society organizations (CSOs) are mobile, fast, and flexible, which gives them significant advantages over slow and rigid bureaucracies. By using their relative flexibility and ability to act quickly, CSOs have been able to shape the agenda, address new priorities, and mobilize public opinion. Consequently, government officials have to use a broad horizontal *policy network,* not just a state hierarchy, if they want to get things done. At local level, a good mayor has to work hand in hand with neighborhood associations, local interest groups, a variety of professional and nonprofessional associations, and local businesses. The same holds true at global level: from poverty eradication to global warming, practically no important global issue can be addressed without the support of many transnational NGOs and their networks.

A Set of Universal Values, Norms, and Standards and a Global Ethic of Common Rights and Shared Responsibilities Seem to Be Emerging.[7]

For the first time in history, universal standards on human rights, environment, democracy, women's rights, freedom of association, and the like have been spelled out and accepted by the vast majority of nations. Enforcement mechanisms remain to be worked out but one simple fact is of great importance: governments, corporations, and individuals at the very least feel embarrassed when they violate those standards. International public opinion — inspired by universal values and standards, informed by global *media,* and mobilized by CSOs — has become a major force in governance at every level.

"A Place for Us"

The new player in governance is civil society. Benjamin Barber calls civil society "a place for us:"

> [A]n independent domain of free social life where neither governments nor private markets are sovereign; a realm we create for ourselves through associated common action in families, clans, churches, and communities; a third sector (the other two are the state and the market) that mediates between our specific individuality as economic producers and consumers and our abstract collectivity as members of a sovereign people."[8]

Let me reiterate five inherent components of Barber's definition, each crucial for understanding the nature and functioning of civil society:

- Civil society is a free or autonomous space of voluntary associations
- It provides mediating structures between individuals and the state
- Through these mediating structures, an individual can become a citizen
- This free space of associational life can accommodate our plural identity (that is, as consumer, family member, and citizen in one person)
- The richer, denser, and more diverse these mediating structures are, the better for society

The important point Barber makes is that civic life is different from both our private lives, where we act as producers and consumers, and our public and political lives, where we usually vote and claim rights. This "place for us" which Barber describes so eloquently is neither public, nor private: it is civic. This civic space offers more direct, intimate, and ongoing participation with more tangible stakes in shaping our lives than the traditional public or political sector can do.

As we all know, civil society is a subtle and complex fabric of institutions and human interactions. Its nonexistence is much more striking and visible than its existence. When it works, we can take it for granted; it makes no news headlines. Only the lack of a civil society makes us understand why it is needed. That is why men and women from South Africa, Poland, Hungary, the Philippines, or Chile, where civic actions were persecuted twenty years ago, can so forcefully testify to the vital importance of civil society today.

Civil society is a bold, radical — but nonrevolutionary — political concept. It is bold and radical because it is not revolutionary. It radically breaks with the politics of war (class, ethnic, whatever). Civic politics, which is about mediating, is an antithesis to the politics of war. At its best, civic politics goes beyond our traditional bipolar or binary thinking, where almost everything is a zero-sum game — "either them, or us." It is no accident that the political heroes of our time are Mahatma Gandhi, Martin Luther King, Nelson Mandela, Václav Havel, and others like them. These very "civil" politicians of the twentieth century emerged as leaders because they were able to overcome the "them-or-us" dichotomy.

"A place for us" was the message of Michnik, Havel, Kundera, Konrad, Sakharov, and others — dissidents in Eastern and Central Europe in the 1980s who revitalized the idea of civil society. They learned the hard way what Adam Michnik once said: "Those who start with storming Bastille will end up building Bastilles." My point is that civil society can enrich our governance by values, style, and approaches that include collaborative ethos, inclusiveness, empathy, tolerance, and consensus seeking.

CSOs: Their Strengths and Weaknesses

Let me hasten to say categorically, however, that civil society cannot and should not be canonized or idealized either. I have come to dislike the quasi-evangelical language we often use when speaking about civil society. I also resent any claim by the sector or its actors to moral superiority over the other two sectors. Too often we use the term "civil society" for things, trends, and groups of which we approve.[9] Civil society has become synonymous with good things. The same applies to civil society organizations (CSOs). Any belief in the "double purity" of CSOs — namely, that they are corrupted neither by power nor by money — is naïve. Surely a few of them are corrupt. But, that does not discredit at all the important and positive role CSOs have been playing locally, nationally, and globally. As always, a realistic, balanced view is needed.

What, then, are the strengths and weaknesses of CSOs in their role in governance? What are the comparative advantages and disadvantages of CSOs vis-à-vis government organizations and businesses? Let's start with the advantages: freedom, flexibility, trust, and legitimacy, "real world" and "hands-on" experience, mobility, and swiftness.

Freedom and Flexibility

As we know, freedom is conducive to creativity. CSOs are less bound than government officials by rules, traditions, interests, and procedures. Therefore, CSOs can more easily engage in social ventures, untested enterprises, and projects involving considerable risk. If they want, CSOs can go against public opinion much longer than, say, elected officials who are more bound by their constituency or electorate. CSOs can be much more creative in bringing together cross-sectoral alliances, issue-related ad hoc coalitions, than governments and their organizations. A great deal of freedom derives from the fact that most CSOs are, by nature, single-issue organizations, which enables them to concentrate their resources on that issue without much compromise or tradeoff. A politician who wants to be reelected has to strike a balance among competing interests, making compromises and tradeoffs all the time.

Trust and Legitimacy

Often driven by issues the public considers worthy causes, CSOs enjoy good reputation and trust among the public. The independence of CSOs from business interests and government influence often gives them a high standing in terms of uncompromising moral and professional authority. The public is more likely to expect impartial information on controversial issues — from human rights violations to environmental pollution — from an independent CSO than from a government agency or a business corporation, which might have other interests than "the truth." In the monitoring and watchdog business, CSOs have comparative advantage because of their professional and moral authority. Of course, we all know how fragile and vulnerable that trust can be. Building that reputation takes CSOs many years, but just one careless act can demolish it.

"Real-world" and "Hands-on" Experience

Especially in the development industry, CSOs, with their grassroots experience, can be invaluable partners for government agencies and businesses. They can provide vital linkages between local communities and funding agencies, because both partners trust them. CSOs can provide development and aid agencies with vital feedback on what works on the ground, and what does not. CSOs with local roots can mobilize indigenous resources otherwise unavailable for development projects.

Mobility and Swiftness

From easy access to information and the capacity to store, manage, and disseminate it with unprecedented speed, CSOs have gained highly visible power in mobilizing public opinion. In fact, there is a perfect match between information technology and the way horizontal CSO networks communicate. With the help of new technology, virtual communities emerge along interest and affinities that cross geographic, political, and cultural borders. People from across the globe can ally and re-ally quickly with distant others on issues they care about. Mobility and swiftness are crucial resources for CSOs in positioning civil society in the global (and local) public policy arena.

Paradoxically, CSOs' strengths can also be weaknesses. Freedom, mobility, and swiftness make their day-to-day operations easier and more efficient. But these same features may also prompt legitimate questions about responsibility, mandate, constituency, accountability, and sustainability — crucial issues from the perspective of governance.

Myths and Misconceptions

Mandate and responsibility are cornerstones of all good governance. CSOs, NGOs, and any other citizen group engaged in public policy deliberations have to be very clear on two things:

- What is their precise mandate?
- To whom do they answer?

Too often, a group claims to speak "on behalf of the people," as opposed to politicians and political parties. Such generalizations — the "we the people" type of claims — are not only false and misleading; they can also undermine a CSO's credibility and seriousness. In addition, these claims suggest that politicians and public officials do not act "on behalf of the people" and that they en bloc are morally inferior to citizen activists. Although we all know of corrupt and immoral public officials, the generalization is false and unjust.

Civil society is a complement, not a rival, to, representative democracy, and participatory democracy goes hand in hand with representative democracy. Civil society is about participation, while parliamentary democracy is about representation. The civic politics of citizen participation and the parliamentary "party politics" of representation have a healthy dynamic of both complementarity and tension. Citizen participation carries its own self-originated legitimacy; it does not need to borrow legitimacy from representation.

Simply put, civil society is not just a new academic fad but a practical reality whose legitimate participation in public life is based on what it does. Thus, it is not only representation of their citizen members that makes a CSO legitimate but the validity of their ideas, the values they promote, and the issues they care about. Civic values and democratic practice distinguish civil society from government, the private sector, and "political society." This is the very special contribution of civil society to governance. Thus, it is not only representation of their citizen members that makes CSOs legitimate, but the validity of their ideas, the values they promote, and the issues they care about.

Unlike public officials, CSO leaders are not accountable to an electorate. Although that limits their mandate — they cannot claim overall representation — this kind of "independence" from the electorate, gives them the freedom, flexibility, and space that constitute the "comparative advantage" of CSOs in governance. In plain English, we need civil society organizations not because they "represent the people" but because, through them, we can get things done better and more quickly.

Frankly, that is why I have some reservations about ideas like the "People's Assembly," a parallel convention "of the people" as opposed to the United Nations General Assembly. I am also skeptical about national and local "civil parliaments." Ideas about a special "civil chamber" of parliaments to "represent "civil society also raise serious questions. In my judgement, these concepts misunderstand the real nature of civil society. They not only confuse participation with representation, by proposing parallel or shadow political structures, they can also undermine the institutions of representative democracy. Fair elections, responsible parliaments, and good, efficient governments cannot be replaced by civic activism.

These Notions Court Three Pitfalls: Parochialism, Lack of Accountability, and Unsustainability

Parochialism

Most CSOs are inherently driven by and focused on a single issue. Usually, it is a strong emotional motivation that compels people to act. Personal commitments, emotional motivations, are the most important resources CSOs can mobilize. Passion and strength that come from strong belief in a cause can multiply the impact of any citizen action. But sometimes the same passion can result in a "tunnel vision" that can hinder a CSO's long-term success.[10] Single-issue CSOs tend to judge everything by how it affects their particular interest. From the perspective of governance, especially, Jessica T. Mathews's warning is right: "A society in which the piling up of special interests replaces a single strong voice for the common good is unlikely to fare well."[11]

Again, the new governance, with its participatory processes and inclusion, will work only if shared values forge a basic cohesion. This holds true for both local and global communities. The challenge of governance — from small town to the global arena — is to ensure diversity and inclusion but to avoid disintegration and fragmentation.

Accountability

Like it or not, we have to make some tradeoffs, between freedom and flexibility on one hand and accountability and responsibility on the other. If public officials are accountable to their electorate and business leaders to the shareholders, to whom are civil society leaders accountable? The easy answer is that a CSO owes responsibility to the "stakeholders." But who are they? Even, if we can come up with some reasonable answers about clients, partners, members, funders, and groups a CSO might work with or for, we know that relations between a CSO and its stakeholders are often loose and difficult to define. Accountability of politicians and corporate managers vis-à-vis their constituency is more direct, contractual, and time-bound. Voters and shareholders have more control and sanction over what governments and businesses do than the constituency of a CSO will ever have over its activities. The different nature of accountability reflects the different role and functions of governments, businesses, and civil society organizations. The best way a CSO can compensate for the natural "accountability gap" is by generating public trust by full transparency and high standards of performance.

Sustainability

The high rate of failure, the short life expectancy in the CSO world, may conflict with the inherent nature of governance, which is about standard procedures, reliability, continuity, and *stability*. The longevity of civil society organizations is an issue here. Partnering is important in the new way of governance: CSOs have to deliver on the commitments they bring into these partnerships. Problems of sustainability can discredit a CSO as a partner.

The New Setting in Governance

Governments remain necessary and trusted institutions of democratic governance, but we are entering a new era in which governing is no longer left only to governments. The emergence of new players reflects the growing interests and capacity of citizens to use new forms of governance, from town hall meetings to transnational NGO networks. This "opening up" makes governance much more complex at every level. Power was accustomed to the language of command and hierarchy. Now, it needs to understand and practice the language of horizontal cooperation. We do not know much about the actors and processes of this new governance setting. Yet, let me try to take stock of some of the institutions and processes with which we appear to govern our lives in the late 1990s. We have:

- global intergovernmental institutions, agencies, and programs such as the United Nations and its family from WHO (World Health Organization) to ILO (International Labor Organization), from IAEA (International Atomic Energy Authority) to UNICEF (United Nations Children's Fund), and the Bretton Woods Institutions (World Bank, International Monetary Fund, and others);

- other global intergovernmental organizations with sectoral responsibility such as WTO (World Trade Organization), OECD (Organization for Economic Cooperation and Development);

- global institutions enforcing global standards and "rule of law" such as the International Court of Justice (the World Court in The Hague);

- global intergovernmental accords, treaties, conventions such as the Kyoto Agreement on Climate Change;

- global policy summits such as the UN Conference on Environment and Development (Rio de Janeiro), the "Social Summit" in Copenhagen;

- more traditional regional intergovernmental organizations such as OAS (Organization of American States);

- multinational corporations and their associations and forums such as the Davos World Economic Forum;

- transnational NGOs such as Amnesty International and Greenpeace;

- media;

- new policy networks and campaigns;
- national and local governments;
- new forms of public deliberations and conflict resolutions town hall meetings, civic forums, roundtables, truth commissions;
- national elections;
- polls, surveys, and referenda;
- CSOs, NGOs, and other civil society initiatives, movements, and campaigns.

Conclusion

In this hybrid world, our options and choices have dramatically increased — individually as well as collectively. That puts us, citizens of this planet, into a much more responsible position than ever before in history. Our capacity to act as citizens has dramatically increased as well. We have fewer excuses for not doing more for a better world.

Much is still uncertain in terms of the future balance of power. Some of the new institutions of governance are yet to emerge. Still, one thing is sure: empowered citizens taking their place alongside government and business will mark the new democratic era. We do not know how the new system of sovereignty will look or what new institutions, rules, and laws will emerge to further empower people. What we do know is that this "new world order," for the first time in history, will be shaped not by a power elite, but by millions of informed, self-conscious, and active citizens.

Even this incomplete list indicates that governance today is a very complex set of interactions that crosses sectors, borders, and hierarchies in breadth and intensity inconceivable twenty to thirty years ago. Separations of sectors and jurisdictions taken for granted for quite a long time are now dissipating, giving way to a much more "hybrid" world.

Case Study on Governance

A World Free of Violence Against Women

On March 8, 1999, the UN Development Fund for Women (UNIFEM), in collaboration with other UN agencies, hosted a global multimedia event "A World Free of Violence Against Women" to end violence against women. Live, two-way video linked human rights activists and policymakers in India, Kenya, Mexico, and Belgium with decision-makers, government representatives, academics, and media representatives. Together, they discussed critical policy directions, steps that must be taken, and successful actions in eradicating violence against women. The event was completely open, people from across the globe could join the meeting as part of an electronic "viewing gallery." As the invitation to the event said, participants were able to gain "a ringside seat to a rare interaction between those working on the ground and those who affect the national and international political and economic support for a world free of violence against women." A worldwide audience had the following options to join in: videoconferencing, the World Wide Web, satellite broadcast.

This event had all the "ingredients" that make up global governance today: (1) an important issue many people across the globe care about; (2) an intergovernmental agency (UNIFEM) understanding the power of global civil society; (3) civil society activists ready to take actions; (4) communication technology making a global dialogue possible.[12]

Notes

1. Miguel Darcy de Oliveira and Rajesh Tandon, eds., *Citizens: Strengthening Global Civil Society* (Washington, DC: CIVICUS, 1994).
2. Jessica T. Mathews, "Power Shift," *Foreign Affairs,* January/February 1997.
3. I relied heavily on a definition produced by the Commission on Global Governance in *Our Global Neighborhood,* The Report of the Commission on Global Governance (New York: Oxford University Press, 1995), p. 2.
4. Jessica T. Mathews, "Power Shift."
5. Jessica T. Mathews, "Power Shift."
6. Jessica T. Mathews, "Power Shift."
7. Commission on Global Governance in *Our Global Neighborhood.*
8. Benjamin R. Barber, *A Place for Us* (New York: Hill and Wang, 1998).
9. A harsh critique of the concept "civil society" is given by David Rieff in "The False Dawn of Civil Society," *The Nation,* February 22, 1999.
10. Jessica T. Mathews, "Power Shift."
11. Jessica T. Mathews, "Power Shift."
12. Source: *e-CIVICUS: Connecting Civil Society Worldwide,* Number 8. (Available from CIVICUS.)

Selected Resources

Yamamoto, Tadashi, ed. *Deciding the Public Good* (Tokyo: Japan Center for International Exchange, 1999).

Rockefeller Brothers Fund. *Inventory of Security Projects, Project on World Security.* New York: RBF, 1997.

14

New Tools — Same Values: Information and Communication Technology to Support Civil Society

Liz Rykert

The latter part of the twentieth century has been characterized by the onslaught of new technologies. Change has been fast, or even furious, at times. Like a descending flock of geese it is hard to see the structure for the cacophony of noise and apparent disorder. It is hard not to feel swooped up in the hype.

As a sector of society, our challenge is to understand these technologies for the benefits they can bring. We need to do this in the context of what we value and strive to achieve as a world alliance for citizen participation. This chapter will explore the benefits and challenges information and communication technology (ICT) poses to civil society organizations. Key examples will demonstrate some principles for making these tools useful in everyday work. Under the surface of each new application are the people for whom it is intended to assist or support. If you start with the needs of the people, then learning to master and apply the technology appropriately will help turn the cacophony into a symphony.

As context, this chapter will emphasize the newer technologies of the Internet, and their capacity to create common platforms for sharing information, building networks, and joining people of common cause for the purpose of change, support, learning and the creation of civil society.

The Benefits

As civil society organizations (CSOs) have ventured into the cacophony we have seen some remarkable uses. From these uses one can draw a list of benefits as a starting point. New applications are emerging daily to be added to the mix including: e-commerce, fund-raising, video, audio, and others. In this case we will concentrate on the examples and benefits which are accessible, relatively speaking, and have proven as useful to furthering civil society and citizen participation.

Shared Information

Perhaps the greatest benefit of information and communication technologies (ICT) is the capacity to share information. We now have the capacity within our sector to join expert knowledge and community wisdom. Sharing information effectively is our challenge.

Two terms you hear regularly in the context of ICT are Knowledge Management and Knowledge Ecology. A trend? Maybe. But at the root of these concepts is the recognition that, with ICT, it is possible to capture and share all the information and experience within an organization, network, or alliance. How often have you agonized over a wrong decision only to learn the person in the next office had critical information that could have saved you time, effort, even great heartache?

Knowledge is the operative word. More than information, knowledge is information in context. It implies experience and wisdom. Knowledge Ecology, borrowing from the biological world, conjures up an image of creating an interdependent system of people and information. For CIVICUS, the system can be networked to improve the quality of our lives and lives of those around us.

Traditional technologies, such as databases, have been holed up inside the walls of agencies and research institutes. We now see these resources moving online for anyone to search at any time. New tools that use database technology are putting the power of web publishing into the hands of non-technical citizens.

Part of the advantage of shared information is the greater equity in access to information and knowledge. Yet the paradox remains between those who have access to technology and those who do not. This will be addressed in the section on challenges. It is a very real concern not to be taken lightly. However, once access is attained, the capacity for greater and more equitable access to information and knowledge is profound.

In *The Web of Life*, Fritjof Capra wrote, "The more we study the major problems of our time, the more we come to realize that they cannot be understood in isolation. They are systemic problems, which means they are interconnected and interdependent."

As an electronic network grows, members increasingly have the capacity to become interconnected and interdependent to find those solutions. As ICT networks grow two social processes are at play:

1. a tendency to flatten traditional hierarchical relationships positively influencing a sense of shared power by working together in new ways; and

2. traditional hub models are shifted to interconnected webs of collaboration.

In traditional models of working together a central group tends to control the flow of information in and out of an organization or group. Once the group is networked electronically the power of centralized control is disintermediated. This is not to say the importance of the central body is lessened. Simply put: the "role of the middle" shifts to take on such activities as facilitation, actively sharing collective knowledge, undertaking analysis and research, and assisting with planning group actions.

In times of reduced resources and hence, greater competition, the capacity to share information adds value. Creating a culture of sharing for the purpose of civil society is one that we must continue to face. We know local knowledge and diversity are critical to the overall health of the sector. In understanding the benefits of shared information through ICT we must learn to value what we have in common and what we need to preserve to ensure that healthy diversity.

Building Shared Partnerships and Collaborations

History tells us we, as a society, have great capacity to build powerful responses to local or global injustice. Two prime examples are women's suffrage and the abolitionist movement. These organizers lacked many of the tools we have today. Perhaps the pace of sharing information was more reflective of the speed by which a mail boat could carry a message. However, the principles and steps were the same, for example:

- The issue is identified and documented.
- The concerns are publicized through local and mainstream media.
- Actions such as advocacy, protest hearings, or court proceedings are planned.

- New laws or legislation are enacted.
- New social norms are established.

Before ICT, civil society organizations used the means and methods they had at their disposal to work toward a just society. Today, we see the same trends:

- A local citizens group attracts two thousand people once a week for three months to fight for local democracy in Toronto. The group uses the Internet to publish the "real" news in the face of media bias. Citizens work together online and in the community to mobilize and prepare more than eight hundred people to present at government hearings and vote in a referendum.

- Anti-landmine activists coordinate their effort by e-mail and on web sites globally to achieve a global anti-landmine treaty and monitor its implementation.

- In 1995, the Beijing Women's Conference introduced e-mail and technology on site at the conference. Women, globally, were able to stay in touch and keep working together to push for implementation of the agenda built collectively.

- Student activists in Indonesia use Internet cafes and anonymous e-mail addresses to coordinate pro-democracy rallies, routinely turning to traditional printing machines to download and share information widely on the ground.

- Human rights activists in Belgrade lose their radio station and within twenty-four hours are broadcasting over the Internet.

- A network in South Africa builds an online database to support local radio broadcasts with programming material.

- Tracking the trends and findings on important issues of the day can be enhanced by the use of ICT. We know there are many points of view when it comes to understanding the issues. As civil society organizations we need the capacity to build on each other's efforts. Our resources are precious and scarce.

As organizations working together for social justice we need to have safe and reliable sources of information. As a sector, we may not all agree on the solutions but we can turn to each other for advice, research, knowledge, and practical know-how on the best approach to issues. We can build on existing lessons of civil society work and jointly explore reasons for variations and local context.

Reducing Costs

ICT has demonstrated a concrete benefit in reducing costs once the barrier of access is overcome. These benefits can include reduced costs for materials, travel, long distance charges for those with local dial-up and access to landlines, printing charges, mailing costs, and administration.

Supporting Participatory Work Processes

E-mail and web-based forums have proven to be useful tools when groups are looking to share work processes to ensure participation by a diverse group of members. For example, groups can:

- draft documents in a distributed way;
- share pre-meeting information or preparatory work;
- offer new learning and teaching venues; and
- create new venues for citizen participation.

The Challenges

Access

ICT is not universally accessible to civil society organizations or the people they serve. This challenge, more than any other, prevents wide use of the technology. A big gap between the "haves" and the "have-nots" exists.

What can CSOs do to address the challenge of access?

- As CSOs gain access to technology they can extend it to members and stakeholders.
- Join local advocacy efforts to ensure universal access.
- Start universal access efforts where there are none.
- Many parts of the world still lack good telephone access. New satellite, digital cellular, and radio signal technologies can assist. Emerging countries don't deserve third-rate technology. The "leapfrog phenomenon" means those just starting out can join developed countries with their level of technology.

If we know the formula for infant rehydration but we only have the capacity to get clean water and teach the methods to some of the world's population, do we withhold the formula until we can reach everyone?

No. We share the information and encourage its use and application, as it is possible. This example demonstrates the need to continue the hard work of creating the circumstances where ICT can be used when possible. It may be a revolution but it is not a priority.

Let's be clear. Technology, in and of itself, will not solve problems. Ethical choices challenge us at every turn as we work for the goals of civil society. Local knowledge has much to contribute to when, why, and how ICT can be applied. Local needs for housing, health, education, governance among others, place demands on available resources. Placing the use of ICT in this context helps one to see the challenge we face. Given the demand on limited resources and our goals as an alliance, we need to face the challenge of building capacity with CSOs to use the technology well.

Mainstream media and corporate agendas would have us believe there is a panacea right around the corner. They would argue "if only we had the technology." Technology is positioned as "either/or." Either you do it online or offline. Either you meet face-to-face or you meet through video conferencing.

As civil society organizations we can challenge this "either/or" agenda. As the radio programming online database demonstrates, the technology is used to supply reliable programming information to local broadcasters so the public can access the information through more traditional means. Or we have the example of pro-democracy activists in Indonesia downloading information and printing it for traditional distribution. Combining old methods with new means enhances our capacity to work together, share our wisdom, and learn from each other. It is the collective capacity, which truly has an impact.

As a membership organization we can agree we will work to extend public access to the technology through our own venues. For example, a community center located in a low-income neighborhood can include public access terminals. Or organizations can create partnerships with local libraries. In settings where CSOs are only emerging themselves, CIVICUS can work with more developed areas to support the integration of public access terminals in more traditional service-based organizations such as community health centers.

We Can Counter the Hype

As an alliance for civil society our first priority is the well-being of people. The information and communication technology revolution may well have introduced a new momentum into our lives — a momentum that is counter-intuitive to the pace of decision-making or daily lives. We can counter the hype. The practical ability to understand how online venues can, in fact, slow or extend a collaborative work process, can be critical to countering the hype.

Building Capacity to Use and Apply ICT in the Sector

To build our ICT capacity as a sector we need to start with what we already know. Our approaches and policies share our values in the actions we take. Moving online means taking what we know and interpreting this knowledge in the new venues.

Building capacity starts with building confidence. Experience has shown our confidence lies in the expertise we already hold about the problems, the solutions, and the methods of engaging and working with people. For example, if you are a good group facilitator offline you already know 90 percent of what you need to know to facilitate groups online.

One of the maxims used in working with groups to create an environment of shared learning is to ask everyone to live by the notion: "If you know a little bit more — you have an obligation to share. If you know a little bit less — you have an obligation to ask."

Capacity building in the ICT sphere happens with experience. Trying new ways of working will bring new insights along with the frustrations. Each new effort brings new lessons. Creating common areas to share what is working and where the challenges exist can help us all to build our capacity locally and among the movement as a whole.

Three examples of web sites and resources that are building capacity include: the Benton Foundation, http://www.benton.org; the Alliance for Progressive Communications, http://www.apc.org and their member networks; and the Bellanet Secretariat, http://www.bellanet.org.

For CIVICUS, we now have an e-mail bulletin and a web site. We need to develop our overall strategy for the use of ICT to support civil society. As we work together we will learn, as we need to, to use these new technologies appropriately in our own corner of the world. Each group and each effort will be slightly different. Learning to apply the technology to accomplish our goals will ensure what we do online is relevant and timely and deeply rooted in the real work we carry out everyday. The local efforts need to be orchestrated into the symphony of change.

Capacity building can include the use of mentoring. As in other areas of civil society work, from supporting new board members and volunteers to teaching programs, mentoring is a respected approach. New online facilitators, for example, can be taught many of the traditional skills of group process, the technical skills required and the general best practices for launching and animating an online dialogue or workspace. The role of the mentor is to quietly look over their shoulder for support, guidance, and insight. Mentors may not be experts but they have been there before. Matching mentors with new facilitators has proven very successful in supporting new online facilitators.

Exchange programs, both formal and informal such as those used by the APC networks, support both technical skill development and the building of relationships to continue capacity building well after the exchange is over.

Managing the Volume of Information

One of the most frequently stated concerns raised as an ICT challenge is learning to cope with the sheer volume of information. Whether we face this as individuals, organizations, or as a movement collectively, setting boundaries and coordinating how we work, can address some of these challenges.

The addition of ICT tools can address the challenge such as:

- refined searches — using customized search tools on web sites, which allow searches to be refined to the needs of the user;

- the creation of search tools for defined web sites — creating predefined portals of information (for example, searching only CIVICUS member sites)

- e-mail filters, assisting individuals to sort e-mail as it arrives;

- well-coordinated zone play, identifying key individuals across geographic or interest specific areas to agree to summarize and report out in a common area the actions or issues emerging.

Other approaches include using online facilitators to summarize the content and post these as digests and sometimes these are based on existing geographic divisions. Sometimes we need to challenge these more traditional divisions and allow ourselves to cluster around topics of interest instead. Either way the symphony works when each section understands and contributes its own unique aspect.

Building an Overall Strategy for CIVICUS

As regional advisory committees, we each develop work plans. Collectively, we could agree to add some minimum ICT applications locally. This could result in allowing the secretariat to weave the resources together. Essentially, you can do three things in any online effort: first, provide information; second, seek information; and third, work together. As a movement we need to ask ourselves: how can technology assist us in addressing these activities?

There is a very different social dynamic underway in an online venue meant for discussion than in one meant for simply storing and retrieving information. Online tools can be configured to strategically capture and support our work.

In the face of continuously changing technological tools, methods, and applications, this simple framework is intended to provide you with an orientation. So you can stop and ask yourself: "What am I trying to accomplish here?" and by understanding the range of tools available, feel more competent and be more able to choose the best approach.

In every case, it can be predicted that these three broad areas will not be operating in isolation; in fact, one should expect to see the convergence of these activities. By their nature, online venues are interconnected and support relationships that tend to be interdependent.

Interpreting Social Process

We need to be sensitive to the differences online venues present. For example:

- working without the regular things that help us to plan, implement, and complete our work;
- interpreting silence; and
- reading the momentum in online venues.

A common error among groups is to see the sharing of text-based information as the "exchanging" of information. Groups routinely enter into dialogue in text-based environments. Hence, if someone posts but no one responds, the silence can feel profound. Interpreting silence as noted above is a key function for leaders in the online dialogue. Similarly, some participants contribute without reading and building upon the contributions of others. In this case, these participants are not listening to the contributions underway. People need help to understand these subtle differences. Online facilitation is key to building this understanding.

Technical Considerations

Keeping in mind the issues discussed under the challenge of access, technical considerations are important to keep in mind. Of particular note, demonstrating sensitivity to those who do not have access to the online tools will be important to ensure the values of civil society are upheld in the context of the transition to using ICT. In some cases people are simply reluctant to move online or to delve into understanding the technology. Seeking agreement up front, and by consensus, means while not everyone will have access you have made a commitment toward building in universal access in your group and planning for bridged activities which can help to close the gap between the "haves" and "have nots."

For example, a citizens group on local democracy routinely used an e-mail bulletin to get information out quickly and cheaply to thousands of people. They also created a telephone hotline with a brief synopsis of the same information that people could call in for if they did not have access to e-mail. They used print newsletters distributed in the subway system and door-to-door to circulate a summary of the real news and were careful to promote the telephone number and the web site on these print materials. For settings where access to landline telephones is an issue the use of the print materials or radio can be critical. Respecting local language and literacy levels can shape the means of access to information.

Specific considerations:

1. For web site development: text-only versions, graphic descriptions, clear language, low graphics use, and limited use of Java applications will ensure people who have limited or no access to the World Wide Web will be able to access the information.

2. Database use: where possible, work with Internet Service Providers who will assist in creating online databases, which can be updated by the stakeholders who collect and have the data or information in them.

3. Online discussion spaces or workspaces: e-mail versus online conferencing. When in doubt, e-mail discussion groups using automated e-mail mailing list software will reach the broadest audience. One challenge we have yet to overcome in working together is coping with multi-lingual environments. Demonstrating sensitivity to language differences and, wherever possible, making resources available in multi-lingual formats extends our capacity to address inclusiveness.

The Unique Qualities of Online Venues

We know the ways and means of engaging in work offline. We can take what we know and interpret the work in new ways if we are well versed in the unique qualities of online venues. Offline venues tend to be synchronous in nature and online spaces tend to be asynchronous.

Synchronicity is present as an influence on social process when people come together to do something at the same time and/or place. A group meeting, a conference, a workshop are all examples of synchronous activities. Technological examples of synchronous environments include a conference call, video conferencing, or Internet Relay Chat (IRC). A precondition for these activities is that each participant must be connected in some way for a given period of time. These interactions are by their nature time limited. Knowledge of local charges, for example, a price per message delivered might also influence tool choices.

Asynchronicity characterizes activities that occur in the absence of time and place. The addition of online spaces allows groups to work together without the barriers of time and place. In a country like Canada this is significant given the costs related to long distance travel or telephone/fax communication for instance.

Asynchronicity as an influence on social process has some interesting impacts. People are no longer limited by the time they have set aside to work together. The work can happen over a period of hours, days, or weeks and at the convenience of the person participating. This shift of control from the group to the individual makes it easier for people to participate in group efforts. Second, it allows people to consider their responses to a discussion that is not contingent on the moment. This means, for instance, the opportunity for sober second thought is available to participants before responding in a group setting.

Asynchronous environments also pose some challenges to group process. Normally, when a group gathers for a period of time, they come with the understanding that there is a beginning, middle, and end to the activity. However, when one engages in group work in asynchronous environments, the notion of a beginning, middle, and end are usually not assumed. Many groups turn to the use of online facilitation to:

- help determine and then set the pace of the work;
- generate time boundaries, if these are critical to the group accomplishing decisions or actions together; and
- create a feeling of momentum or movement within the online workspace.

For example, the Association of Progressive Communications (APC) routinely holds online meetings with their global members. A meeting, generally, takes place over a two- to three-week period. The agenda is drafted online. The online facilitator(s) opens the meeting and members sign in. The first agenda items are discussed and the meeting proceeds until all agenda items have been reviewed and deliberated. The online facilitator of the meeting then summarizes the points and posts the final minutes.

Finding the Snug Fit

A "snug fit" between online and offline activities ensures that online resources are rooted in activities that are relevant to the participants. To maximize a snug fit, the people who are generating the information should be responsible for the preparation and posting of it online — whether this is in a discussion area, on a web site, or in an online searchable database. Where online efforts are not completely rooted in the "real" work of groups, they are seen as add-ons. Approaching the addition of online resources as a separate activity can result in web sites that are not updated regularly, in discussion areas that are barren of participants, and databases that are full of out-of-date information.

Any effort will require online management to continuously monitor the relationship between the literal (tangible in time and place) and the virtual venues (those spaces or activities not limited by time and place). The responsibility for management should be designated to an individual or core group who are considered part of the overall organizing group. Assuming the goal of seeing every participant connected and actively contributing, the considerations for managing the initial transition may be somewhat different than what may be expected over the long term.

A designated online manager works with the big picture in mind. His or her role includes:

- matching online activities with existing work flows;
- coordinating traditional communication activities with the electronic venues; and
- helping staff or participants to understand the value of the online venues.

Online Facilitation

Facilitation online means paying attention to the social processes of the people you're working with electronically to enable the group to achieve its goals. The facilitator is the person or team that provides leadership in the group to get things going and keep them going. Just as in face-to-face facilitation, online facilitation can involve:

- helping your group articulate its goals;
- creating a forum for discussion;
- enabling broad participation;
- promoting constructive debate;
- when possible, moving shared ideas into action;
- when not possible, acknowledging differences without debilitating the group working through specific activities (that is, meetings, document development, information sharing, etc.);
- and the many other responsibilities, which engage your skills with people, with group dynamics, and with mobilization.

Managing discussion and information-sharing on a mailing list is quite different from doing it in person. You do not have the same tools at your disposal as you do in a face-to-face meeting, such as a finite agenda or timekeeper. How much control you exert online really depends on the nature of what you're trying to achieve. If you are using your list to hold online meetings, you'll need to facilitate more actively than if the purpose of your list is general, less time-sensitive information sharing and collaboration. A first priority should be to help everyone achieve an online comfort level. That may mean giving up rigorous adherence to rules of how, where, and what gets posted. The last thing you want to do is scare off a new participant by telling them they've posted something incorrectly.

Experience shows using two facilitators, rather than one, can greatly increase the success of your online discussion space for working together. Roles of online facilitators vary. Typically, two people serving as facilitators can help each other out. For example, one can fill in for another during vacations. Similarly it can be very useful to have one person who concentrates on the topic under discussion from a content point of view. This leaves the other person free to focus on the interpersonal dynamics within the group.

Defining boundaries within and without the organization can help to create a sense of order to the messy overlapping world of online resources. As a movement we need to know who is in and who is out. What is intended for the public and what is intended for our members to further our work in influencing public processes?

CIVICUS, as a world alliance for citizen participation, has a vision. We see our world as a place that will be better when the opportunities for citizens to engage are many and the efforts of this engagement work towards better circumstances in the lives of those around us. ICT introduces abilities for our collective minds and hearts to move from working in isolation to working together.

We can extend our reach, our ability to tap into our collective knowledge, and our capacity for change, by joining together. To date, we have done this in a limited way. We cannot count on a central place to do this for us. We must each, in our own way, understand how we can put these tools together to support our own efforts locally. As we do this we will over time build our ability to find each other, to join in a more closely orchestrated effort, and, to turn what feels like the cacophony into the symphony.

Selected Resources

James, Maureen and Liz Rykert. *Working Together Online*. Toronto: Web Networks, 1997.

James, Maureen and Liz Rykert. *From Workplace to Workspace*. Toronto: IDRC, 1998. http://www.idrc.ca/books/848.

Lipnack, Jessica and Jeffrey Stamps. *Virtual Teams*. New York: John Wiley & Sons Inc., 1997.

15

Civil Society at the Millennium

Kumi Naidoo and Rajesh Tandon

Imagine a time when there were no formal institutions. Imagine a time when there were no governments, no civil society organizations, and no businesses. Imagine a time when there were no national boundaries. Then, imagine that it was nevertheless a time of human existence. It was an era with its own sets of rules and regulations, even though they were never written down. Nevertheless, there was governance. It was a time when social organization depended on a very deep sense of community. It was a time when responsibilities were shared by community members, when conflict resolution strategies prevailed, and when there was less of a sense that some sectors of society were beneficiaries while others were providers. Clearly, we cannot turn back the clock to this era, but reminding ourselves where we come from as humanity, should help us better imagine the potentiality that lies in the future.

The preceding chapters have explored both the promise of civil society and the challenges it faces in the new millennium. In this closing chapter we seek to reinforce the centrality of the citizen in our conception of civil society. We then explore a few key trends that emerge from the essays in this publication and simultaneously explore a future agenda for civil society globally.

A key question for the future role of civil society is how it will participate — from the level of grassroots citizen organizations to global alliances such as CIVICUS — as a legitimate partner in the processes and institutions that will govern world affairs in the new millennium. Since the fall of the Berlin Wall, we have heard of the arrival and promise of a "New World Order." At the same time, the effect of "globalization" has increasingly dominated discussions of the future, focusing primarily on two issues. The first of these is global security and the need to address threats of disease, narco-terrorism, environmental disaster, and ethnic conflicts, all of which spill across borders, destabilize populations, and bring on unimaginable suffering. The second is the ascendance of a global system of free markets with trade regimes and investment flows that know no borders and promise economic prosperity. Increasingly the reality, however, often produces more losers than winners.

Amidst all the recent talk and writing on globalization — not to mention its actual reality — has been a growing discussion concerning the role and functions of a new set of "supranational" institutions of governance (regional and global), or the revamping of older ones. Increasingly, these institutions are involved in making policy — social, economic, and environmental — the effect of which has been and will continue to be felt by citizens at the very lowest level of governance. In this regard, it is somewhat ironic that just as millions of citizens have finally attained political enfranchisement and achieved the right to participate in national affairs, the locus of decision-making in many critical areas of public life has moved beyond their immediate reach. A key challenge, then, that confronts civil society is how does it mediate national sovereignty and the emergence of globalization, and with it a range of supra-national power centers.

It is not surprising, therefore, that civil society is now confronted with defining its own role in this rapidly evolving global system of governance. Having only recently gained a degree of acceptance and legitimacy as participants in national-level policymaking, most civil society organizations (CSOs) have given little thought as to how to promote and defend the interests of their members beyond the national level. Although several international CSO networks and movements have successfully influenced policies with an international dimension, there is still a considerable way to go before we attain a coherent and articulated strategy developed by civil society that defines its role and functions in this newly emerging global order.

The danger in civil society of not taking up this challenge is to leave the other principal international actors, specifically intergovernmental institutions and multinational corporations, with an open field to define the appropriate role for civil society in global public life. It is not hard to imagine such a scenario leading to the role of civil society undertaking a "safety-net" and welfare function at the international level that mirrors the role played at the national and regional levels in years past. The difference in the future — and we are already witnessing it — is that CSOs could just as likely be expected to deal with entire countries instead of specific population groups.

Or, as some have suggested, because of civil society's prominent role in the promotion of democracy, its real function may be seen as being the unwitting accomplice in promotion of liberal market capitalism as the dominant ideology of the post-Cold War era.[1] To counter such views, however, requires that CSOs firmly engage these other actors in defining the nature of its future role in global as well as local affairs. In helping to define this role, we examine a set of issues and propose possible solutions as a starting point for the broader discussion that must take place.

A Call to Citizen Action

Civil society is a representation of collective citizen action, whether to advance mutual interests, solve common problems, or promote shared aspirations. Civil society and its organizations provide an alternative means for citizens to participate in designing and creating a healthy public life in their own image. Civil society has no existence apart from and is no stronger than the citizens that compose it. This is as true for the older northern democracies as it is for newly democratizing countries of the transitioning East and developing South. In the former countries, the quantity and quality of citizen participation in political and civic life has steadily declined during the past three decades; while in the latter countries citizenship and its rights and obligations are still fairly tentative. Improving the quality of public life, whether at the local level or in arenas of global governance, will require greater citizen involvement in the organizations they create to represent them in relevant decision-making arenas.

Better Defining Civil Society's Role in Governance Matters

In a democracy, civil society has both demand- and supply-side governance functions. On the demand side, civil society monitors the state's exercise of power and broadens citizen participation in public policymaking. On the supply side, civil society shares the function of implementing public policy with state institutions (co-production and management of public goods and services) and undertakes this function outside of but with the sanction of state institutions (self-governance). These governance functions pertain both to grassroots citizen organizations vis-à-vis local governments and to alliances of citizen's organizations with a mandate to act in global fora.

Building a Global Institutional
Infrastructure to Support Civil Society

If we can identify the attributes that make up a strong CSO — and the corresponding capacity building interventions that will lead to one — can we not also begin to conceive of the attributes of civil society itself at the national, regional, and global levels? Nation states have created a range of intergovernmental organizations — from international financial institutions to an international court of justice as well as evolving rules structure, that include treaties and conventions — that govern relations between countries. Business actors have created regional and global organizations that represent them in the official intergovernmental bodies and provide information. To be able to act as *effective partners* in governance, what would strong civil societies look like at the national, regional, and global levels? What are their capacity building needs and what might CIVICUS's role be in building these capacities?

Building the Legitimacy of Civil Society

Democratically elected governments are able to claim legitimate representation of their citizens. Civil society organizations also claim to speak on behalf of citizens, with the link between membership and representation in grassroots citizens' organizations being the principal factor of legitimization. However, the farther away we move from the grassroots and from "citizen" organizations, the more difficult it is to claim legitimate citizen representation. CSOs like CIVICUS that want to facilitate greater civil society participation in global governance matters must be able to demonstrate their legitimate right to act on behalf of citizens in regional and international decision-making fora.

Negotiating an International Social Contract

Underlying any rule of law or constitutional arrangement is an agreement between the governed and governors that defines their rights and obligations. So far, the newly emerging institutions and processes of global governance have had no direct representation of citizens in their conception let alone their implementation. What are the fundamental agreements that would need to be made between the members of a global society — that is, between intergovernmental bodies, regional and global actors in civil society, and multinational market organizations — to develop a system of governance that ensures adequate checks and balances and citizen participation and representation in supranational institutions?

This is where the argument must be made for civil society's legitimate right to participate as a partner in making and implementing global decisions and policies.

The key challenge then is: how do we ensure that we focus on ways to connect local civil society action with national and global civil society actions? Here we should not emulate the manner in which governmental and intergovernmental bodies and multinational corporations operate globally. For the former a system of representative elections and for the latter a hierarchy of profits and sales are the organizing principles for linking local to national and global. For civil society action, neither of these two principles is likely to work. National and global civil society action should learn from the principles of local civil society action. Those principles are based on shared vision and norms, mutual support and linkages, horizontal accountability, and collective responsibility. These principles should also guide civil society action at the national and global levels. Therefore, global formations of civil society must become the voice of citizens at global fora without getting bogged down with the formalistic and bureaucratic patterns of representation. This is likely to be an important issue for citizens and CSOs to address in the new millennium.

Emerging Trends, Achievements, and Challenges

There is a new paradigm alive in the world. No longer are we dealing with a single nation state that dictates the nature of societal development. The notion of the nation state in its current form and its ability to solve local, national, and global problems is seriously diminishing both in perception and reality. As several preceding chapters illustrate, the power of the central state has been reduced in terms of defining societal needs and in meeting them. This does not necessarily eradicate the important role and purpose of the state. Alongside this phenomenon, there has been a growing rise of the importance of civil society in meeting these needs. The emergence of new centers of power both at the global and national level is a reality with which civil society must contend.

The chapters in this volume reflect the reality that there is no crystal clear unanimity about what we mean by civil society, what its role is, and who composes it. Definitions will continue to remain fluid, even though some basic fundamentals need to be established. While not seeking to establish and impose a new orthodox definition, we think it is appropriate to extrapolate the common denominators that cut across the various competing definitions of civil society.

Some of the common ideas about civil society are hardly surprising.

One of the most powerful is that the citizen is the basic building block of civil society. Civil society is the citizen acting collectively through networks and associations that she or he joins voluntarily to address a common problem, advance a collective cause, or defend a shared interest.

Civil society is not value-free either as a concept or in reality. Likewise it is not a neutral space, notwithstanding the fact that there is strong recognition of the diversity of civil society and recognizing that this diversity is a strength. An important distinction exists between the concept of civil society and that of associational life. While an important component of civil society is the promotion of an environment that encourages citizen-initiated voluntary associations, it does not necessarily follow that all such associational forms fall within the rubric of civil society. Here we take the oft cited example of citizen-initiated associations that overtly promote racism, intolerance of whatever kind, and exclusion based on race, religion, ethnicity, and gender — the Ku Klux Klan and neo-Nazi groups come readily to mind. So, civil society is an arena where citizens collectively exercise civic values and continue their quest to promote the common interests of community without threatening the rights of others.

Informal or traditional associations and networks compose the majority of civil society's density and diversity. You do not need to have an office and a fax machine to be an important and valued member of civil society. So when a parent participates in his or her parent-teacher association meeting, it is a manifestation of civic action whether it is in Burundi or Belgium. Furthermore, people working in government and the private sector also have a stake in civil society, because when all is said and done, they too are citizens. The communities in which they live, the schools their children attend, their places of worship, and the playgrounds and community facilities where they find recreation are all arenas where the fabric of civil society is woven.

It is important to acknowledge that certain groups have been marginalized because of societal hierarchies and social attitudes. Here we refer to the elderly, youth, women, Indigenous Peoples, people with disabilities, and special groups such as people living with HIV/AIDS. Meeting the challenge of inclusion of these marginalized groups is critical to the maintenance of a healthy public life and sustainable human development. Contributions to this volume assert that civil society, more so than the private sector or government, is in the forefront of meeting the challenge of fostering inclusion and tolerance—civil society is the domain of civic norms. However, what our authors suggest almost unanimously is that these attempts still fall short of meeting the huge challenges that lie ahead. What we can safely say is that the unfinished business that we in civil society leave behind in this millennium will be waiting right there for us in the coming one.

The emergence of a global civil society brings with it inherent dangers of representation and legitimacy. It is sometimes a temptation for those within civil society — who acquire access to institutions of local, national, and global governance — to assume the role of information and opinion gatekeepers. The righteousness of their cause — not necessarily driven by bad intentions — can sometimes lead them to ignore the realities of citizen struggles in everyday life. There is a real danger of disconnectedness between an emerging elite in civil society and the base units of civil society, where the voices of millions of people are expressed. Not only are elites in civil society talking to their counterparts in the state and the market, but they sometimes have more in common with these other elites than they do with their own members whose interests they seek to advance. While there are no absolute solutions to this conundrum, it is imperative that CSO leaders remind themselves constantly from whence they came and of the inherent contradictions that exist in the complicated interrelationships that constitute the web of global humanity. Civil society organizations can also be exclusionary, even though this is rarely intended.

We raise these issues not to be alarmist or negative but to encourage the greatest possible honesty and transparency in the way CSOs confront the challenges that await the new millennium.

Challenges to Be Faced by Global Civil Society in the Coming Millennium

As we approach the new millennium, millions of citizens, even in long-standing democracies, feel a deep sense of alienation and distance from the social, political, and economic life of their societies. Many have been deprived of their sense of self-worth and believe that they cannot have an effect on the society around them. This sense of alienation can be found among nearly all citizens, young and old, from the wealthy North to the impoverished South. Each citizen feels that the political systems in his or her country are failing. As citizens, they do not feel their efforts will lead to improvements in their lives. In Chapter 2, Colin Ball and Barry Knight argue that the world is in a mess and that too many efforts leave out the "people." They conclude that a civil society development strategy for the future will be more effective if it targets people who have a strong mission for change, and then only uses organizations as delivery vehicles. In short, they say that it makes less sense to build the delivery vehicles and wait for the people to come along and drive them.

Historical injustices that have passed on from generation to generation and that inhibit a society and its members from realizing their true potential for development need to come under civil society's microscope, which should magnify social justice and human rights. Caren Wickliffe in Chapter 4 on the situation of Indigenous Peoples or First Nations captures an important and painful part of the human legacy. She explores the unique location of Indigenous Peoples who, while having their own inherent forms of civil society, see themselves as having to engage not only a "mainstream" state and market but a mainstream civil society as well. This is a distinctive challenge that humanity needs to confront in the new millennium, uncomfortable as it might be, so that historical injustices can be redressed in such a manner that we can all find our humanity.

Religion has been a civic and non-civic force throughout history. More wars and violent conflict have been fought in the name of religious views than for any other reason. Yet, as Fritz Anhelm shows in Chapter 8, religion has also been one of the principle forces for peace and justice throughout the history of humankind. This dichotomy of religion and its role remains a major challenge. However we choose to meet this challenge, we cannot and must not ignore the deeply pervasive nature of religious influence, religious networks, and its overwhelming power of social influence.

At the time of writing, the world has been shocked by the horrible tragedy in Colorado, United States, where two young students took their own lives as well as those of a dozen of their schoolmates and teachers. While it might be more comfortable for us to dismiss this event as a random and isolated act of a few mentally unstable kids, the reality is different. There have been far too many similar incidents and disproportionately so in the developed world. Will the same mass culture that has popularized Coca-Cola and the Big Mac extend this new phenomenon of youth alienation and marginalization to the rest of the world? This is not a Northern problem, as the equally unfathomable but real phenomenon of the "boy soldiers" in Africa becomes part of our daily lexicon and imagery.

Far too often, adults view young people as a problem or "issue" rather than as a positive resource to be harnessed. Adult society needs to value the energy, creativity, and other traits that most young people can bring to promoting the public good. Civil society needs young people to ensure that strong volunteerism, social cohesion, citizen participation, and organizations reflect the rich diversity within society and sustain it into the future. Civil society needs young people to bring in new ideas and to adapt the old ones to our changing world.

As Jane Foster, Kumi Naidoo, and Marcus Akuhata-Brown argue in Chapter 6 concerning youth empowerment and civil society, engaging youth in civil society has become a super-urgent priority, not nice to do, but critical to do. In short, this is a demographic imperative.

It is only citizens and their grassroots organizations that can protect and secure the environment for future generations. This concern is of huge importance in a world of diminishing natural resources that we have become accustomed to and have taken for granted. CSOs have led the fight to protect the environment, and we can suggest that without CSO interventions, we would be in even more serious trouble than we are now. Oscar Rojas, in his examination of civil society's role in promoting sustainable development in Chapter 7, predicts that in the new millennium, CSOs' roles in this arena will no doubt intensify and will call for even greater courage and innovation on their part.

Civil society must find an approach to foster greater partnership in solving this societal challenge with the participation of its counterparts in the state and market. Likewise, we need to recognize that we are living in a world of growing inequality that is exacerbating poverty. Poverty eradication has to be one of the highest priorities for civil society in the new millennium. We also need to link poverty eradication and sustainable development more closely. In Chapter 11, Caitlin Wiesen, Geoffrey D. Prewitt, and Babar Sobhan make a convincing case for strengthening the efforts around poverty eradication on the basis of it being a moral imperative, that it makes good business sense, and that it will help fulfill an important human right and social obligation. Here again, the forces of globalization will shape the contours of economic, environmental, and cultural intervention at the local, national, regional, and global levels. Their notion of building a new "social architecture" as part of a strategy to eradicate poverty is a powerful idea and one that places civil society fore-square in the endeavor.

Even though women are major participants in CSOs and in civil society generally, this has not been reflected in leadership roles. While this problem may be much more acute in the private sector and in government, this should not be reason for civil society to consider itself absolved of its own failure in this regard. As we begin this new millennium we recognize that the level of women's leadership is just over 5 percent in the government and business sectors. Amani Kandil in her discussion on the role of women in civil society in Chapter 5 cautions that the limited gains made by women in the last three decades of the twentieth century could be jeopardized in many countries by the current economic crises and on-going structural adjustment policies. We therefore need to commit ourselves to the goal that when future generations gather at the end of the coming millennium, there will be full gender equity in leadership roles — hopefully it will not take another one thousand years to achieve this fundamental global societal goal.

In meeting these challenges we are lucky to have additional tools for expressing citizenship. Information technology infrastructure, while still underdeveloped in many parts of the world, does enhance the possibilities for transmitting the values we have been discussing above. The tools of citizenship will be dependent on peoples' technology, and should broaden ownership of CSOs and hence their legitimacy. As Liz Rykert illustrates in Chapter 14, CSOs have successfully used emerging information technologies to promote and further civil society action. She cautions, however, that it is critical that access be promoted to the billions of people who do not yet have access to such technologies nor even access to a telephone, which in the North is taken for granted. Unless we heed this warning, some of us will speed away on the information super highway, leaving millions more marginalized in their potholes or dust.

Margaret Bell's discussion on volunteering and civil society in Chapter 3 is timely with the UN having declared 2001 the International Year of the Volunteer. In this discussion, we are reminded of the important power in what CIVICUS describes as "private action for the public good." These citizen energies increasingly are proving indispensable in saving our planet from a range of social, economic, political, and environmental disasters. In taking forward the empowering agenda of voluntarism, she is concerned that we avoid the trap of any form of imperialism or fundamentalist thought that might create unhealthy dependencies and promote cultural domination — that inhibit the ability of citizens to exercise their right of volunteering.

There remains the need to continue the important work of promoting an enabling architecture for civil society and to build a strong worldwide movement committed to promoting citizen participation. To improve the architecture of civil society and the organizations that comprise it, we need to ensure an enabling legal and fiscal environment, promote resource mobilization opportunities and strategies, and enhance its visibility and understanding.

There has been intensive worldwide discussion about the legal and tax environment confronting civil society organizations. This trend will prevail for at least the next decade, with the likelihood of legislative interventions in a wide variety of countries. CIVICUS stands ready to support and mobilize its global network whenever and wherever members report threats to the legal and fiscal frameworks crucial for a healthy civil society. We need to catalyze such learning processes among CSOs worldwide. In those countries where fresh interventions are being considered, they should have the benefit of global experience. In doing this, we must be mindful of falling into the "one size fits all" trap. What constitutes an appropriate legislative framework in one country might be extremely unsuitable in another.

A key challenge facing most civil society organizations today is the question of financial sustainability. As we fashion a global civil society movement, we need to recognize and deal with the contradictions and commonalities between the North, who are mainly seen as donors, and the South, who are mainly viewed as aid recipients of a wide variety. Volker Then and Peter Walkenhorst, in Chapter 10 on foundations and civil society, invite our specific attention to the growing importance of charitable foundations and similar grant-making bodies, who while being the funders and sustainers of CSOs are themselves very much part of civil society. The relationship between service delivery and advocacy CSOs on the one hand and grant-making CSOs on the other also raises important questions of independence, accountability, and transparency. Indeed, this is another challenge that awaits the new millennium.

Globalization has made corporations a dominant force in determining many of the trajectories of public life. Undemocratic political systems have given way to open democratic ones, while citizens and civil society have emerged as legitimate actors alongside the state and business sector. Within this late millennium paradigm, as Miklós Marschall points out in Chapter 13, the role of the central state is changing to provide an environment where local governments, civil society, and the private sector can engage in public problem-solving collectively.

There is no doubt that the free market is and will remain for the foreseeable future the central if not dominating feature of economic organization. It is in this context that corporate citizenship must be considered. While some corporate entities have invested significant resources in thinking through how they can give expression to their corporate citizenship and have begun to consciously engage civil society, many remain aloof to these important innovations. CSOs themselves increasingly recognize that they cannot wish away the private sector and that by engaging them in creative ways, the public good can be enhanced. This does not mean abdicating the civil society's right to be critical of policies and practices of the private sector, in the same way that relating to government does not subordinate its right to be an independent voice of society's interests.

As civil society faces the promise and challenge of globalization, promoting corporate social involvement is essential to its health and effectiveness on a worldwide basis. This does not imply that the interests and objectives of the corporate sector and civil society are common. In fact, their prime purposes differ. From a civil society perspective, business not only can, but also should do more to contribute its considerable resources to build a more just and humane world. This is a learning process as much as it is one of principle, and we expect that there will be vigorous debate and interaction both within civil society and between it and the business community.

In Chapter 12 Isagani Serrano highlights, with concern, the dual impact that globalization is having on civil society. He cautions that while globalization can promote greater cohesion and solidarity among CSOs, a key challenge in the future will be how to ensure that the tendency for humanity to "come apart" in an explosion of special interest fragmentation does not take place. While not negating the reality of globalization, he suggests that attention needs to be paid to the "activist idealists" who are seeking to curtail the negative aspects of globalization.

Finally, in Chapter 9 Ezra Mbogori and Hope Chigudu gesture to a continuum of possibilities in their discussion about civil society and government relations. In tracing the sharing of power between the state and other non-state actors, they suggest that the notion of "co-governance" represents the first time in 350 years that power is no longer concentrated in the state. By continuing to extend the sphere of influence of nongovernmental actors beyond confrontation with government, and into the arena of actual governing, there is the possibility of transforming what we have known in the twentieth century as the third, nonprofit, or voluntary sector to a true civil society partner in the coming millennium.

Not Merely Voters Nor Simply Consumers, but Citizens

The challenge of broadening the understanding of the challenges and opportunities facing civil society globally requires special attention. Initiatives such as the proposed CIVICUS Index on Civil Society should capture the achievements and threats to the health of, as well as trends in, civil society generally. The time has clearly arrived where some of the conceptual challenges — such as who's in and who's out — that were put on the back burner will need to be addressed. We should not be intimidated by these challenges, neither should we become obsessed by them.

Enabling the reinsertion of citizens and their organizations as a central and dominant feature in the public sphere is an important part of the agenda for the new millennium. Over the next decade, we are likely to see greater efforts at enhancing citizen participation in such areas as poverty eradication initiatives, the leadership role of women in civil society, youth participation in civil society, and corporate citizenship. In proposing a worldwide campaign to develop a global citizen commitment, CIVICUS and various other civil society partners will give expression to the notion of the citizen as the basic building block of civil society. In taking forward this initiative, we need to see people not merely as voters nor simply consumers, but as citizens.

The coming millennium will clearly bring with it many challenges and opportunities. We should resist the temptation of premature triumphalism about the state of humanity as we embrace the coming era. Much remains to be done to ensure that social and economic justice prevail, that sustainable environmental and development strategies are pursued, and that participatory democracy reigns supreme. While we have good reason to celebrate the attainment of formal electoral democracy during the last decades of this concluding millennium, we will have to confront the reality that electoral democracy will perhaps face its biggest challenges in the coming decades. With growing citizen alienation from the public arena and public processes, reflected in part by frighteningly low voter turnouts in elections in many countries, electoral democracy on its own runs the risk of becoming simply a preordained elite legitimization process. Put differently, we will have the form of democracy without the substance.

We urgently need to put the citizen back into the center of the public arena both locally and globally. We need to ensure that we can foster a notion of democracy that is understood as an ongoing sense of ownership of the public arena and the right to citizen participation opportunities that are ongoing, perhaps even daily. Why do we return again and again to this issue of civil society and its relation to political life? Because civil society, like the citizen and democracy to which it is intimately tied, is not only a political concept but has once again become a political reality, much as it was two centuries and two millennia ago.

Our new slogan should be "think both locally and globally and act both locally and globally," since the realities of globalization now deprive us of the luxury of national parochialism. As we attempt to mediate the pros and cons of globalization, we should once again ensure that we are driven by an agenda that puts the majority of humanity at the center of our thoughts and deliberations. Whether we succeed or not will depend, to a large extent, on the capacity of leaders in CSOs, government, and the business sectors, to listen and to learn from the experiences and aspirations of the vast majority of the poor and marginalized peoples throughout the world. We ignore these voices and concerns at our own peril.

Notes

1. David Rieff, "The False Dawn of Civil Society," *The Nation*, February 22, 1999.

About the Contributors

MARCUS AKUHATA-BROWN chairs the Youth Caucus of the Commonwealth Youth Programme. In 1998, he represented the Programme at the Committee of Management, the Second World Youth Forum of the United Nations System in Braga, Portugal, and the United Nations meeting of Ministers Responsible for Youth in Lisbon, Portugal. Mr. Brown also served as the New Zealand youth representative to the Commonwealth Youth Ministers meeting in Edinburgh, Scotland, and the Commonwealth Youth Ministers Meeting in Kuala Lumpur, Malaysia. He graduated in 1994 from the University of Waikato with a degree in teaching and education.

FRITZ ERICH ANHELM has more than twenty years professional experience exploring issues related to church and society. Since 1994, he has served as Director of the Protestant Academy Loccum in Germany. Previously, he served as General Secretary of the Protestant Academies in Germany (1979–94) and of the Ecumenical Association of Academies and Lay Centres in Europe (1985–94). Dr. Anhelm has authored numerous books and articles on church and society and edited the 1995 Loccum publication, *Theology and Civil Society*. His educational background includes university studies in social and political science, German literature, and education.

COLIN BALL is currently Deputy Director of the Commonwealth Foundation in the United Kingdom. Previously, he worked as a consultant and researcher in the fields of enterprise education, youth enterprise, youth service, and vocational training programs for the unemployed and community development in numerous developed and developing countries. He was also one of the founders of COMMACT, the Commonwealth Association for Local Action and Economic Development and served as its inaugural chair from 1990 to 1996.

MARGARET BELL was a founding board member of CIVICUS and is Regional Director of CIVICUS in Asia Pacific. She has served on the Prime Minister of Australia's Round Table Business/Community Partnerships and has led organizations such as Volunteering Australia, the Volunteer Centre, New South Wales (NSW), Australia, and International Association for Volunteer Effort. She founded the NSW School of Volunteer Management. Ms. Bell holds a baccalaureate degree in social welfare and a Masters of Art in educational psychology. She was recognized by the United States Presidential Summit on America's future and the United Nations as "a world leader in volunteering."

HOPE CHIGUDU is an advisor to the United Nations Industrial Development Organization (UNIDO). Based in Harare, Zimbabwe, Ms. Chigudu works towards integrating gender issues in the tanning and leather industries in eight countries in East and Southern Africa. Ms. Chigudu has written several discussion papers on gender issues for the Zimbabwe Women's Resource Center. Ms. Chigudu holds a B.A. from Makerere University in Kampala, Uganda, and an M.A. in Development Studies from the University of Illinois, USA.

JANE FOSTER is Special Adviser and Head of Youth Affairs for the Commonwealth Youth Programme at the Commonwealth Secretariat in the United Kingdom. She has more than twenty years experience working in youth affairs and youth empowerment. Ms. Foster holds a Bachelors Degree in Social Research from the University of Central England and a Masters of Business Administration (MBA) from the University of Westminster.

AMANI KANDIL is the Executive Director for the Arab Network for NGOs, located in Egypt. She serves on the CIVICUS Board of Directors and as a regional contact for CIVICUS in the Arab Region. In addition, she is an expert on public policies at the National Center for Social and Criminological Research in Cairo and lectures at Cairo University on the Faculty of Economics and Political Science. Dr. Kandil earned her Ph.D. in political science from Cairo University, Egypt, in 1985.

BARRY KNIGHT is Secretary to the Foundation for Civil Society in the United Kingdom, and a consultant to a number of international development organizations, including the Commonwealth Foundation and the British Council. Mr. Knight has written extensively on social policy and practice. He has coauthored several books including: *The Delinquent Way of Life* (1977), *Voluntary Action* (1993). Mr. Knight has a background in work with NGOs and civil society development both in the UK and internationally.

MIKLÓS MARSCHALL was the founding executive director of CIVICUS (1994–98). He served as deputy mayor of the city of Budapest, Hungary, between 1991 and 1994. He was an early advocate of the third sector in Eastern and Central Europe and serves as chairperson to several prominent nonprofit organizations in Hungary, including the Budapest Festival Orchestra Foundation and the Nonprofit Information and Training Center (NIOK). He has written and lectured extensively on governance issues. Dr. Marschall earned his doctorate from the Karl Marx University of Economic Sciences in Budapest in 1984.

EZRA MBOGORI serves as the Executive Director of MWENGO and on the CIVICUS Board of Directors. He has worked with both national and international NGOs since 1979, including serving as the Director of the Undugu Society in Nairobi and the first Chairperson of the NGO Council of Kenya. More recently, Mr. Mbogori has focused his energy on initiatives that build the capacity of NGOs to implement innovative development programs and to engage in policy advocacy. He was educated at the University in Kenya.

KUMI NAIDOO joined CIVICUS as Secretary General and CEO in 1998. Previously he was the founding Executive Director of the South African National NGO Coalition, the umbrella agency for the NGO community in South Africa. Dr. Naidoo initiated and led a wide range of education, development, and social justice initiatives within South Africa, including the National Men's March Against Violence on Women and Children, the National Campaign on the Apartheid Debt, and the Electronic Media in Education Forum. He is currently a member of the Commonwealth Foundation's NGO Advisory Committee. Expelled from school in South Africa at the age of fifteen as a result of his anti-Apartheid activities, Dr. Naidoo is a Rhodes Scholar and holds degrees in politics and law. He holds a doctoral degree in political sociology at Oxford University.

GEOFFREY D. PREWITT has worked with UNDP in various capacities during the past four years. Currently, he is the Programme Officer of the CSO and Participation Programme within the Bureau for Development

Policy. Previously, he worked overseas for several years, including two years with the international NGO, Africare, in Malawi. He holds a Masters Degree in International Development from Cornell University.

OSCAR ROJAS is Vice President for Social Development of FES, a Colombian nonprofit foundation, and serves on the CIVICUS Board of Directors. He has combined university teaching, public service, and work with the Colombian NGO sector during the last twenty-five years. Past positions include Vice President of the Colombian NGO Carvajal Foundation and Vice Minister of Health of Colombia. He has served as temporary advisor to multilateral organizations such as WHO, the World Bank, and the Inter-American Development Bank. Dr. Rojas holds a medical degree (M.D.) from Universidad del Valle in Cali, Colombia, and has a Masters in Public Health (MPH) from the London School of Hygiene and Tropical Medicine at London University.

LIZ RYKERT is a community development worker and project manager who has worked extensively with community-based groups to help them engage participants and enhance their project outcomes through the Internet. Along with a colleague, she coauthored *Working Together Online* and *From Workplace to Workplace*. Her recent work on online democracy has drawn attention from the press and is considered a model of citizen engagement. She is an occasional panelist on Canadian Vision TV's Starlight show, addressing the ethical implications of New Media.

ISAGANI R. SERRANO is Senior Vice President of the Philippine Rural Reconstruction Movement (PRRM) and works on development policy and advocacy. His works include a collection of essays on the environment and development, including *Pay Now, Not Later* (1994), *On Civil Society* (1993), and a poetry collection, *Firetree* (1985). He also coauthored *Bataan: A Case of Ecosystem Approach to Sustainable Development in the Philippines* (1991).

BABAR SOBHAN is currently working as a consultant with the CSO and Participation Programme in UNDP. Previously, he worked for a number of NGOs and International Agencies in Bangladesh and in the United Kingdom. Mr. Sobhan holds a M.Phil. in Economics from the University of Cambridge and is currently working towards a doctoral degree.

RAJESH TANDON is the founder and coordinator of the Society for Participatory Research in Asia (PRIA), a nongovernmental organization based in New Delhi, India. He serves as President of the Asia-South Pacific Bureau of Adult Education, an Asia-Pacific regional NGO; Chairperson of CIVICUS (1997–99); and as an Asian Vice President of the International Council for Adult Education. Dr. Tandon holds a Ph.D. in Organizational Behavior from Case Western Reserve University in Cleveland, Ohio. He has written extensively on participatory research and development strategies in the Third World.

VOLKER THEN is Director of Philanthropy and Foundations of the Bertelsmann Foundation, Germany. Previously, he has served at the Foundation as Director Cultural Orientation (1995–98) and Program Manager Cultural Orientation (1994–95). He is a member of the National Advisory Committee of the Initiative to Promote the Growth of Philanthropy in the US and serves on the editorial board of *Alliance,* a publication of the Charities Aid Foundation. Dr. Then holds a Ph.D. in history from the Free University of Berlin.

PETER WALKENHORST has served as a Program Manager (1997–98) and Director of Philanthropy and Foundations (1999) of the Bertelsmann Foundation in Germany. Mr. Walkenhorst holds a Masters of Art from the University of Massachusetts, Boston. He has also studied history and public law at Freiburg and Bielefeld Universities and at the University of Massachusetts.

CAREN WICKLIFFE is currently a Commonwealth Fund for Technical Cooperation Fellow in Human Rights Education, based at the Institute of Justice and Applied Legal Studies, University of the South Pacific, Suva, Fiji. She is from the tribal nation of Ngato Porou, Aotearoa/New Zealand and has served as an indigenous rights lawyer for Maori tribes and communities in Aotearoa/New Zealand. She holds a Bachelor of Laws and Masters of Laws from Victoria University, New Zealand.

CAITLIN WIESEN has fifteen years experience working on issues of poverty and civil society. As Poverty Advisor for the United Nations Development Program (UNDP) Africa, she worked in Senegal, Malawi, and in Southeast and West Africa. More recently, she has been the Manager of the Civil Society and Participation Program Unit within UNDP's Bureau for Development Policy. Ms. Wiesen holds a Masters Degree from the Fletcher School of Law and International Diplomacy at Tufts University.

CIVICUS
World Alliance for Citizen Participation

Mission: CIVICUS is an international alliance dedicated to strengthening citizen action and civil society throughout the world.

Our vision: A worldwide community of informed, inspired, committed citizens engaged in confronting the challenges facing humanity.

Our purpose: CIVICUS is dedicated to pursuing a world such that:
- citizen action is a predominant feature of the political, economic, and cultural life of all societies;
- private action for the public good is expressed by a rich and diverse array of organizations operating sometimes apart and sometimes in dialogue with government and business; and
- a healthy society is one in which there is an equitable relationship among citizens, their associations and foundations, business and governments.

CIVICUS's special purpose, therefore, is to help nurture the foundation, growth, protection, and resourcing of citizen action throughout the world and especially in areas where participatory democracy, freedom of association of citizens, and their funds for public benefit are threatened.

Our activities:
- *Strengthening tri-sectoral partnerships.* Promoting partnerships between governments, businesses, and non-governmental organizations. Strengthening the role of civil society organizations in these partnerships.
- *Protecting the ideals and institutions of civil society.* As a global network, CIVICUS and our members advocate for a healthy fiscal and regulatory environment.
- *Telling the story of civil society.* Publications, a bimonthly newsletter, a weekly e-mail bulletin and our web site, help tell the story of civil society.
- *Bringing people and information together.* Biennial World Assemblies and regional meetings bring civil society organizations and citizens together to share information, ideas, and inspiration across geographic boundaries.

For more information on our activities, visit our web site at www.civicus.org or e-mail info@civicus.org.

6543